Women's Human Rights and Migration

PENNSYLVANIA STUDIES IN HUMAN RIGHTS

Bert B. Lockwood, Series Editor

A complete list of books in the series
is available from the publisher.

WOMEN'S HUMAN RIGHTS AND MIGRATION

Sex-Selective Abortion Laws in the United States and India

Sital Kalantry

PENN

UNIVERSITY OF PENNSYLVANIA PRESS

PHILADELPHIA

Published by
University of Pennsylvania Press
Philadelphia, Pennsylvania 19104-4112
www.upenn.edu/pennpress

Printed in the United States of America on acid-free paper

10 9 8 7 6 5 4 3 2 1

Library of Congress Cataloging-in-Publication Data

Names: Kalantry, Sital, author.
Title: Women's human rights and migration : sex-selective abortion laws in the United States and India / Sital Kalantry.
Other titles: Pennsylvania studies in human rights.
Description: 1st ed. | Philadelphia : University of Pennsylvania Press, [2017] | Series: Pennsylvania studies in human rights | Includes bibliographical references.
Identifiers: LCCN 2017001726 | ISBN 9780812249330 (hardcover)
Subjects: LCSH: Abortion—Law and legislation—United States. | Abortion—Law and legislation—India. | Sex of children, Parental preferences for—United States. | Sex of children, Parental preferences for—India. | Sex preselection—Law and legislation—United States. | Sex preselection—Law and legislation—India. | Immigrants—United States—Social conditions—History—21st century.
Classification: LCC K2000 .K35 2017 | DDC 342.5408/78—dc23 LC record available at https://lccn.loc.gov/2017001726.

To my boys (Eduardo, Sidhartha, and Jai Julio)

CONTENTS

PREFACE

A few years ago an Indian American undergraduate student at the University of Chicago asked me to moderate a film discussion about a documentary on sex-selective abortion in India and China. The screening of the film, *It's a Girl: The Three Deadliest Words*, was sponsored by a well-regarded human rights center on campus. Before I agreed to host the film discussion, I wanted to know a little bit about the movie. Through an online search I learned that many women's groups, including the National Organization for Women, were screening the film across the country. The film was also an official selection for the Amnesty International Film Festival, and it appeared in *Ms.* review of feminist movies. Given the support it had from feminist organizations, I agreed to moderate the discussion even though my initial Google search did not reveal any background about the people and organizations that made the movie.

However, when I watched the movie, I was troubled by the narrow story it told about sex selection in India. The movie began with a poor Indian woman from a village pointing to where she buried the infant girls she had killed; it depicted the violent removal of a fetus from the womb as part of a cycle of violence against Indian women; and it ended with an interview with a Caucasian American woman activist who said that she helps women in other countries because they cannot help themselves.

The characters in this film were exactly the offensive caricatures identified by human rights scholar Makau Mutua nearly two decades ago in his critique of human rights work.[1] In this movie, Indians were savages, female fetuses were victims, and Caucasian American women were saviors. Nonetheless, much like the feminists who lauded the movie across the United States, the largely pro-choice audience for whom I moderated the film discussion did not challenge the film or its message.

Through a series of interviews with policymakers, advocates, and women who sex-select, the film framed sex-selective abortion as a cycle of violence against girls and women in India. Having spent many summers in India with my grandparents, through the academic and activist work I have done in India over the last decade, and having lived there as a Fulbright scholar, I know firsthand that many women obtain sex-selective abortions because of societal norms that demand a male heir, and not as a result of overt physical or emotional coercion. There is no doubt that some of these women also face domestic violence for their failure to produce a male heir. The film, however, depicted no possibility other than violence.

Upset by the disconnect between my discomfort with the film and the general acceptance of its message by the people with whom I watched it, that very evening I stayed up late into the night trying to find out information about the filmmakers and the film's funding sources. The film was expensive to make as it was shot on location in India and China. But unlike other films with such generous funding, the film credits did not list any funding sources. I thought I was at a dead end when I made it to the final page of the Google search results and uncovered nothing.

As a last resort I traced the ownership of the domain name of the website for the movie. By doing this, I found that the director of the film worked for an organization that makes gruesome anti-abortion videos. On the website that promotes the film, he is described only as a filmmaker who makes movies on human rights issues—there is no mention of any of his prior works. The director later admitted to me in an interview that some of his funding came from people whom he had met through that anti-abortion organization.[2] Had the director's background and funding sources not been so cleverly hidden, then perhaps the American feminist community would have been more skeptical of the story he was telling about India and China.

In May 2013, I published an article in *Slate* about my discovery.[3] Shivana Jorawar, Reproductive Justice Director at the National Asian Pacific American Women's Forum (NAPAWF) at the time, read my article and told me that the promoters of *It's a Girl* asked her organization to co-sponser a screening of the film on Capitol Hill for congressional representatives in Washington, D.C. This was all happening at the same time that a bill was pending in the U.S. House of Representatives to ban sex-selective abortion in the United States.[4] The bill's preamble states that its purpose is to stop the widespread practice of abortions of female fetuses by Indian and Chinese people living in the United States. Bills like this were also sweeping across state legislatures. By 2016, half of all state legislatures in the United States had voted on bans on sex-selective abortions, purportedly to address the behavior of Asian Americans. Seven states enacted the bans during this wave of legislative activity. Two states had adopted them decades ago.

Americans went to India and China, made a film depicting the "culture" of "son preference" and violence against women, and brought it back to the United States to support claims that Asian Americans sex-select and to lobby for laws that burden the reproductive rights of all American women. The rub of it is that they are convincing pro-choice feminists that the ban promotes women's equality.

Moreover, anti-abortion legislators and movement actors deceptively used advocates concerned about women's equality in other countries to further restrictions on reproductive rights. For example, Sabu George, a well-known activist against sex selection in India, was invited to testify and did testify at a hearing organized by Representative Chris Smith, a staunch opponent of legal abortion rights, for the U.S. House Foreign Affairs Committee. The purpose of the hearing was to push the U.S. government to stop funding family planning services in India because of sex selection.[5]

The legislative discussions about sex-selective abortion uniformly contend that the bans address a widespread practice among Asian Americans.[6] As someone whose scholarship and clinical work involve India and who has a personal connection to both the United States and India, I was skeptical of both the film and the empirical claims made by the proponents of the sex-selective abortion bills. Many of the factors that motivated my aunt who lives in India to abort a female fetus after she had already given birth to two girls did not exist for my other aunt who lived in the United States. As someone who was raised by Indian immigrants in the United States, I was aware that the "culture" of immigrant communities evolves from the "culture" in the places from which they migrated.

I teamed up with movement leaders to study the issue further. An important voice for Asian American and Pacific Islander women, the National Asian Pacific Women's Forum (NAPAWF), under Miriam Yeung's direction was working to defeat the bans. I also worked with Sujatha Jesudason who is an expert in the field. Under the auspices of the International Human Rights Clinic at the University of Chicago Law School, which I directed at the time, we investigated the issue from empirical, comparative, legal, and medical perspectives. As part of our team were economists Arindam Nandi and Alexander Persaud; law students Kelsey Stricker and Jeff Gilson; and Brian Citro, a fellow in the clinic; as well as health experts at ANSIRH (Advancing New Standards in Reproductive Health), a reproductive health organization based at the University of California–San Francisco. Economists on our team analyzed U.S. demographic data from 2008 to 2012 from the American Community Survey and found that in some cases, Asian Americans had a girl preference. When some Asian Americans had two prior boys, they were more likely to have girls than were Caucasian Americans. These findings, together with the contextualized and comparative perspective presented in this book, suggest that a few Asian Americans may use some method of sex selection (not necessarily abortion) to obtain a family with gender balance. That is a family that has at least one boy and at least one girl.

We released a report in June 2014 documenting the empirical findings and disproving other misrepresentations made by supporters of sex-selective abortion bans in the United States.[7] Since the report was released, no bill banning sex-selective abortion has been adopted by any state except Indiana. However, a federal judge in Indiana has blocked the enforcement of the Indiana law.[8] This book builds on my collaborative as well as my own individual work on sex selection.[9]

Introduction

Some of the most hotly debated issues about women's human rights today relate to practices undertaken by immigrants in their country of destination. When someone migrates to another country, she may replicate some of the cultural traditions and customs prevalent in the country of her origin. If she decides to settle permanently in the country of her destination, her children also may decide to continue those traditions. These customs can include celebrating certain holidays, eating distinctive food, and speaking a language other than the one spoken in the mainstream society. While most of these practices are unobjectionable, some practices of immigrants seem to be contrary to women's equality and rights. In some cases, feminists, human rights advocates, and other stakeholders push for legal prohibitions on this behavior with the goal of advancing women's rights. But these legal prohibitions themselves raise human rights concerns.

This book uses sex-selective abortion laws in the United States as a site to develop a transnational feminist approach to sort through questions about women's human rights. Laws prohibiting sex-selective abortion, which are spreading like wildfire in the United States, are an example of laws designed to prevent a practice that is (erroneously) thought to be prevalent among people of Asian descent living in the United States. Since 2009, nearly half of the state legislative bodies in fifty states have considered laws to stop women from terminating their pregnancies if they are doing so because of the sex of the fetus. Nine states have passed sex-selective abortion bans. In May 2016, Vice President Mike Pence signed the most recent sex-selective abortion ban while he was governor of Indiana.

In regulating practices of immigrants, advocates, legislators, and even some pro-choice feminists (erroneously) draw conclusions about the scope, motives, and impact of a practice based on their (mis)understanding of how the practice is undertaken in the country of origin of certain immigrants. In some cases, if a practice is thought to be discriminatory against women and girls in the country of origin of the migrant, it is assumed that the practice will have the same impact on women in migrant-receiving countries. Policymakers, feminists, and other stakeholders often draw conclusions about the magnitude of the practice based on their understanding of its scope in the country of origin of the immigrant. Additionally, some people in the migrant-receiving countries assume that immigrants who undertake the practice do so for the same reasons as people in the country of origin of the migrant.

This phenomenon, which I refer to as decontextualization, can be observed in the discourse around bans on sex-selective abortion in the United States. The dominant narrative used to justify these laws is that: (1) people in Asia prefer sons and that is why they abort female fetuses, (2) Asians have emigrated to the United States and many of them obtain sex-selective abortions, (3) Asian Americans obtain these abortions because (like Asians) they have a sexist preference for sons and an aversion to daughters, and (4) sex selection in both the United States and Asia is discriminatory and harms women.

In the increasingly global world of communication, news and knowledge travel quickly and at a massive scale across borders. Sometimes the knowledge about people in the migrant-receiving country may itself be distorted and lack nuance. This knowledge is filtered through media sound bites and dominant stereotypes about foreign peoples. The popular perception in the United States is that women in India who sex-select are largely physically or mentally coerced to do so. A story about one woman who was coerced by her in-laws to abort her twin fetuses, which she refused to do, circulates around the media and the legislative discussions about the bans. On the other hand, an in-depth study of India presented in this book suggests that women sex-select for many reasons other than direct coercion.

Sex-selective abortion bans are part of a larger strategy by anti-abortion groups to pass a variety of state-level bills restricting abortion. Anti-abortion groups frame sex-selective abortion bans in women's equality terms. This puts some pro-choice feminists between a rock and a hard place. They oppose the bans because the laws burden the right to choose, but they also believe that it is sexist for a woman to terminate her pregnancy just because she does not want to give birth to a girl. As a result of this tension, it appears that some pro-choice feminists support the legislation while others express no view about it. With some notable exceptions, pro-choice organizations have not devoted significant resources to opposing the bans even though the sex-selective abortion bills were the second most often introduced anti-abortion legislation in 2012.

There appears to be a Rawlsian "overlapping consensus among some pro-choice and pro-life people in the United States in regard to" sex-selective abortion bans. Pro-life people oppose sex-selective abortion because they oppose abortion for any reason. Pro-choice people in the United States oppose sex-selective abortion because they are concerned about equality for women and girls. The title of an article by Noah Berlatsky, a writer for *The Atlantic*, observes this consensus. In his article, "Neither Pro-Life Nor Pro-Choice Can Solve the Selective Abortion Crisis," he suggests that sex-selective abortion in the United States is an issue that both proponents and opponents of legal abortion rights should work together on.[1] An analysis of legislative voting records presented in Chapter 3 suggests that pro-choice legislators in a few states voted in favor of prohibitions on sex-selective abortion. Another indicator of the overlap in positions between the two factions is the fact that the term "gendercide," coined decades ago by a staunch feminist supporter of abortion rights,[2] is now the rallying cry for anti-abortion movement actors.

I argue that scholarship that informs these questions—feminist legal theory and international human rights theory—has not considered questions of this nature and thus does not provide adequate tools in sorting through the competing rights. Both of these theoretical perspectives support a universal view of practices and rights. None of the many variants of American feminist legal theory have conceived of practices that so radically change meaning that they may be oppressive to women in one country, but not repressive when undertaken by women in another country. Though it should be noted that recent scholarship has been attuned to the view that different regulatory approaches may be necessary in regard to a practice based on the context in which the practice emerges.

The lines in the sand are even more firmly drawn in international human rights theory and practice on these questions. Modern international human rights theory is built on the premise that all rights are "universal"—everyone everywhere has the same substantive human rights. If a practice violates human rights in one country, it is also thought to violate human rights in another country. On the opposite pole of universality is cultural relativism. The extreme form of cultural relativism is problematic because it uses culture and religion to shield practices that are oppressive to women. The strong force of universalism of human rights is necessary to counteract the extreme forms of cultural relativism.

I endeavor to create a conceptual space between these two poles. In contrast to this universalizing messages in both feminist legal theory and international human rights law, I argue that whether or not bans on certain practices of immigrant women promote women's rights should be ascertained using an evidence-based understanding of the practice in the context in which it occurs. I develop the framework of a new approach to evaluating regulations on the practices of migrants. This transnational feminist legal approach is a methodology that emphasizes both the context of the immigrant-sending and migrant-receiving country in evaluating bans on women's behavior.

I argue that in evaluating whether or not a practice is oppressive to women, we should be open to the possibility that when the practice emerges in a new context, it has a different human rights impact. The universal approach to human rights is not adequately skeptical of claims that practices have the same negative human rights impact across multiple country contexts. Once a practice is thought to be contrary to human rights in one country context, it is assumed to also be discriminatory in another country context. In contrast, I suggest that policymakers in migrant-receiving countries should not leap to this conclusion.

In examining the behavior of people who trace their origin to another country, some people in migrant-receiving countries also assume that immigrants will undertake similar practices as people from their country of origin because they overemphasize the role of "culture" in shaping behavior and underestimate the role of the larger societal structures and context in influencing behavior. In contrast, I call for a careful empirical analysis that ascertains the scope of the practice in question in immigrant communities, the motives for the practice, and the impact the practice is likely to have in the migrant-receiving country.

The politics and discourse surrounding sex-selective abortion bans in the United States provide a rich case study for critiquing shortcomings in existing feminist legal theories as well as in developing a new methodology, the transnational feminist legal approach. Using the general principles of the transnational feminist legal approach that I develop in Chapter 1, I propose a specific framework in Chapter 2 that can be used to evaluate and resolve the competing rights in question when bans on sex-selective abortion are considered.

In proposing bans on sex-selective abortion, anti-abortion advocates have successfully argued that the bans are necessary to protect fetuses from sex discrimination. Pro-choice feminists and scholars have not successfully rejected this framing. Indeed, some advocates have tacitly accepted it. The context-based legal approach I propose frames the competing rights in question as women's reproductive rights, on one hand, and the harm that sex selection may cause to girls and women living in a society, on the other. I start from the proposition that reason-based restrictions on the right to choose during the pre-viability period—including sex-selective abortion bans—do burden women's reproductive rights, but they may be justifiable if women in any given society are exercising their rights in a way that harms women as a group.

In India, for example, many women want to have at least one male child, but they also want to have fewer children. This has led to fewer girls and women in society than there would be had women not aborted female fetuses. There is a consequent male surplus. Emerging empirical studies in India suggest that violence against women is associated with a male surplus.

On the other hand, there is no evidence in the United States that sex selection is widespread. However, the national discourse in the United States on sex-selective abortion has been driven by misinterpretations and misrepresentations of empirical studies of (now) old data on the children born to Asian American women. Indeed, the anti–sex-selective abortion bans in the United States were fueled by an article by economics professors Douglas Almond and Lena Edlund published in an influential multidisciplinary science journal in 2008. They found that when Chinese, Indian, and Korean families in the United States have one or two girl children, they are more likely than Caucasian Americans to have a boy as their next child. Their study was based on a 5% representative sample of the U.S. Census of 2000, which contained only 324 Asian American families with three children. They found that a small subset of these Asian American families select for boys. Yet, proponents of sex-selective abortion bans in state legislatures misrepresented these findings (and subsequent studies) as proof that "[s]ex-selection abortions have the effect of diminishing the representation of women in the American population."[3]

It is no surprise that the anti-abortion movement was successful in exaggerating the findings of this technical article—even the media blew it out of proportion and claimed that it proved "son preference" among all Asian Americans. The article lent itself to these types of misrepresentations because the authors suggested that the magnitude of sex selection among Asian Americans was the same as among people who live in Asia.[4] The authors attempted to contain the can of worms they unleashed by clarifying to media sources that they did not mean to suggest that sex selection occurs among "all" or even "most" Asians.[5] But the damage was already done.

I present a new empirical analysis of sex ratios of Asian Americans, but also critique existing quantitative empirical studies using a critical race theory lens in Chapter 4. I argue that these studies rely too heavily on the ratio of girls to boys born to Caucasian American parents as a baseline to measure whether or not Asian Americans are sex-selecting. Some researchers also make unjustified comparisons to the behavior of Asian Americans and the behavior of people living in Asia. Finally, stereotypes that Asian Americans have a "son preference" foreclose interpretations of the data in ways that challenge that narrative.

I present an analysis of new demographic data about the sex of children born to Asian Americans from 2008 to 2012, which was developed in collaboration with economists Alexander Persaud and Arindam Nandi. Our analysis of this data suggests that a very small number of Asian Americans may be using some method of sex selection to ensure that they conceive a fetus of the opposite sex to the two prior children they already have. Survey data of attitudes of Asian Americans suggests that more than any other racial or ethnic group, Asian Americans desire to have gender-balanced families—families with at least one boy and one girl.

The national rhetoric on sex-selective abortion bans, including the draft federal legislation, consistently makes reference to the practice in foreign countries as a way to advance a domestic agenda. Although in understanding the significance of sex-selective abortion practices among immigrant communities, the country context of their country of origin should not be overemphasized, it is still relevant. I undertake a comparative analysis with the situation in India in Chapter 5.[6] I examine how the practice became widespread in certain parts of India, the societal and personal factors that contribute to women's desires to have at least one son and at the same time have fewer children, and the efforts made by the Indian government to curb the practice. Through this in-depth comparative study, it becomes clear that many of the societal institutions that contribute to sex selection such as dowry, reliance on sons for support during old age, significantly fewer economic opportunities for women as compared to men, as well as other factors are not present in the United States.

I use empirical and comparative methodologies to shed light on the practice of sex-selective abortion in the United States. From the information developed through this analysis in Chapter 6, I consider the practice of sex-selective abortion in the United States through the lens of the legal framework I articulated. Are women practicing it in society in great numbers? What are the consequences of the practice? Bans on sex-selective abortion in the United States will lead to racial profiling of Asian American women, place access restrictions on women seeking nonselective abortions, and potentially open the door to many other pre-viability restrictions. Few women abort fetuses because of their sex in the United States, and the practice is not driven by the discriminatory societal institutions that contribute to a desire to have at least one boy child (as it is in some other countries). Unlike in parts of India, where there is some emerging empirical evidence that a male surplus leads to violence against women, there is no larger societal impact of sex selection in the United States. Instead, prohibitions on sex-selective abortion in the United States do no more than harm women's equality.

The transnational feminist approach can also provide a useful lens to examine other practices of immigrants in other countries. Finding that the full-face veil worn by some Muslim women in France was oppressive to those women, France passed a law to prohibit it. A French woman brought a claim to the European Court of Human Rights arguing that ban violated her right to religious expression (among other things) under the European Convention for the Protection of Human Rights. I examine the discourse surrounding the full-face veil in France in Chapter 7, and suggest that much like the national discourse on sex-selective abortion in the United States, many policymakers, feminists, and other stakeholders made assumptions about veiling based on their impression of its causes, motives, and consequences in foreign countries. They failed to give sufficient weight to the French context. Some women who wore the veil in France claimed it was an expression of their identity as a minority.

Multidisciplinary Approach to Sex Selection

Much of the work on sex-selective abortion has been undertaken in silos—focusing only on specific geographies (India or China, for example) or using only one methodology such as feminist theory, quantitative analysis of sex ratios, or biological perspectives. In contrast, this book examines sex selection globally and through multiple disciplinary lenses.

I present a quantitative empirical analysis of sex ratios to determine whether Asian Americans sex-select (while at the same time critiquing this methodology) and conduct a political analysis of the sex-selective abortion bills in state legislatures. I also engage in a comparative study of the politics, causes, and consequences of sex-selective abortion in India. I conduct a legal doctrinal analysis of reproductive rights jurisprudence in the United States to assess whether or not the United States Supreme Court would uphold sex-selective abortion bans if the issue were to reach the Court.

I use sex selection as a lens to enter and make contributions to several contested issues in multiple disciplines. Responses to sex-selective abortion expose a gap in feminist legal theories. None of the dominant strands of thinking are able to make sense of both sex-selective abortion practices among Asian Americans and among people living in Asia. They are unable to adequately grapple with how to react to fact that the practice as undertaken in the United States is significantly different from the way in which it is carried out in foreign countries.

I compare legal responses to sex selection around the world and examine the spectrum of ethical views on the issues from a feminist lens. While traditional approaches to sex selection pit the rights of women against the right of the fetus, my framework places women's equality on both sides of the equation. The framework I propose can be used across multiple jurisdictions. It can be used to evaluate restrictions on sex-selective abortion both in countries where large segments of the population sex-select in favor of one sex and in countries where it is not practiced in that way.

By focusing on sex selection in both immigrant communities in the United States and among people in India, I examine questions about culture and change through the lens of critical legal theory. Explanations for sex selection that focus only on culture fail to recognize that the contextual factors (such as economic opportunities for women, a system of support for senior citizens, and fertility patterns) influence sex selection practices as well. The discourse on sex-selective abortion bans also often imagines culture as fixed rather than dynamic and changing both in India and among Indian American immigrant communities.

In attempting to assess the harms of sex selection to women as a group, I enter decades-old debates among feminists, medical ethicists, and economists regarding the societal impact of imbalanced sex ratios. Some theorists suggested that a male surplus would benefit women; others suggested that it will harm women. Today we have data to test those theories. There is a shortage of women in India as a result of the selective abortion of female fetuses, which began to occur in great numbers in the 1980s. Some believe that even if India's sex ratio returned to normal, by 2050 the country would still have 30% more single men hoping to marry than single women.[7] I examine empirical studies emerging from India and other countries to help determine the impact of sex selection on living women.

This work will be of interest to feminist legal theorists and will push new perspectives forward within that field. This work will also be informative to pro-choice people and others who are concerned about women's rights in the United States and other migrant-receiving countries. Canada,[8] Australia,[9] and the United Kingdom[10] have also considered bans on sex selection to address the perceived behavior of migrants. The transnational feminist legal approach sheds light not only on sex-selective abortion, but on other practices of migrant women that implicate women's rights concerns, such as veiling. Additionally, the contextual lens is relevant to judges who have jurisdiction over cases across many different countries, such as those who sit on the European Court of Human Rights. Finally, this work will also be useful for the many United Nations bodies that issue policy recommendations across diverse country contexts.

Chapter Overview and Methodology

It is not an easy task for people in migrant-receiving countries to determine whether or not a practice violates human rights when there are competing human rights claims involved. Banning a practice can impinge on women's right to religion, for example, but permitting it may be contrary to women's equality more broadly. The problem is that national debates often rely on decontextualized information about the scope, causes, and consequences of practices of immigrants without examining the practice within their own context.

The deep contextual examination that I propose would require scholars and policymakers to undertake the following task: First, scholars and policymakers should evaluate the practice in their own country context and resist the tendency to decontextualize. Second, they should seek to understand the magnitude and motives of the practice in the country of origin of the relevant immigrant communities. Third, they should compare and appropriately distinguish the causes and consequences of the practice in their own country from the causes and consequences in the country of origin of the immigrant. Fourth, they should examine the practice from a perspective that places women's rights at the center of the competing claims. This book follows this methodology in examining sex-selective abortion bans in the United States.

In Chapter 1, I explain the limitations of feminist legal theory and international human rights in evaluating the women's rights implications of bans on certain practices of immigrant women. These theories are not generally open to the possibility that practices that are oppressive to women in one country context may not have a negative impact on women in another country context. I also analyze the discourse around sex-selective abortion bans to demonstrate how decontextualized arguments have been deployed by supporters of bans in the United States. As a result of decontextualized arguments, legislators, voters, and judges inaccurately evaluate and weigh the competing harms at stake and, consequently, make decisions that harm women's equality while intending to promote it. I draw from more recent feminist legal scholarship that fixes its gaze on the global.

In Chapter 2, I use the insights about context to develop a framework that is specifically aimed at evaluating sex-selective abortion bans across multiple countries. I present the wide spectrum of moral and ethical positions on sex selection and explain how my legal approach builds upon and differs from existing viewpoints. Predominant approaches to sex selection focus on the harm to the female fetus, but fail to focus on the harms that sex selection causes (or does not cause) to living women. On the other hand, I argue that when jurisdictions ascertain whether or not banning sex-selective abortion will promote women's equality, they should weigh the restrictions on women's reproductive rights against the harms that sex-selective abortion of female fetuses causes to living women and girls.

Chapter 3 provides more background information on sex-selective abortion bans in the United States. Why are state legislators considering and passing the bans? Are the bills adopted in response to the fact that Asian Americans are the fastest growing immigrant community in the United States? Why are the laws difficult to enforce? This chapter maps the views of pro-choice legislators, pro-choice organizations, and voters to explain why some people who oppose other abortion bans support sex-selective abortion bans or remain silent about them. Although sex-selective abortion bans gained momentum in state legislatures, I explain why their close relative, race-selective abortion bans, have fallen out of favor.

Chapter 4 explains how empirical data and its misuse has driven the flurry of sex-selective abortion laws in state legislatures. I demonstrate that some authors of key studies on sex ratios of Asian Americans have decontextualized behavior and motives. I question why the sex ratios of Caucasian Americans are used as the baseline to measure whether or not Asian American sex ratios are "normal." Studies have found that there are natural variations in sex ratios across geographic regions and among racial groups. I present new and original empirical research on the sex ratios of Asian Americans from 2008 to 2012. While prior studies use data that is more than fifteen years old, our study of new data suggests that Asian Americans desire both girls and boys and not just boys. Survey data from a national survey confirms that Asian Americans are more likely to desire families with gender variety than any other racial or ethnic group surveyed.

I provide a detailed examination of the sex ratios, the causes of sex selection, and the consequences of sex selection in India in Chapter 5. I demonstrate how "culture" is used as a blanket explanation for sex selection, while other factors such as changes in fertility and economic changes are often neglected. Through this country study, it is clear that most factors that lead to sex-selective abortion in India are not present in the American context.

Having laid out the U.S. context in Chapters 3 and 4 and the Indian context in Chapter 5, I apply the legal approach to sex-selective abortion that I outlined in Chapter 2 to analyze the validity of sex-selective abortion bans in both contexts. Using this feminist legal approach, I argue in Chapter 6 that sex-selective abortion bans restrict rather than enhance women's rights in the United States.

In Chapter 7, I demonstrate the relevance of the transnational feminist legal approach to another practice arising in a different migrant-receiving country—veiling in France. I examine the debates around France's ban on wearing full-face veils and the European Court of Human Rights decision that upheld that ban. I analyze how debates about the full-face veil ban decontextualized behavior and motives.

CHAPTER 1

Transnational Legal Feminist Approach to Cross-Border Practices

The transplantation of people from one country to another has given rise to hotly contested questions about women's human rights. When Muslim women migrate to France, some may wear a veil to cover their bodies and faces. Many in France view the veil as a symbol of inequality. France presently bans the full-face veil. Yet, some veil-wearers in France argue that the veil is emancipatory. The debate raises a number of questions: Just because the practice of veiling in another country reinforces women's inequality, should we assume that it has the same impact in France? Some immigrants from Asia in the United States may abort fetuses because they do not want a child of that sex. While sex-selective abortion is thought to violate human rights in India, should we assume that it also contravenes women's equality in the United States? Should sex-selective abortion, which is banned in some countries, also be prohibited in the United States? How relevant is the context where the practice arises in making that decision? Using sex-selective abortion as a case study, I propose a methodology to evaluate similar practices that emerge across borders.

Practices such as veiling and sex-selective abortion are often examined by scholars and advocates through the lens of feminist legal theory and international human rights law. In the United States, feminist legal theories worked dynamically to push for legal and policy changes to further women's equality. However, when American feminist legal theory developed it did not have to contend with a world with such massive migration of people who also brought practices with them from one place to another. Those theories were largely aimed at assessing and addressing women's inequality in one country context.

The dominant paradigm among international human rights scholars and practitioners is that rights are "universal." In other words, if a practice violates a right (such as the freedom from gender discrimination) in one country, that same practice undertaken in another country is also deemed to violate human rights. Cultural relativism is often contrasted with universalism in human rights discourse. A strong cultural relativist would argue that human rights are relative and as such, traditional or religious practices, even if they deprive women of autonomy and equality, should not be prohibited. While I disagree with cultural relativism, I think that the universalist perspective also has limitations in evaluating bans on practices that are brought from one country to another by immigrants. I call these practices "cross-border practices." Scholars should do more work to explore the possibility of a legitimate theoretical space between cultural relativism and universality.

Largely as a result of the dominant universalist paradigm, scholars, policymakers, judges, and other important actors may not adequately contextualize cross-border practices. Some who believe that an act has the same harms across borders may assume that motives for and consequences of a practice in one country context will be the same or similar in another country context. Because of these assumptions, they might also fail to give significant recognition to how the social context where the practice emerges informs whether or not a practice is discriminatory. In this chapter, I demonstrate that policymakers who are considering bans on sex-selective abortion rely heavily on their understanding of the practice as it occurs in the immigrant's country of origin. I refer to this as "decontextualization." I also observe how decontextualization occurs in the debates on the veil ban in France, which I describe in Chapter 7.

I use sex-selective abortion bans in the United States to make the case for why we need a new legal approach to examining whether or not cross-border practices contravene women's equality. I propose a methodology that prioritizes women's rights, is context-sensitive, and uses comparative methodologies to evaluate cross-border practices. Few Americans are aware that a wave of legislation to restrict sex-selective abortion began sweeping through state legislatures in 2009. More than half of state legislatures since that time have voted on such bills. Seven states recently adopted them. Two states had enacted them decades ago. As recently as April 2016, the judiciary committee of the U.S. House of Representatives held a hearing on a federal bill to prohibit sex-selective and race-selective abortion.[1] A similar bill was introduced again in January 2017 in the U.S. House of Representatives.

These bills prohibit abortions if they are being undertaken because the fetus is not of a sex that the parents desire. The bills are part of a strategy of anti-abortion groups in the United States to limit access to abortion. Anti-abortion advocates target issues that appeal to people who otherwise support legal abortion. They justify the bills by arguing that sex-selective abortion is widespread among Asian Americans and occurs at similar rates in the United States as other countries.

Sex-selective abortion bans are not the only anti-abortion statutes that have been justified in terms of women's rights. The U.S. Supreme Court in *Whole Woman's Health v. Hellerstedt*[2] found restrictions on access to abortion that claimed to promote women's health unconstitutional. The Texas statutes in question in that case required abortion clinics to satisfy the same standards as surgical care centers and required medical professionals working at those clinics to meet other unobtainable requirements.[3] The Court found that those restrictions did not actually improve women's health and instead severely limited access to abortion services in Texas.[4] It is easier for pro-choice Americans as well as the majority of the U.S. Supreme Court justices to see the disingenuousness of arguments in favor of the Texas statutes. It is harder to immediately recognize the disingenuousness of arguments in favor of sex-selective abortion bans.

In the section "Decontextualization in Debates on Sex-Selective Abortion Bans in the United States," I describe how the debates on sex-selective abortion bans in the United States referred to the magnitude and impact of sex selection in other countries in making conclusions about its scope, motives, and consequences in the United States and explain why that is problematic. The section "Culture vs. Context in Understanding Immigrant Behavior" demonstrates why decontextualization occurs in popular discourse as well as some feminist writings. When evaluating immigrant behavior, there is a tendency to overestimate the role of culture in shaping behavior and to underestimate the role of context. In the section "Context in Feminist Legal Theories and International Human Rights Law," I discuss the role context plays in traditional American feminist legal theories as well as in more recent work that focuses on the global. The section "Transnational Feminist Legal Approach to Cross-Border Practices" proposes a methodology, the transnational feminist legal approach, to evaluate legal regulations on immigrant women's behavior. I first define "sex selection" and the methods that can be used to achieve it.

Methods of Sex Selection

I use "sex selection" to mean the process whereby people intervene with nature in an attempt to give birth to a child of their desired sex. Some authors refer to the selection of the sex of a child as gender selection. I prefer to use "sex selection" in recognition of the fact that "gender" is both a biological as well as a sociological construct. A person's sex does not necessarily determine his or her gender. When one or more parents attempt to preselect the sex of their child using medical technology, they are unable to control the future gender of the child.

Some people who engage in sex selection do so to achieve gender variety in their families—in other words, they want at least one boy and at least one girl. This is known as "family balancing." There are several methods of sex selection, which I categorize as pre-implantation or post-implantation methods.

There are two pre-implantation methods of sex selection: (1) sperm sorting combined with artificial insemination (also known as intrauterine insemination, or IUI), and (2) in vitro fertilization (IVF) combined with pre-implantation genetic diagnosis (PGD). Sperm sorting involves sorting sperm into those that carry the X-chromosome and those that carry the Y-chromosome. If a girl is desired, then the woman will be artificially inseminated only with sperm bearing the X-chromosome. If a boy is desired, then the woman is inseminated with Y-chromosome-bearing sperm.[5]

Dr. Ronald Ericsson developed a method for sperm sorting in the 1970s. By the 1980s, it was available in the United States.[6] MicroSort recently developed another method of sperm sorting. According to the company, this technology is proven to be 93% effective for selecting girls and 82% effective for selecting boys.[7] The MicroSort process works by exposing spermatozoa to a fluorescent dye. The sperm are passed through a flow cytometer, which is able to sort the sperm on the basis of cell fluorescence. Sperm with an X-chromosome (indicating a girl) glow more brightly.[8]

The Food and Drug Administration (FDA) banned MicroSort from continuing to conduct clinical trials for family balancing purposes, but allowed it to continue trials for sex-linked diseases. With this seemingly insignificant regulation, the FDA has weighed in on the ethics of sex selection in the United States without any public process.[9] In places outside the United States, MicroSort advertises its services for people who already have at least one child and want to have another child of an "underrepresented gender in the family."[10] Thus, MicroSort will deny its services to a family that wants only girls or only boys. Although MicroSort is not legally available in the United States for family balancing purposes, other methods of sperm sorting are available and are being advertised. One clinic in the United States offers sperm sorting for $1,300 to $2,500.[11]

Once sperm are sorted according to X-chromosome and Y-chromosome, the selected sperm are inserted into the uterine cavity, but artificial insemination does not result in a pregnancy every time. Indeed, its success rate is only approximately 20% per cycle.[12] The procedure may need to be repeated several times to achieve pregnancy. In addition, no sperm sorting procedure is 100% effective in properly sorting the sperm according to X- and Y-bearing chromosomes. Thus, even when pregnancy is achieved through artificial insemination, it is possible that the sperm-sorting process failed and the child will be of a sex other than the one that was desired.

There is, however, another procedure, widely available in the United States that is more effective for sex selection: in vitro fertilization (IVF)[13] combined with pre-implantation genetic diagnosis (PGD).[14] PGD is used to test the genes of an embryo to identify genetic diseases, but it can also be used for sex selection purposes.[15] In the IVF procedure, medical professionals remove eggs from a woman and fertilize them outside of the body.[16] One or two cells are removed from the embryo three days after fertilization, and the sex of the embryo is determined through chromosomal analysis of the removed cells using PGD.[17] Only the embryos of the desired sex are implanted in the uterus. Although more than one embryo is typically inserted into the woman's body, IVF does not always result in pregnancy. Indeed, its success rate for achieving pregnancy is less than 50%.[18] Thus, a woman may have to repeat the procedure. If a pregnancy is achieved, however, then it is certain that the embryos placed in the uterus will be of the desired sex.

IVF costs approximately $15,000 to $20,000 for each round in the United States. IVF is typically used mainly by infertile couples, but there is enormous profit potential for providers to market their services for sex selection. These procedures are legally available in the United States and, indeed, some fertility clinics actively promote them for sex selection purposes.[19] Incidentally, none of the proposed or enacted bills attempts to prohibit the use of sperm sorting or PGD for sex selection purposes.

The post-implantation method of sex selection is abortion, which I refer to here as "sex-selective abortion." There are several ways to identify the future sex of a fetus. The most commonly used test for sex determination is the ultrasound. In an ultrasound test, a medical professional uses a machine that emits and receives high-frequency sound waves to create an image, also known as a sonogram, of a woman's uterus.[20] A medical professional can observe the anatomy of the fetus and detect its future sex at around eighteen weeks of gestation. About 90 percent of abortions occur in the United States well before the future sex of the fetus can be known using an ultrasound.[21] Even at eighteen weeks of gestation, medical professionals cannot detect the sex with 100% accuracy, particularly if the fetus is not in an appropriate physical position to allow for such a determination.[22]

Amniocentesis and chorionic villus sampling are other tests that can determine the sex of the fetus.[23] Amniocentesis involves withdrawing amniotic fluids and testing them for the sex of the fetus; this procedure can be conducted during or after the fifteenth week of gestation. Chorionic villus sampling involves the insertion of a needle into the pregnant woman's uterus and the removal of a sample of the chorionic villi from the placenta for testing.[24] This test can be performed between the ninth and twelfth weeks of gestation. Both of these tests involve a risk of miscarriage. As a result, less than 2% of pregnant women in the United States undergo an amniocentesis or the chorionic sampling test.[25]

Finally, blood tests, a rapidly evolving technology, are relatively inexpensive and easy to administer. A pregnant woman can simply prick her finger and send a sample of her blood to a lab for analysis. One study found that blood tests to determine the sex of the fetus are very reliable around seven weeks of gestation, with accuracy rates between 95% and 99%.[26] Having defined sex selection and the methods by which it can be accomplished, I now turn to a discussion about decontextualization in the discourse around the bans on sex-selective abortion in the United States.

Decontextualization in Debates on Sex-Selective Abortion Bans in the United States

In our increasingly global world more people are moving across borders and settling in new countries. Information is also increasingly global. An important news event in India reaches the United States almost instantaneously. Media in one country may often report on human rights abuses in another country. But the knowledge that is conveyed across borders is usually a snapshot of the nuanced reality.

People in migrant-receiving countries sometimes use the limited knowledge they have about certain groups of people in foreign countries and see migrants from that country through the lens of that knowledge. Advocates and policymakers may inadvertently assume that many migrants will undertake practices for the same reasons as people who are from the country of origin of the migrant. I identify three ways in which decontextualizaton occurs—behavior, motives, and harms. To assume that people who live in one country behave in a certain way and for the same reasons based on knowledge of people in another country is like stereotyping across borders. Those who decontextualize incorrectly assume that women who trace their origins to a particular country share similar characteristics as people who have been raised and live in another country. As further explained in the next section, some people who assume that first- and second-generation immigrants share the same patterns of behavior as people from the country of origin of the immigrants overemphasize culture rather than context in explaining behavior.

Additionally, advocates and legislators sometimes incorrectly suggest that harms that ensue from a practice that is the subject of the ban are similar to the harms and impact of that practice in the foreign country. Theories that accept that the substantive content of rights are universal are not able to articulate a significant basis to resist this type of decontextualization. Using the lens of decontextualization, below I examine the discourse surrounding laws to ban sex-selective abortion, which have mushroomed in state legislatures in the United States.

Supporters of bans on sex-selective abortion decontextualize behavior when they assume people in India and China abort female fetuses and, therefore, most Asian American[27] women do too. Bills to ban sex-selective abortion have been introduced in the U.S. Congress for many consecutive years and the text is almost identical across the various versions. The federal bill introduced in 2016 asserts that Asian Americans practice sex-selective abortions in the United States in the same way that people in Asia do: "Evidence strongly suggests that some Americans are exercising sex-selection abortion practices within the United States *consistent with* discriminatory practices common to their country of origin, or the country to which they trace their ancestry."[28] In Chapter 4, I explain why this conclusion is unfounded.

Advocates for sex-selective abortion bans also decontextualize motives. They assume that Asian American women who sex-select do so with the same motives as women in their countries of origin. They argue that a preference for boys in India and China causes Asian American women to abort female fetuses to avoid having a female child. For example, a report by the Judiciary Committee of the House of Representatives, undertaken in connection with the federal legislative ban on sex selection, states that "the selective abortion of females is . . . the intentional killing of unborn females, due to the preference for male offspring or 'son preference.' "[29] The report explains why "son preference" exists in other countries: girls are a financial burden and do not carry the family name.[30]

The report further suggests that the motives of Asian American women are the same as those for women in Asia. Our study of recent U.S. Census data, however, finds that Asian Americans do not necessarily have a son preference; they want to have both sons and daughters. Indeed, both a new analysis of sex ratios in the American Community Survey from 2008 to 2012 and a poll of Asian Americans suggest that a few Asian Americans appear to be attempting to balance their families so they have one boy and one girl rather than sex-selecting due to a preference for boys. The results of a national survey of Asian Americans presented in Chapter 4 supports this conclusion.

Supporters of sex-selective abortion bans also decontextualize harms. Based on their understanding of its harms in India and China, they argue that sex selection is harmful in the United States in three ways. First, they believe that because sex-selective abortions have resulted in a significant number of "missing women" in India and China, it will have the same impact in the United States. For example, the federal bill that would ban sex-selective abortion states that "sex-selective abortions have the effect of diminishing women in the American population" and that "sex-selection abortion results in an unnatural sex-ratio imbalance."[31] The magnitude, however, is not the same in the United States. One article found that sex-selective abortions occurring among Asian Americans has resulted in at most 1,000 "missing women" in the United States from 1983 to 2002, which is approximately 50 per year.[32] On the other hand, estimates in India reach as high as 700,000 "missing women" per year.[33]

The preamble further notes, "an unnatural sex-ratio imbalance gives rise to . . . human trafficking . . . kidnapping and other violent crime."[34] While some empirical studies have indeed found that societies with a surplus of men are marked by more violence and instability, there is no such surplus of men in the United States. In Chapter 6, I discuss in greater detail the consequences of a sex-ratio imbalance in India.

Second, advocates for the bans believe that most women in India are forced to undergo sex-selective abortion through physical violence and mental abuse. They assume Asian American women are under that same pressure. The problem here is not only that the harm is decontextualized, but also that the understanding of what actually occurs in India is itself distorted. With globalization, information travels quickly across borders but that information is only a snapshot of the complex reality of the situation in other countries. The media often packages information in sound bites that are filtered through stereotypes about foreign peoples.

The mainstream understanding in the United States among anti-abortion advocates and pro-choice voters alike is that most women in India—through physical or emotional coercion—are forced to abort female fetuses. This coercion narrative prevails in the documentary *It's a Girl*.[35] This film, funded by anti-abortion advocates, has received accolades from *Ms. Magazine*, the National Organization for Women, and Amnesty International. The filmmakers extensively interview and depict the life of Mitu Khurana, a pediatrician who left her husband because he physically abused her after she refused to abort her female fetuses.[36] The film, however, fails to depict what more commonly occurs in India: women make the choice to abort female fetuses without physical violence or overt coercion. There is no doubt that some women in India are coerced through violence, but the documentary presents no other narrative.

The depiction of women in India as coerced is then projected onto Asian American women. The federal bill to ban sex-selective abortion extensively cites from a study by Puri *et al.* in which she interviewed 65 South Asian immigrant women recruited from a clinic that provides sex determination tests.[37] One-third of the 65 women cited past physical abuse and neglect related specifically to their failing to produce a male child.[38] But while it is true—and disturbing—that many of the women experienced domestic violence, the emphasis on the women who cited coercion neglects the fact that two-thirds of the women in the study did not cite coercion. Moreover, the sample was not representative of all Indian American women; it consisted of women who specifically sought sex determination tests. The federal bill also highlights the work of the photojournalist Walter Astrada, whose documentary tells the story of a woman from India who was pressured to abort her twins, but resisted that coercion. It turns out that this is the same woman featured in *It's a Girl*—who bravely refused to abort her twin girls despite her husband's threats.[39] Some state sex-selective abortion bills specifically include prohibitions on coercive abortions, sanctioning the view that coercion is a part of most sex-selective abortions.[40]

However, direct physical coercion is not the only explanation for sex selection in India. Women may choose to sex-select to gain status in their household. They may have empathy for the unborn girl: they do not want a girl to endure the gender-based discriminatory society they have had to endure. In Chapter 5, I describe the Indian context in greater detail to compare and distinguish it from the United States. This nuanced narrative is absent from the mainstream American media.

Third, proponents of sex-selective abortion bans point out that sex selection is discriminatory when practiced in the United States. In his submission to a House committee, U.S. Representative Lamar Smith stated: "The reason for opposing sex-selection is uniform: the desire to combat discrimination."[41] The preamble to the congressional bill to ban sex-selective abortion also notes that it is needed to promote equality.[42] However, social institutions, history, and other contexts are relevant in defining something as discriminatory, and sex-selective abortion reflects social institutions in India that perpetuate inequality. Many of those social institutions are not prevalent in the United States even though other forms of gender equality still persist.

Moreover, empirical evidence in the United States suggests that the practice of sex selection as carried out in the United States by a few people does not appear to be significantly gender-biased, as discussed in Chapter 4. Some may believe that sex selection is wrong for eugenic, moral, or for other reasons—but it should not be considered discriminatory to women and girls in the United States just because it is carried out in a discriminatory manner in India and reflects unequal social norms and institutions.

Decontextualization is problematic because it homogenizes people in a number of ways. First, the discourse does not adequately distinguish between the situation in various foreign countries. For example, "son preference" is assumed to drive behavior in both India and China. Adequate consideration, however, is not given to the historical and contextual differences between those countries. For example, the one-child policy has historically influenced the behavior of Chinese parents, but India has never had such a drastic policy.

Second, the discourse assumes that all Asian Americans share the same behaviors. This is problematic, because it fails to understand the differences in behavior and values among this group. Asian Americans include Indian Americans, Chinese Americans, Korean Americans, and others. Each of these groups is influenced by different religious, linguistic and cultural patterns. "Asian American" is a common label in the United States—it is used by scholars, advocacy organizations,[43] and social organizations.[44] Many universities have departments called "Asian American Studies."[45] I use "Asian American" to include people who have recently immigrated from or whose parents, grandparents or other generations have emigrated from a country in Asia. It should be noted that there is disagreement about what groups should be included under the umbrella "Asian American," and whether the category should be abandoned altogether given the plurality of people who are swept into that category.

Third, discussions of sex-selective abortion also fail to portray a more nuanced story about what occurs in foreign countries. India is a religiously and linguistically diverse country. Indeed, many states in India do not have male-skewed ratios at all. In the Indian state of Kerala, for example, the ratio of males born to females is close to the natural range. This suggests that parental sex-selection is not occurring. There is no one fixed "culture" that prevails throughout India as the discourse implies. However, there is no recognition of intracountry variation in sex- selection practices in the mainstream American discourse.

Fourth, the discourse assumes that the "culture" of people who live in Asia is the same as the "culture" of Asian Americans. It assumes (1) people in Asia favor sons over daughters, (2) this preference is caused by culture, and (3) these same cultural patterns replicate themselves among Asian Americans. The extreme version of this viewpoint ignores the role of context in shaping people's behavior. It fails to acknowledge that specific social norms such as dowry or employment opportunities for women also influence behavior.

Finally, the discussions relating to the bans fail to recognize and distinguish between first- and second-generation immigrants. People from Asia first came to the United States as slaves and laborers in the late eighteenth century. Later, there was an influx of Chinese immigrants during the gold rush.[46] Today, 79% of Asian American adults are foreign born.[47] Most of the remaining 21% are likely second-generation immigrants, which means that they were born and raised in the United States. While recent immigrants may have cultural traits in common with people from their country of origin, the longer that immigrants live in the United States, the more they are likely to take on characteristics of the mainstream culture. This is often referred to as "assimilation." Our research on sex ratios bears this out. When my coauthors compared the ratio of male to female children born to second-generation Asian Americans and Caucasian Americans in the American Community Survey from 2008 to 2012, we found no significant differences in the sex ratios for these two groups.

Certainly both first-generation and second-generation Indian immigrants share similarities with people living in India. They may celebrate the same religious holidays and share common values, foods, and traditions. The sex-selective abortion debate takes the comparison too far—it fails to see any distinctions between the two groups. Yet, people of Indian descent living in the United States clearly recognize these distinctions. Second-generation immigrants derogatorily refer to recent immigrants as "FOBs" or "fresh off the boat." Indian Americans born in the United States are sometimes referred to as ABCDs or "American Born Confused Desis." *Desi* derives from *desh*, which means nation or country, and a *desi* is a person from that country. It is used colloquially to mean someone from the homeland.[48] These labels reflect Indian Americans' own understanding of themselves as a diverse group.

A crude theory of assimilation would posit that the longer an immigrant has lived in another country, the less likely she is to share cultural characteristics with people from her country of origin.[49] Of course, there are exceptions to this rule. Amish people retain their distinctive traditions and language even though they have lived in the United States for generations.[50] They are able to do this because they remain geographically isolated, do not send their children to American public schools, and limit their interactions with contemporary society.[51] While some Indian Americans live in predominately Indian American communities, they are not isolated in the same way as the Amish.

Adopting laws based on decontextualized knowledge is problematic not only because it means that a law is adopted without properly reflecting on whether it addresses a problem in the jurisdiction where it is adopted, but also because there are other potential negative consequences. Indeed, the bans will lead to the profiling of Asian American women who are seeking abortions. The bans will create access barriers to all women who in some states now have to answer a battery of questions in order to obtain an abortion. Finally, if ruled constitutional, the bans will open the door to a host of other "reason-based" pre-viability restrictions, which would further limit the right to choose even during the first trimester.

Legislative representative advocates voting for the ban might assume that a practice that is prevalent in the country of origin of the migrant will also be replicated among immigrants when they move to their new home. This is because they may think that the practice is ingrained in the culture of the immigrant, which culture they believe to be the same or similar to the culture of people living in the country of origin of the migrant. This view is incorrect because culture is not fixed—it changes over time. In addition, there is an overemphasis on culture in understanding the reasons for an immigrant's behavior and an underemphasis on context, as I explain in the next section.

References to the situation in other countries may simply be a strategic move by anti-abortion advocates. Those arguments are used to justify their primary goal—placing restrictions on abortion. Yet their advocacy sways people who do not normally support their goals (e.g., pro-choice people). In fact, many pro-choice state legislators have voted for these bans—I discuss this in Chapter 3. I argue below that assumptions about the behavior of Asian Americans made by some pro-choice feminists rest on a mistaken view about culture.

Culture vs. Context in Understanding Immigrant Behavior

In migrant-receiving countries, the role of culture is often overemphasized in explaining the behavior and acts of immigrants and their progeny. If "son preference" is thought to be part of the culture of people living in Asia, then it will be assumed that it is a widespread sentiment among Asian Americans if mainstream communities believe that culture is fixed and unchanging and that it is what drives the behavior of immigrants. On the other hand, too little emphasis is given to context in shaping behavior.

There is no agreed-on definition of "culture" across disciplines. I use "culture" to mean not just customs, usages, traditions, or habit clusters, but a set of control mechanisms for the governing of behavior.[52] When I refer to "context" I mean factors that are outside of a person that guide and shape behavior. While a particular behavior can be motivated largely by "culture," it could also be shaped by the specific situation and norms that the person encounters. Along the lines of what Knop, Michaels, and Riles call the "post-essentialist critique" of culture, I accept the view that a person's culture is not fixed; it is dynamic and may change in response to his or her surrounding context.[53]

Uma Narayan observes how many people in the United States define the behavior of people who live in India by their culture. She points out how the media and popular American views frame murders of married women in India as products of Indian culture ("dowry death"), while murders by abusive domestic partners in the United States are not framed in cultural terms.[54] Narayan points out how a similar incident (the murder of a wife by her husband) when it emerges in a foreign country is painted as more heinous and attributed to culture whereas in the United States that murder would simply be seen as an isolated crime. Sex-selective abortion discourse in the United States goes further and paints an incident in the United States in the same way that it is perceived to occur in a foreign country.

Legal scholar Leti Volpp's article published in 2000, "Blaming Culture for Bad Behavior," further points out that not only is culture blamed for the behavior of immigrants, but the understanding of culture is fixed and unchanging. To illustrate her point, she compares the dominant American discourse about underage marriage between Caucasian Americans and Mexican Americans. In the context of Caucasian Americans, underage marriage is generally viewed as outside of the norm, whereas underage marriage among Mexican Americans is attributed to culture.

Volpp's work explains why this disparate treatment occurs. First, Volpp explains that the dominant American paradigm assumes that immigrant culture is fixed while mainstream American culture is fluid:

> We sometimes assume culture to be static and insular, a fixed property of groups rather than an entity constantly created through relationships. This assumption is made much more frequently for outsider communities such as communities of color. Culture, for communities of color, is transformed into what Paul Gilroy calls a "pseudo-biological property of communal life." Under such a paradigm, culture for communities of color is a fixed, monolithic essence that directs the actions of community members. Racialized culture thus becomes an essence that is transmitted in an unchanging form from one generation to the next.
>
> We can contrast this racialized culture to culture that is considered to be "hegemonic"—the culture established as the norm. Hegemonic culture is either experienced as invisible or is characterized by hybridity, fluidity, and complexity.[55]

Much of the discourse on sex-selective abortion among immigrant communities assumes that the culture of immigrants is fixed. It does not leave any room for the possibility that behavior changes with context as well as over time.

Second, practices of immigrants are assumed to be "rooted" in their culture while practices of Caucasian Americans are not. Volpp points out that "[t]hese visions of culture influence our perceptions of individual acts. For communities of color, a specific individual act is assumed to be the product of a group identity and further, is used to define the group."[56]

Third, by grounding the practices of immigrants in their culture, the practices are framed as misogynistic and contrasted with the practices of Caucasian Americans. Volpp writes:

> Even while voluntary or forced adolescent marriages occur within white American communities, we do not conceptualize these practices as cultural phenomena characterizing white America. Rather, this undesirable behavior is projected beyond U.S. borders and characterized as an abhorrent practice imported by immigrants that undermines enlightened Western norms. This projection allows the United States to maintain a self-image as a progressive state with a progressive culture—especially in the arena of women's rights—by naming as "other" the source of backward behavior.[57]

Volpp further points out that contrasting immigrant culture with mainstream American culture "has the effect both of equating racialized immigrant culture with sex-subordination, and denying the reality of gendered subordination prevalent in mainstream white America."[58] Thus, if parents from the mainstream culture were to abort a female fetus because they want a boy, people would not automatically assume that they are misogynistic.

Anna Korteweg, a Canadian-based sociology professor, observes a similar phenomenon. She studies honor-related violence, which she defines as a "family-initiated, planned violent response to the perception that a woman, as wife or daughter, has violated the honor of her family by crossing a boundary of sexual appropriateness."[59] Identifying the dichotomy between how immigrant culture and mainstream culture is viewed, she notes that "discussions of honor killing and honor-related violence stigmatize and racialize immigrant communities while positioning immigrant-receiving societies as free of 'barbaric' violence in contrast."[60]

In her study of Great Britain, the Netherlands, and Germany, she also points out the overemphasis on culture in discussions about violence within immigrant communities. She notes that media reports suggest that once a girl from certain immigrant communities has done something to disgrace her family, they must resort to murder. These accounts fail to describe situations where solutions outside of murder are sought.[61]

Korteweg rightly argues that culture is important in understanding the practice of honor killing but cautions against viewing it as a "monolithic, deterministic force."[62] She warns against giving too much weight to culture in understanding the behavior of Asian and other immigrants. She also emphasizes context and points out that many immigrant children are often exposed to a different social context at school and in their homes.[63] However, she does not explain how the concept of honor killings itself gains meaning from context. The context-based lens I propose here provides a new perspective.

In a small rural community in Pakistan, a family may feel a very strong sense of honor/dishonor if their daughter violates a community norm, for example by dating a boy (or another girl). In Canada and other migrant-receiving countries, the situation is different—immigrant families do not always live in close proximity to one another. Many do not have to encounter on a daily basis people who consider what their daughter did to be shameful. Moreover, in parts of Pakistan, communities may condone the murder of that girl. There is no similar mainstream community in Canada that would condone this behavior.

Thus, the murder of a daughter by her father in Canada for having premarital sex where the crime is not done in reaction to the "community" carries a different meaning than if the crime is committed in Pakistan where it may be encouraged and/or condoned by the community and done to preserve the father's honor in that community. To put it another way, a crime is considered to be a "hate crime" (which usually means the criminal liability is escalated) only in reaction to the context where the crime occurs. A crime that is considered a "hate crime" in Pakistan should not be considered a "hate crime" in Canada just because the perpetrator is of Pakistani descent. This is not to say that honor as a motive does not exist in any circumstances in a murder of a daughter by her father for the breach of a cultural or religious norm.

In the early 1990s debates erupted about the use of the "culture defense" in cases where Asian immigrants were being tried for criminal offenses. Those discussions provide useful examples of how immigrant culture is treated in mainstream discourse. The core question in feminist legal literature on this topic was: against what standards should Asians be judged—the standards of the dominant American culture or the standards of the culture of people in Asia? For example, if a Hmong man kidnaps and rapes a woman as a way of marrying her—a practice undertaken in their country of origin—should he be able to refer to his culture in his criminal trial? Take another example—should a woman who attempted to kill herself after she killed all her children to escape domestic violence be able to present evidence about a similar practice of parent-children suicide in the country she emigrated from?

Doriane Coleman argued against the introduction of culture in criminal trials. She contends that the behavior of immigrants in the United States should be judged against American standards and not by the standards of the immigrant's country of origin.[64] Leti Volpp acknowledges that it is a problem for feminists if men use "culture" as an excuse for causing physical or mental harm to women. But she further argues that the cultural background of the defendant should play a limited role in a trial.[65]

If we understand culture and context to be separate, we gain insight into both the debates over the culture defense in trials and the debates on bans of purportedly harmful practices of immigrant women. Rather than refuse to admit evidence of culture, courts should admit and consider information about the culture of the country of origin of the immigrant only to the extent it was shown that this culture actually influences his or her behavior. This way, we do not presume that a homogeneous and unchanging culture accompanies migrants as they cross borders and remain in another country. Yet, the context of the United States should also be given weight.[66] This approach is not blind to the problems inherent in attempting to identify what encompasses culture. This solution recognizes that both culture and context shape the behavior of Asian Americans as well as other immigrant communities. Clearly the culture of the country of origin might be more relevant for understanding the behavior and motives of first-generation immigrants rather than second-generation immigrants.

Professors Knop, Michaels, and Riles's insightful article proposes another flexible framework to resolve what they frame as the debate between Okin-style feminists who claim that women's equality (as defined in Western feminist terms) should trump multiculturalism and multiculturalists who give priority to culture.[67] They draw from principles courts use in resolving conflicts of laws to determine when courts should consider foreign cultural and other norms and when they should not.

They explain how the conflict of laws approach would work by applying it to a hypothetical case that involves a father in Japan and a daughter living in California. The father transfers shares of a California subsidiary of a Japanese parent corporation to the daughter, but his intention is not to transfer actual control but only to transfer the stock in "name only," which is a common practice in Japan to prevent potential disputes between siblings. The question is how relevant should the Japanese cultural norms and traditions be to an American judge deciding the case.[68] Their proposal to use a modified conflict of law framework allows a decision-maker to use one normative system for one purpose and another normative system to resolve another issue.[69]

Context in Feminist Legal Theories and International Human Rights Law

There has been a dynamic relationship between American feminist legal theory and practice. Feminist legal theorists shaped litigation and advocacy strategies to promote women's equality and the practice influenced how the theories evolved. These theories are often used in evaluating laws from the perspective of women's equality. The perspectives were used by feminist lawyers and advocates to evaluate whether a law promotes, inhibits, or has a neutral impact in respect to women's equality. When American legal feminism theories emerged to address inequalities in one domestic context—the United States. These theorists did not face a world with massive immigration. Today practices like sex selection, veiling, and female genital cutting move beyond borders more than ever. Recent feminist scholarship has begun to address women's rights issues across multiple countries. It observes that country context is relevant in determining the human rights implications of immigrant practices. I discuss geographic context in traditional and emerging feminist legal theories and international human rights law and theory below.

Context in Traditional Feminist Legal Theories

Contemporary legal feminism traces its roots to the 1970s when early feminist activists struggled against laws that were formally unequal. They pushed for women to be able to engage in traditionally male-dominated activities. Prior to the 1970s, many laws contained sex-based distinctions. For example, only women could receive alimony, only men could be drafted, and the age of majority was different for men and women.[70] Essentially, laws were motivated by the idea that a woman's appropriate role was in the private sphere of home and family. The form of feminism, which reacted against such laws, is often referred to as "liberal feminism."

In the 1970s, court victories erased many formal gender-based distinctions in the law. One prominent example is the case of *Reed v. Reed* where the U.S. Supreme Court found a statute that permitted only men to be executors of an estate unconstitutional.[71] It should be noted that liberal feminists would advocate changing not only laws that seem to benefit only men, but also laws that benefit only women. For example, they helped in eradicating the "tender years rule" that gave women preference in child custody cases.[72] These feminists emphasized women's similarity to men. Most liberal feminists would not push the law beyond formal equality with men.

In liberal feminism, context is not very relevant in questions about laws and women's equality. Making laws gender neutral and ensuring formal equality is assumed to promote women's equality regardless of their impact on society. That is, liberal feminists assumed that giving women the same rights as men would translate into women's equality. It was difficult for them to contend with biological differences where equal treatment could be disadvantageous to women.

Taking feminism in new directions, scholars emerging in the 1980s emphasized women's differences from men and proposed that any evaluation of laws and policies should take that fundamental notion into account. Taking their cue from Carol Gilligan's work, cultural feminists found that women's behavioral differences were tied to their sex.[73] Critics of cultural feminism argue that sex "essentializes" women's behavior.[74] While these feminists took into account social context, it was mostly fixed—all women shared certain traits and they were different from those of men.

Anti-subordination legal theorists also emphasized the difference between men and women. Men's and women's different roles and privileges in society contributed to women's inequality. If men and women were not equal in society, then treating them the same in the law would not necessarily promote equality. These scholars believed that gender was socially constructed rather than fixed. According to a prominent anti-subordination theorist, Catharine MacKinnon, women's inequality in society was the result of oppression by men, not biology. MacKinnon's approach rejects the idea that men and women should be treated identically. Instead, she believes that in some cases identical treatment can lead to subordination. These theorists would be willing to deviate from formally equal laws if they will benefit women in practice.

Even though the impact of laws must be evaluated within the social context, MacKinnon's theory did not imagine social context to vary so significantly. Her theory is animated by the assumption that society is defined by male dominance over women. In her view, the legal system was principally designed to perpetuate male dominance over women. Sexual abuse and sexual relationships were the fundamental ways in which women were oppressed. Consequently, even under dominance theory, if a policy promotes women's equality in one country context, then it would be assumed to have the same impact in a different country context.[75] Thus, these feminist legal theories did not seem to conceive of the possibility that a practice could be oppressive to women in one context, but not oppressive to women or neutral to women's equality in another geographic context.

The anti-essential feminist theorists' critique of the dominant strands of feminism in the 1990s is also relevant here. Those theorists have argued that the dominant feminist understandings were shaped by the concerns and goals of a very specific class of women. Some feminists called this essentialism "false universalism," where the unstated norm is the white, middle-class, heterosexual woman.[76] Angela Harris, for example, argued that Catharine MacKinnon's understanding of rape ignored the experiences of black women for whom rape is linked with gender and race.[77] She also argued that the motherhood experience varies for women of different races.[78] Other scholars have pointed out that mainstream feminist legal theories have largely ignored lesbian women and assumed that their experiences are the same as those of heterosexual women.[79] These theorists' basic point is that women differ on the basis of race, sexuality, class, and other things. To treat them the same is problematic for a host of reasons, including the fact that policies developed around white middle-class women's experiences do not necessarily apply to all women.

Race is the lens often used for analysis and critique in critical legal studies, but Indian American women and Indian women living in India are arguably of the same "race." Scholars have pushed anti-essentialist feminist theory further to acknowledge that even those two groups of women should be distinguished. Consequently, an anti-essentialist feminist view would posit that a policy solution designed to address women living in India would not necessarily be appropriate for women living in the United States who are of Indian descent.

Context in Critiques of Governance Feminism

Janet Halley, Chantal Thomas, Hila Shamir, and Prabha Kotiswaran's main goal in their groundbreaking article in 2006 was to describe a trend in international and humanitarian law where a certain form of American feminism (primarily dominance theory) infuses international institutions, as well as the discussions and negotiations of international treaties. They label this type of feminism "governance feminism." Their critique does not explicitly argue that governance feminism is problematic because it is insensitive to country context, but the threads for this argument are present in their work. I develop those threads in support of my argument that a practice can call for a radically different response in different country contexts.

Critics of governance feminism do not necessarily oppose the influence of domestic feminism on the international realm; rather, they appear to disapprove of the fact that only a certain form of feminism is elevated to the international realm. Their critique is important because it is the first to identify how feminism (and specifically a certain brand of it) has been exported from the United States to international institutions and then transposed to the domestic level in other countries.

Although the critics of governance feminists do not expressly point to the importance of context in designing policy solutions on women's rights, it is clear that they view geographic context as important. First, Halley points out that it is problematic to use radical feminist understandings of rape, which were developed in a non-war context, in war situations. She argues that the *Kunarac* case before the International Criminal Tribunal for the former Yugoslavia is an example of where this was done. The defendant in that case was convicted for the rape of a woman he transported out of detention. The court assumed that she did not consent to the sex, because it occurred in a war-like setting. Here Halley sees the imprint of radical feminists, who "have long argued that, in rape trials, force, resistance, and consent/non-consent are the wrong issues of coercive circumstances."[80] Imposing what she calls radical feminist views in the war context could lead to overenforcement, because any sex in a war setting could be considered rape.

Second, Shamir's case study suggests that regulations on sex work might be appropriate in one context but not in another. She notes that governance feminism, "well-intentioned as it may be—is pre-loaded with a strong tendency to overlook or underplay the costs it might cause to some and fix its gaze on the benefits gained by others."[81] She expands on this by arguing that it is necessary to focus on the impact a policy has on many groups in determining whether or not to adopt it; she then analyzes the policies of several different countries on sex workers in those countries.[82] Shamir applies a cost/benefit analysis to evaluate policies concerning sex workers in three different countries. Engaging in this type of balancing test assumes that policy solutions to women's equality issues are not fixed and can vary with the context.

Third, Thomas's case study of the negotiations of the international agreement on trafficking (Palermo Protocol) can be interpreted to illustrate the problems that ensue when feminist approaches to laws in one country context are transposed to another country context. Thomas describes the dominant strands of feminist thought on sex work and observes how they have manifested themselves in the negotiations of the Palermo Protocol.[83] These feminists, drawing inspiration from MacKinnon, argued that all sex work is trafficking because it enforces subordination of women by men. Thomas describes these views as follows:

> Women are prostituted precisely in order to be degraded and subjected to cruel and brutal treatment without human limits; it is the opportunity to do this that is exchanged when women are bought and sold for sex. . . . [L]iberty for men . . . includes liberal access to women, including prostituted ones. So, while for men, liberty entails that women be prostituted, for women prostitution entails loss of all that liberty means.[84]

On the other end of the spectrum are the individualists who believe that sex workers frequently exercise choice in choosing to perform sex work. They therefore believe that not all sex work is trafficking. The individualists disfavor a definition of trafficking that fails to recognize that some sex work is undertaken by choice and thus is not trafficking.[85] Another, less vocal, camp framed sex work as simply the right to work, a form of wage labor.[86] The view pushed by the Clinton administration "conceptualized prostitution and trafficking as distinct; envisioned the possibility of non-coerced prostitution; it also emphasized the centrality of human rights."[87] This liberal framework emphasized autonomy.[88] Ultimately, Thomas notes that both the liberal and structuralist feminist views prevailed in the treaty language that was eventually adopted.[89]

MacKinnon's view is that prostitution is detrimental to women's equality and should be outlawed everywhere. I argue against this universal approach to women's equality and rights. In some countries like India, many sex workers would not be able to provide the basic necessities like food and shelter for themselves and their children if they were not able to undertake sex work. There are few alternative jobs available to sex workers, particularly in a place like India, where sex workers are shunned by society. While there certainly are sex workers in the United States who engage in sex work just to have enough money to eat, most do not operate at that level.

While the harms of sex work might be the same across countries (dignity harms, greater risk of violence, etc.), the costs of a ban will not be. A ban in a place like India could result in the inability of many women to support themselves. In other countries, a woman is more likely to avoid costs like ostracism and may be able to find other paid work. Like Shamir, I believe that in weighing competing rights at stake in banning sex work, the legal outcome could be different in a country like the United States than a place like India.

Governance feminism seems to push for policy solutions developed in one country context to other country contexts. Typically, it pushes a more developed country's policies onto a less developed country. This harkens back to the law and development work undertaken in the early 1960s and 1970s, where Western lawyers and advocates embarked on reforming and strengthening regimes in emerging economies.[90] The problem was that the model laws they proposed were developed in Western countries and they neglected to tailor the laws to the specific context of the destination country, and in many cases the transplanted laws did not work to accomplish their goals.[91]

Sex-selective abortion bans are in a way a reverse transplantation of laws—from a less economically developed country to a more developed country. Advocates for the bans in the United States often argue that because India and China ban sex selection, the United States should also do so. This reverse transplantation is problematic for many of the same reasons that the law and development movement has been criticized.

Context in Karima Bennoune's Work

Professor Karima Bennoune's groundbreaking work more explicitly foregrounds context in evaluating bans on practices that are thought to be harmful in one context, but then emerge in other country contexts largely through human migration. She examines veil bans and argues that whether or not they are appropriate depends on the context. As she notes, her proposal provides "an innovative contextual approach to assessing the legality of bans in public schools on 'modest' garments claimed to be required by religious beliefs of Muslim women."[92]

She elaborates that a contextual analysis of bans on modest dress of Muslim women would involve examining a number of factors, including:

> [T]he impact of the garments on other women (or girls) in the same environment; coercion of women in the context, including activities

> of religious extremist organizations; gender discrimination; related violence against women in the location; the motivation of those imposing the restriction; Islamophobia, if relevant, or religious discrimination in the context; the alternatives to restrictions; the possible consequences for human rights both of restrictions and a lack thereof; and whether or not there has been consultation with impacted constituencies (both those impacted by restrictions and by a lack of restrictions on such garments), and, if so, what their views are.[93]

She examines two court decisions—the European Court of Human Rights (ECHR) judgment in *Sahin v. Turkey* (2004)[94] and the British House of Lords judgment in *Begum v. Headteacher*. In *Sahin*, the ECHR found that Turkey's ban on the headscarf in universities did not violate the European Convention on the Proection Human Rights' Convention guarantee of religious expression. On the other hand, in *Begum*, the House of Lords upheld a school's ban on the *jilbab*, which is a long cloak covering everything but the head, hands, and feet.[95] While she appears to be open to the possibility that veil bans are permissible in some countries but not in others, Bennoune finds the bans to be justified in Turkey and the United Kingdom.[96]

In *Sahin*, the issue before the ECHR was whether the Turkish ban violated a women's right to free expression under the Convention.[97] Under the Convention, this right can be limited in order to protect the rights of others.[98] Bennoune believes that the Turkish ban was appropriate because "[e]ven to the extent that for some women, the choice to wear a headscarf is their own, and is for them an expression of religious belief, this limitation on that choice is necessary in context to protect the rights of others."[99]

She also concludes that in *Begum* the ban in the United Kingdom on the more restrictive clothing was appropriate in a situation where a less restrictive headscarf was still available and where there was evidence that some girls would have felt coerced into wearing the restrictive dress if it were not banned.[100] Bennoune points out that her conclusion that the bans were appropriate in both the Turkey and United Kingdom cases hinges upon the fact that they were in public educational institutions, which shape the identities of future generations and forge the public consensus about gender roles and equality.[101]

On the other hand, she argues that while bans in Turkey and the United Kingdom were appropriate, it would be inappropriate to ban it in the American law school where she teaches because so few women wear them.[102] The magnitude of the practice in the context in which it occurs appears to be an important consideration in determining whether to ban it. Even though she believes bans in both Turkey and the United Kingdom were appropriate, her contextual approach to evaluate bans leaves open the possibility that in some contexts, veil bans may not be appropriate. I build on this idea in developing the methodology I describe in the next section.

Bennoune also briefly discusses France's 2004 law restricting religious dress in schools, but does not draw any conclusions about its legitimacy. She notes that the "the French law perches in between as a truly hard case."[103] In Chapter 7, I discuss France's full-face veil ban adopted in 2010, three years after the publication of Bennoune's article.

Context in International Human Rights Law: Universality vs. Cultural Relativism

The debate about whether international human rights should apply universally across cultures and countries or whether they should vary based on culture is age-old.[104] A "strong" cultural relativist would "assert that culture is the sole or primary source of the validity of a practice or claim to a moral right."[105] The supporters of universalism often draw upon natural law and reason and argue that there are objective standards by which to judge human conduct and to create law. Universalism "assumes that there is law that is so basic, so 'natural,' that it exists in all communities."[106]

In the early 1990s, this binary frame for human rights also elicited much debate about women's rights. What Western feminists might consider oppressive, Western relativists consider cultural preservation.[107] Take, for example, the practice that some call female genital mutilation while others label female genital cutting, which is a more neutral term. Feminists have debated whether or not the practice is oppressive to women in Africa or an acceptable cultural practice.[108]

Tracy Higgins, a feminist and international human rights legal scholar, observed decades ago the parallels in the critiques made by anti-essentialist feminists against mainstream feminism to the critiques made by relativists to universalism.[109] She notes that:

> . . . anti-essentialist feminists have attempted to rethink both the various descriptions of gender oppression that have been offered and the assumption that gender oppression can be described meaningfully along a single axis. Instead, they have focused on local, contextualized problems of gender oppression. In this sense, anti-essentialism's criticism of general accounts of women's oppression parallels cultural relativism's critique of universal theories of human rights. Like cultural relativism, feminist anti-essentialism seems to lead to the conclusion that gender inequality cannot be explained cross-culturally.[110]

These observations recognize the intersection between feminist legal theory and international human rights law and practice as I do here.

Professor Higgins further observed the challenges in resolving the debate between the universalists and relativists. She pointed out that:

> Confronted with the challenge of cultural relativism, feminism faces divergent paths, neither of which seems to lead out of the woods of patriarchy. The first path, leading to simple tolerance of cultural difference, is too broad. To follow it would require feminists to ignore pervasive limits on women's freedom in the name of an autonomy that exists for women in theory only. The other path, leading to objective condemnation of cultural practices, is too narrow. To follow it would require feminists to dismiss the culturally distinct experiences of women as false consciousness.[111]

I think there may be a narrow road between the two broad paths she lays out between the rejection of a common notion of gender equality and the rejection of all "cultural practices."

While those feminist debates in international human rights are relevant here, I am not asking the same question they struggled with. Those conversations were about whether or not a seemingly sexist practice should be permitted in a country because it is part of the religion or culture of the country in which it is practiced. Rather, I am asking whether a practice that is considered to be oppressive in one country context should be automatically deemed oppressive in another country context. For example, the question I am wrestling with is whether the veil is oppressive to women in

France or Belgium where it has not been traditionally worn and is worn by a relative few number of women. I am not asking whether or not the veil is oppressive to women in Iran where it is required by law or in a country where social norms dictate it. Few have seen these as separate questions, and I argue that they are not only separate questions but that they should be analyzed differently.

Of course whether the veil is oppressive in countries where it is mandatory or dictated by social custom is not totally unrelated to the question about whether the veil is oppressive to women who wear it in France. In order to understand whether or not a cross-border practice is harmful for women's rights in the country of destination of a migrant, we must understand the reasons, scope, and consequences of the practice in the country of origin of that migrant. In this process of comparison, we may learn that the motives, consequences, and impact of the practice are entirely different in the country of origin of the immigrant than in the country of destination. We may also learn that they are similar. In its current state, international human rights practice and theory has left little room to consider whether or not cross-border practices change meaning when transported to another context—such that a practice can simultaneously be seen to violate human rights in one country context but not in another. Questions about these narrow sets of practices (i.e., brought from one country to another by migrants) get swallowed up by the larger debate about whether all human rights are universal or culturally relative.

Universality has largely won the day in international human rights law and practice. Today, international human rights organizations are reluctant to deviate from the principle of universality because (among other things) it gives their positions great moral authority. They may also feel uncomfortable taking conflicting positions on the same practice (e.g., that veil bans are appropriate in one country, but not in another). Scholars and advocates resist deviating from universality as it implies the acceptance of cultural relativism, the only other alternative currently available. Thus, the thrust of international human rights discourse also leaves little room for finding that a practice is a human rights violation in one context, but not in another. In the next section, I outline a context-based feminist proposal to evaluate whether or not a practice that raises women's rights concerns in one context also contravenes women's rights when it is practiced in another country context.

Transnational Feminist Legal Approach to Cross-Border Practices

As Professors Bowman and Schneider explain, there is a deep engagement and positive feedback between feminist legal theory and lawmaking. Feminist legal theory was used to push for changes in laws to guarantee equality in the 1960s and beyond.[112] For example, feminist arguments that pregnancy was an issue of gender equality led to new legislation known as the Pregnancy Discrimination Act.[113] Litigation strategies and advocacy were also reflected in the work of feminist legal theorists. Catharine MacKinnon's book, *Sexual Harassment of Working Women*, reiterates the legal theories about the harms of sexual harassment that had already been litigated by feminist lawyers.[114]

Liberal equality theory, dominance theory, and cultural feminism each had an important role in addressing and changing different types of discriminatory laws or in pushing for the enactment of laws to address women's inequality where there were none before. Each of the strands of legal feminist theory was used to evaluate a law for the purpose of determining whether or not it promotes women's position in relation to men's position. While theorists might disagree about whether or not a law promotes women's equality based on their perspective, their categories of analysis were typically men and women. Anti-essentialist feminist theorists soon pointed out that "women" as a category was too broad in conducting this type of legal analysis—it included women of many races, sexualities, and so on. Consequently, they argued that just because a law was thought to enhance equality for one group did not mean it would have that same impact on another group. I believe that to assume that similar policies would promote equality for women who are living in multiple country contexts is also to essentialize women.

Since the evolution of American feminist legal theory, the foreign-born population in the United States has grown significantly from fewer than 4.7% in 1970 to 13.1% in 2013.[115] Migration is on the rise globally as well. Three times the number of people live outside their birth country in 2016 than did in 1960.[116] Migrant-receiving countries are increasingly adopting regulations to address the behavior (or perceived behavior in the case of sex selection) of women immigrants and their progeny. Often knowledge of the practice as it is carried out in a foreign country informs policy decisions in migrant-receiving countries. But this knowledge is far from complete—it is packaged into sound bites sometimes filtered through stereotypes about the power dynamics between men and women in some foreign countries.

Feminist legal theory was created and evolved in the context of the United States. Liberal feminists pushed for facially gender-neutral laws and thought they would serve to equalize women's position vis-à-vis men's. Dominance feminism, on the other hand, is highly sensitive to the impact of a particular law in the context where it is adopted. Yet its methodology still calls for examining only the context where the law was adopted. Similarly, law and society scholars have long argued that context is important in understanding how law has developed, how it is enforced, and how it changes.[117] But their focus generally was also on the context where the law was proposed to be adopted and not on any other context.

Cross-border practices push us to examine contexts beyond the one where a law is being proposed to be adopted. In understanding cross-border practices, I argue we must gain a better understanding of the country context where the practices originate through in-depth empirical analysis. It is only through broadening our gaze to these multiple contexts that we can recognize how practices change meaning with context. Professor Bennoune as well as the critics of governance feminism recognize that context can radically change the human rights impact of a practice and therefore the legal response to a practice should differ depending on the circumstances. For example, a practice like the veil, according to Bennoune, should be banned to promote women's equality in one context, but need not be banned in another context for that reason.

Another theoretical lens that informs how social justice advocates understand cross-border practices is international human rights law. There is a growing movement in the United States to use international human rights norms and accountability mechanisms to push for social change.[118] Nongovernmental organizations increasingly participate in UN institutions by writing shadow reports, hosting panels and speakers alongside major UN conferences, and writing reports that utilize international human rights laws and norms. In other countries like France, which I discuss in Chapter 7, regional human rights conventions provide an even stronger basis for individuals to challenge domestic laws.

While American feminist legal theory would focus on the context where a regulation is being considered, in evaluating cross-border practices through the lens of international human rights law, one might be tempted to focus on the context of the country of origin of the migrant. The universal perspective of rights suggests that once it is determined that a practice violates human rights in one context, it will be a rights violation (since rights are constant across geographies) when it emerges in another context. Indeed, the UN's major policies on sex-selective abortion address it only in contexts where it first emerged like China and India and not in the United Kingdom or the United States where migrants from Asia are thought to practice it.[119] The international human rights perspective does not necessarily encourage scholars and policymakers to deeply examine the migrant-receiving country context in evaluating regulations on cross-border practices.

On the other hand, the insights of the field of transnational law can be used to draw attention to the importance of both the migrant-receiving and migrant-sending context in evaluating whether a regulation on immigrant women's behavior will promote equality or contravene it.[120] Since Philip Jessup conceptualized "transnational law" in 1956, a vast literature within that field has emerged.[121] Harold Koh's insightful article explains that transnational legal process is the interaction of domestic norms with international norms.[122] Carrie Menkel-Meadow describes "transnational law" as the study of legal phenomena, including lawmaking processes, rules, and legal institutions, that affect or have the power to affect behaviors beyond a single state border.[123] The concept encompasses a growing web of global connections. Transnational law, however it is defined, is certainly distinct from international law, which governs the relationships between states/countries.

In a way it may be fruitless to attempt to define the substance of transnational law. Professor Zumbansen's recent work describes transnational law more as a methodology. He notes:

> Going beyond early work in international legal theory and partly drawing on the insights from transnational commercial law, we can begin to understand transnational law primarily as a methodological approach and less as a distinctly demarcated legal field, such as contract or administrative law. Transnational law, from this perspective, emerges foremost as a methodological lens through which we can study the particular transformation of legal institutions in the context of an evolving complex society.[124]

Drawing on this understanding of transnational law, I propose a transnational feminist legal methodology. This methodology provides a way to sort through questions about women's equality on a global scale. It proposes a global framework that can be utilized to provide local solutions. Professors Knop, Michaels, and Riles's proposal was also to develop a feminist methodology to resolve the debate they describe as one between equality and multiculturalism. Although I frame the debate differently than they do, like them I do not come up with a resolution to the debate but rather develop a methodology for evaluating what equality means in relation to cross-border practices.[125] I call it a feminist methodology because it focuses on women in evaluating the competing rights that are often in question in bans on immigrant women's behavior.

When people, practices, and knowledge move across borders fluidly and quickly, we need to consider multiple contexts to design appropriate regulations to these cross-border practices. As noted above, American feminist legal theory might point to one context (the country of destination of the immigrant) while international human rights law may suggest another (the country of origin of the immigrant). A transnational legal methodology, because of its emphasis both on the international and the domestic/local, —encourages us to focus on multiple contexts in evaluating a ban in one country. Transnational law highlights the interactions of domestic laws and contexts in the increasingly global web of connections among people, corporations as well as goods, services, and knowledge.

To evaluate whether or not a practice is discriminatory or oppressive to women in the migrant-receiving country, we must examine that context. Social institutions, historic subjugation and inequality, and other factors give meaning to the practice as discriminatory to women. Researchers should investigate why the practice is considered to be discriminatory or repressive to women. Is it because the practice is widespread or is it because of unequal social institutions? What are the social institutions that reflect gender inequality? In addition, the scope and magnitude of the practice should be determined.

In order to properly understand the human rights consequences of a practice as it emerges in a new country, I suggest also studying the practice in the context where it first emerged. How widespread is the practice migrant-sending country? What are the individual motives of the women who undertake it? What societal institutions contribute to the practice? As I have noted, perceptions about cross-border practices are informed by knowledge often channeled through the sound bites of media rather than by in-depth studies in the country of destination of the migrant.

After understanding the practices in the two contexts (the migrant-receiving country and migrant-sending country), I propose a comparative study of these contexts. Do women undertake the practice at the same rate in both countries? Do the same social institutions give rise to the practice in the country of origin of the migrant exist in the country of destination? What (if any) societal factors present in the migrant-receiving country that give rise to the practice are absent in the migrant-sending country? Are there different factors in the migrant-receiving country that explain the reasons for the practice? Through this comparative study, we can better determine the human rights impact of the cross-border in the migrant-receiving countries.

Both quantitative and qualitative approaches are necessary to understand the practice in context. Even though traditionally feminist scholars had rejected quantitative methodologies,[126] I embrace them and structure my own research in a way that takes into account the criticisms of the critical race scholars in regard to quantitative empirical study. Ascertaining the scope of the practice (i.e., how many migrants actually undertake the act) can best be done by quantitative methodologies. On the other hand, qualitative methods help understand the reasons why people engage in an act. The intent behind a person's behavior is relevant to determine whether or not their behavior is discriminatory or violates human rights. To the extent that we can get honest responses, the best way to ascertain motives for behavior is by asking the people who undertake the behavior. This can be done through individual interview-based methods or through surveys of people that are representative of the entire group. Researchers may fail to undertake this survey-based research if they believe that the motives of immigrants in undertaking cross-border practices are the same as the motives for people who undertake similar practices in the country of origin of the immigrant.

Looking at the practice across multiple contexts helps to ascertain its human rights implications and also makes it possible to develop a legal test that can be used to evaluate bans across borders. The legal test should be transnational in its applicability, but must also be able to be used locally to implement solutions suitable to the context. Unlike universalist approaches, a transnational feminist legal approach is open to this possibility that a practice that appears to be harmful or discriminatory to women in one country context may not have that impact in another country context.

From an in-depth study of the context of the foreign country, it may also become clear that the knowledge and information about the foreign country is itself distorted. Knowledge is channeled through sound bites and stereotypes of foreign cultures as misogynist. In this narrative, women in some foreign countries are believed to be forced by men to undertake the practice and are viewed as being unable to make their own decisions or participate in any way in the decision-making process. Using comparative and empirical analyses, we gain accurate information about the multiple contexts in which a practice emerges.

My proposal is a pragmatic and realist approach that argues that a cost/benefit analysis be undertaken when there are competing rights at stake. When two competing rights are at stake, weighing the costs and benefits of bans may sometimes lead to the most meaningful solutions. The transnational feminist legal approach sees women's rights through the global lens rather than the parochial domestic lens, but also proposes solutions that can be utilized in domestic policymaking.

The consequences of failing to contextualize and compare are grave. Policymakers will inaccurately understand and weigh the competing rights at stake in banning women's practices. By emphasizing harms caused by a practice in another country, policymakers will overestimate the benefits of banning it in their own country. As a result, they undervalue the costs of a ban. Additionally, by relying on decontextualized explanations, policymakers fail to investigate the unique reasons and consequences of certain practices undertaken by immigrants. If policymakers examine the context in which the practice occurs and resist relying on the behavior and motives of people in other countries and the harms caused by practices in other countries, they will adopt policies that are more fair. If they do not, then they will adopt laws that harm women's rights rather than promote them.

This book utilizes the transnational legal feminist methodology proposed in this section to evaluate bans on one cross-border practice—sex-selective abortion—from the perspective of women's equality. Using the general principles of a transnational feminist legal approach that I articulated above, I develop a specific legal framework to assess bans on sex-selective abortion in Chapter 2. The goal of this legal test is to determine whether or not a ban on sex-selective abortion in any given context will promote women's equality. My proposal is a feminist framework because it places women and girls at its center. I argue that the competing rights at stake in legal prohibitions on sex-selective abortion are the reproductive rights of women, on the one hand, and the harm that the widespread practice can cause to women as a group, on the other hand. The approach is contextual because it requires an evaluation of the way the practice is undertaken and its consequences in the geographic context where it is emerges. Under the framework, a ban might promote women's rights on the whole in one country, but restrict it in another country.

In developing an approach to evaluate bans on sex-selective abortion, I engage with the spectrum of ethical views on the subject. Some oppose sex-selective abortion because they oppose abortion altogether. According to that perspective, no woman should have the right to an abortion, except in rare cases such as if it is necessary to save her life. Anti-abortion advocates see sex-selective abortion as sex discrimination against the fetus. Liberal feminists argue that sex-selective abortion should not be banned in any country since it impedes women's autonomy. At the same time, they also believe that sex-selective abortion reflects discrimination in society against women and girls. Other feminists argue that while it should not be prohibited, it is morally problematic because those who obtain sex-selective abortions fail to acknowledge the distinction between gender and sex. Those who advocate for the right to procreative liberty argue that parents should be permitted to select (including by in-vitro fertilization and sperm-sorting) the appropriate gender balance of their families. I do not support the practice nor do I support a right to sex-select, but rather view the bans to be problematic because (among other things) they burden women's ability to exercise the right to choose for non–sex selection purposes.

To contextualize the practice, I use evidence-based empirical methodologies to understand immigrant behavior and motives. In furtherance of this, I have collaborated with economists to examine sex ratios of Asian Americans. Contrary to popular belief, we found that sex selection among this group is very limited and nowhere near the scale found in India. In addition, a few Asian Americans appear to have a preference for family balancing rather than just a son preference. These findings are discussed in greater detail in Chapter 4.

Furthermore, as noted above a transnational legal feminist approach calls for a comparative and detailed examination of the situation not only in the country of destination of the immigrant, but also in their country of origin. In Chapter 5, I closely examine the practice of sex-selective abortion in India and its potential harm to demonstrate the fallacy of the "coercion narrative" and to argue that the harm in India of sex-selective abortion is on women as a group. Abortion of female fetuses by individual women on a massive scale has led to a sex ratio imbalance. This has led to a surplus of unmarried men in India. A sex ratio imbalance threatens to harm living women—for example, by increasing violence against women. In Chapter 6, I apply the transnational feminist legal framework to sex-selective abortion bans to conclude that the bans in the United States serve only to restrict reproductive rights and could also lead to other negative consequences without any potential benefits for the rights of women and girls.

The principles of a transnational feminist legal approach I articulate here are relevant to evaluating not only sex-selective abortion bans but also other bans on practices of immigrants in migrant-receiving countries that are thought to be harmful to women. In Chapter 7, I demonstrate how the debates on the full-face veil in France also made decontextualized arguments in support of the bans and failed to examine the harms in context. Using an evidence-based contextualized feminist approach to the question of veil bans in France would lead to better legal decision-making.

CHAPTER 2

Transnational Legal Feminist Approach to Sex-Selective Abortion

In contrast to the universal approach to human rights in Chapter 1, I proposed a context-based transnational feminist legal approach that suggests that we should be open to the possibility that a practice that is discriminatory or otherwise harmful to women's rights in one country may not necessarily be contrary to women's rights when undertaken in another country.

In this chapter, I develop a legal framework to evaluate bans on sex-selective abortion that is animated by the principles of the transnational legal feminist approach developed in the prior chapter. This approach to sex-selective abortion is transnational because it is useful to examine bans on sex-selective abortion that exist across multiple jurisdictions. I argue that a country should prohibit sex-selective abortion or sex determination tests only to the extent that women in that society are practicing sex selection in a way that harms other women and girls living in that society. I agree with liberal feminists that prohibitions on sex-selective abortion burden reproductive rights and can have unintended negative consequences like restricting abortion access more generally. However, I argue that the restrictions may be justifiable in certain contexts. It is appropriate to limit sex selection in countries where there is evidence that sex selection is so widespread that it is harming other women and girls. But where such negative consequences from sex selection are not present, then bans serve no purpose in promoting women's rights.

In the section "Reproductive Rights of Individual Women and Harm to Women and Girls in Society," below, I develop a legal framework drawing insights from the transnational feminist legal approach proposed in Chapter 1. I explain how my framework builds upon existing feminist and nonfeminist approaches to sex-selective abortion in the section "Ethical and Legal Perspectives on Sex-Selective Abortion." Next, I provide an overview of "International and Comparative Laws." I conclude in the section "Operationalizing a Transnational Feminist Legal Approach to Sex Selection" by describing some of the challenges in applying my proposal to sex-selective abortion. I then propose methods to overcome those challenges.[1]

Reproductive Rights of Individual Women and Harm to Women and Girls in Society

In Chapter 1, I explained that prevailing feminist legal theories take a universal position on cross-border practices. If a practice is thought to be contrary to women's equality in one country, feminists (as well as non-feminists) assume it will have a similar impact in another country. In line with this view, liberal feminists take a universal position toward sex-selective abortion—it should not be prohibited in the United States or in any other country. They generally view prohibitions on sex-selective abortion as a burden on a woman's right to terminate her pregnancy. They refuse to deviate from this view even in countries like India where many women obtain sex-selective abortions to the detriment of other Indian girls and women living in that country.

I agree with the liberal feminist position that restrictions on sex-selective abortion impinge on women's reproductive liberties. However, unlike the liberal universal feminist position, I argue for a perspective that allows for certain restrictions on sex-selective abortion—for example, restrictions on sex determination tests—if the practice harms girls and women in a particular society. When many women in a country abort female fetuses to give birth to sons, a surplus of men results. An excess of men and shortage of women can have negative consequences for the women and girls in that society.

Indeed, emerging empirical studies about sex selection in India have concluded that a shortage of women is associated with an increase in violence against women. On the other hand, studies suggest that some women are able to marry into higher castes and social classes when there is a shortage of women. I discuss these consequences in greater detail in Chapter 6 when I evaluate the situation in India in light of the legal framework I propose here.

April Cherry, an American law professor, first articulated the need to consider how the practice of sex selection harms women as a group. Cherry states that "[m]y construction of a radical feminist analysis moves away from a view of the procedure as one of individual choice, and acknowledges sex-selection as an issue affecting women as a class."[2] While Cherry does not explicitly say so, it seems that she does not propose that sex-selective abortion should be banned, but denying women information about the sex of the fetus could be permissible in certain situations.[3] However, she does not go further to develop a framework or a feminist legal approach using those observations. Farhat Moazam also suggests that, in the context of India, a strategy that looks toward and utilizes the power of the state to further a wider goal of public welfare may have a more realistic chance of achieving gender equality than unbound reproductive autonomy.[4]

The approach I propose to sex selection also takes into account harm to women as a group and allows for limitations on individual autonomy if it promotes the well-being of the group. This view draws from the logic of public health regulations. Take the example of regulations on vaccinations for children. Many childhood diseases occur at low rates in the United States because parents are required to vaccinate their children. Some parents think that there are risks associated with vaccines, such as developing autism, and as a result they strongly oppose childhood vaccination.[5] If only a few parents fail to vaccinate their children, there will likely be no societal impact. However, if many parents refuse vaccinations for their children, then those childhood diseases that are now rare would become widespread again. This would harm the greater good of society. Therefore, to prevent harmful consequences for all children, state laws typically require children entering school to be vaccinated. Similarly, it is appropriate to place limitations on the individual's right to autonomy if—and only if—sex selection is being practiced in a way that harms women or has the potential to harm women in society as a whole.[6] Ruth Macklin, a biomedical ethicist, is among the few voices who have also suggested that the harm caused by sex selection should be decided through utilitarian methods rather than abstract thought.[7]

The challenge in operationalizing an approach that takes into account the consequences of a practice on women as a whole is how one determines whether sex selection is being practiced widely and whether it harms girls and women in a society. One way to measure the magnitude of sex selection is by reference to sex ratios in society. The sex ratio (the ratio of boys to girls) is an indicator of the level of sex selection. From looking at the at-birth sex ratios (if most births in the country are properly recorded) or the sex ratio of children (if the birth-recording system is inadequate), we can tell whether or not sex selection is widespread in that society. There is a genre of academic literature that discusses the consequences of imbalanced sex ratios in a society. In the section "Operationalizing a Transnational Feminist Legal Approach to Sex Selection," I describe several sex ratio theories in greater detail and assess their ability to accurately predict potential consequences of imbalanced sex ratios.

Another difficulty in applying the transnational feminist framework is how one determines when the harm to women and girls in a society is great enough to outweigh the costs. Any method that requires balancing costs and benefits is inherently challenging for the reasons I discuss in "Challenging, Justifying, and Operationalizing a Consequences-Focused Framework." Notwithstanding these problems, judges regularly articulate and apply balancing tests. Indeed, the Supreme Court of the United States did just that in *Whole Woman's Health*, its most recent case on abortion rights. It articulated the "undue burden standard" as a cost/benefit test.[8] The Court found that requiring doctors who perform abortions to have admitting privileges at local hospitals and requiring abortion clinics to meet the same stringent regulations as those imposed on surgical centers had too great a cost on a woman's right to access abortion and virtually no health benefit to women.

I call my framework "feminist" because it places women at the center. There are strong voices who oppose sex selection for reasons other than a concern for women's rights. Some authors believe sex selection should be prohibited because they think it is a slippery slope to other forms of manipulation of the traits of a child. Others oppose sex selection on the grounds that a fetus has the right to life under all circumstances. The framework I propose does not address positions that do not directly take women's rights into account. My framework is meant to determine whether or not a ban on sex-selective abortion is necessary to promote women's equality in any given society.

This framework is not formulated around the jurisprudence of any specific country. On the contrary, this feminist framework can be used to evaluate restrictions on sex-selective abortion in any country where access to abortion is otherwise legal. In many countries women have no right to obtain an abortion except to save their own life. The approach I propose would not be relevant to those countries.

In debates about the legality of abortion in the United States, the fetus's right to life is juxtaposed against the reproductive rights of the woman. This framing unconsciously seeps into discussions about prohibitions on sex-selective abortion even within feminist writings. Pro-choice feminists are reluctant to support any prohibitions on sex selection because they think such support would validate the view that fetuses and embryos have an independant right to life.

Indian feminist scholar Nivedita Menon's view exemplifies this dilemma. She writes:

> [W]e cannot hold simultaneously that abortion involves the right of women to control their bodies, but that women must be restricted by law from choosing specifically to abort female foetuses. We seem to be counterposing the rights of (future) women to be born against the rights of (present) women to control over their bodies.[9]

Based on her framing of rights, she concludes that sex-selective abortions and sex determination tests should not be prohibited.[10]

Observing the need for a new understanding of sex-selective abortion bans, Mallika Kaur Sarkaria argued that the way sex selection is practiced in India challenges the Western concept of "choice" and must be reevaluated from a global feminist perspective.[11] The framework I propose is a fundamental shift in feminist thinking about sex-selective abortion. Feminists are caught between a rock and a hard place in regard to sex selection—they want to preserve a woman's right to choose, and, at the same time, they do not want to take positions that suggest that a pre-viability fetus or embryo has a right to life. The approach I suggest resolves this tension by changing the parameters within which the debate has been occurring.

In line with the observations I made in Chapter 1 about the use and misuse of context in evaluating cross-border practices, policymakers, advocates, and others applying the transnational feminist approach should focus only on empirical evidence in the country context where the policy is proposed and resist drawing conclusions based on how sex-selective abortion is practiced in other countries. In the next section, I lay out the spectrum of existing ethical and legal positions for both pre-implantation sex selection and sex-selective abortion. In describing each viewpoint, I explain how my proposal builds upon or deviates from each position.

Ethical and Legal Perspectives on Sex-Selective Abortion

Parents have long tried to intervene to produce children of a specific sex. The list of advice to women on this front is nearly endless. Aristotle is said to have told women to lie on their right sides after intercourse to increase the chances of having a boy.[12] An ancient Egyptian manuscript states that if the face of a pregnant woman has a greenish cast, then she is certain to bear a son. More often than not, it was thought to be the woman's responsibility to produce a male heir. In some cultures, failure to do so gave rise to the husband's right to divorce the woman and marry another woman.[13] Even today in many parts of the world (such as India), women are ostracized if they do not produce a male heir. This occurs despite the fact that scientific evidence tells us that the sex of the embryo will be determined by whether an X-chromosome–bearing sperm or Y-chromosome–bearing sperm unites with the egg.[14] Women always contribute the X-chromosome, and as a result it is the man's sperm that determines the sex of the fertilized egg.[15]

Advocates as well as scholars from many disciplines have expressed strong and often conflicting views on sex selection. Some people urge for its legality, and others fiercely oppose it. Some would prohibit sex-selective abortion but would accept the use of pre-implantation technologies for sex selection. I discuss each of these viewpoints and how they diverge from or inform my proposal. While the perspectives I describe below are largely from American authors, I also draw on European and Indian perspectives. I discuss works by legal scholars, philosophers, and medical ethicists. I divide positions on sex selection into three broad categories: (1) feminist and women-centered perspectives, (2) anti-abortion views, and (3) eugenics concerns.

Feminist and Women-Centered Perspectives

Western Feminist Positions

With the advent of in vitro fertilization (IVF) and pre-implantation genetic diagnosis (PGD), a number of American feminists wrote about sex selection in the 1980s. They feared it would lead to a shortage of women in the United States. Some decried the practice because they believed it manifests sexism. Tabitha M. Powledge's view exemplifies this position:

> I want to argue that we should not choose the sexes of our children because to do so is one of the most stupendously sexist acts in which it is possible to engage. It is the original sexist sin. This argument applies to both pre- and post-conception technologies. To destroy an extant fetus for this reason is more morally opprobrious than techniques aimed at conceiving a child of a particular sex, but they both are deeply wrong. They are wrong because they make the most basic judgment about the worth of a human being rest first and foremost on its sex.[16]

Rosalind Petchesky also argued that it was "blatantly sexist" for a woman "to get an abortion on the grounds that they prefer a different gender."[17] Along these lines, Mary Warren, a strong proponent of a woman's right to abortion (including late-term abortions), simply maintained that it was morally wrong to "deprive a sentient human being of its life because of its sex," but not because she thought it was sexist to do so.[18]

In more recent feminist writing on sex selection, the view that the practice is inherently sexist still prevails. I identify three variants of feminist objections to sex selection. First, feminists informed by postmodern and queer theories oppose sex selection because it supports the idea of gender as a binary category—male or female. These activists have argued that sex selection is inherently sexist because the practice "reject[s] the idea that gender is fluid" and is premised on the assumption that "sex and gender can be classified into two distinct male and female forms."[19] This view draws on the fundamental principle of postmodern feminism that gender is socially constructed.[20] However, even if we assume that our ideal society is one where everyone believes that gender is fluid, preventing people from sex-selecting will do little to make people less sexist.

Second, another feminist argument against sex selection is that people who sex-select are more likely to force their children to conform to traditional gender expectations and roles. Berkowitz and Snyder have argued that parents who sex-select will have expectations that their children's behavior will conform to a specific gender.[21] Another commentator notes that "[i]f you're going through the trouble and expense to select a child of a certain sex, you're encouraging gender stereotypes that are damaging to women and girls . . . What if you get a girl who wants to play basketball?"[22] It is, however, inaccurate to assume all or most people who want to select for a certain sex desire to constrain their children to traditional and oppressive gender roles.

Another author posits that it is sexist for a man who has two girls to select for a boy just because the man thinks that a boy would give him certain pleasures like playing ball or fishing. This man is thought to be sexist because he assumes that he could not have those pleasures with girls.[23] Yet preventing this man from having a boy would not change his views and would not make it more likely that he would give his girl children more opportunities.

Let's take a few other examples. What if a woman who has two boys desires a girl because she wants to have someone to have manicures and pedicures with? Is that sexist? And would this harm the girl she gives birth to? Should parents who want two daughters so that they can grow up sharing a bond with each other be permitted to sex-select? Should two gay men who want to have a boy because they feel they could relate to him better be permitted to sex-select? These are harder and less clear-cut cases to resolve than the ones used by feminists who argue that sex selection is inherently sexist.

Third, some people argue that by sex-selecting, parents make a statement that one sex is superior to another. The American Congress of Obstetricians and Gynecologists opposes sex selection on these grounds. The organization concludes that even sex selection for family balancing purposes "violates the norm of equality between the sexes."[24] Incidentally, this association of American obstetricians and gynecologists justifies its policy position by reference to UN guidelines, which invariably only refer to countries where sex selection is practiced in favor of only boys. In societies where sex selection is practiced largely in favor of one sex, one could argue that this reflects a society that believes one sex is superior. On the other hand, in societies where parents select for both boys and girls in equal numbers, the practice does not necessarily violate the norm of equality between the sexes.

The feminists in the 1980s who vociferously claimed that sex selection is sexist argued with similar force that there should be no legal restrictions prohibiting it. This is because the push to make abortion legal was a prominent feature of the 1960s women's movement in the United States. Powledge argued that "[t]o make it illegal to use prenatal diagnostic techniques for sex choice is to nibble away at our hard-won reproductive control, control that I think most of us believe is the absolute rock-bottom minimum goal we have got to keep achieved before we can achieve anything else."[25] To be sure, feminists opposed these bans not because they viewed sex selection as a separate right, but rather because they thought of the bans as restrictions on abortion rights.[26]

Feminist authors writing in the 1980s did not have to contend with widespread sex-selective abortions in India and China. At that time, ultrasound technology was not widespread and as a result abortions of female fetuses were not that common even in India and China. Thus, their opposition to restrictions on sex-selective abortions were formulated before many people were aborting female fetuses. Nevertheless, even after women in India and other parts of the world started to sex-select in great numbers, liberal feminists continued to oppose limitations on sex selection under any circumstances. In the article "Sex Selection: Treating Different Cases Differently," Bernard Dickens, Rebecca Cook and their coauthors point out that there is an "ethical injustice" in treating sex selection in a place like Canada as if it is the same as in a country like India.[27] Consistent with my argument for contextualization of cross-border practices in Chapter 1, the authors argue that sex-selective abortion should not be regulated in Canada based on how the practice is undertaken in India.[28]

While the authors correctly suggest that sex selection in Canada should not be banned because it is not as widely practiced as in India, they also conclude that it should not be prohibited in India.[29] Their view about regulations in India seems to stem from a general opposition to any restrictions on reproductive rights. Instead of passing prohibitions on sex selection, they argue that the problem that should be addressed is discrimination against girls. While I too distinguish the situation in the United States from that in India, the framework I propose allows for the possibility of restrictions on sex-selective abortion where abortions of female fetuses are harming living women and girls.

In line with the liberal and universal feminist perspective, the Center for Reproductive Rights, a preeminent international reproductive rights organization, opposes sex selection bans in every country, including India.[30] Instead of regulating sex-selective abortion, it proposes the same solution articulated by Rebecca Cook, an honorary trustee of the center: The Indian government should focus on stopping discrimination against girls and women in society instead of limiting abortion rights.[31] Rachel Rebouché describes this perspective as the "anti-discrimination" approach.[32]

In the United States, two theoretical perspectives have been offered to justify abortion rights—the individual autonomy perspective and the equality rights perspective. *Roe v. Wade*,[33] the U.S. Supreme Court decision that prohibited states from restricting pre-viability abortion access, articulated a framework based on autonomy and privacy. Decisions about abortion are private, and abortion restrictions limit the exercise of individual autonomy rights.[34]

Starting in the 1980s, scholars began to justify abortion access in terms of equality. In an essay, Justice Ginsburg argued that the discussion about abortion "is not simply one between a fetus' interests and a woman's interests . . . [i]n the balance is a woman's autonomous charge of her full life's course . . . her ability to stand in relation to man, society, and the state as an independent, self-sustaining, equal citizen."[35] Drawing upon Catharine MacKinnon's work, Sylvia Law argued that abortion access should be protected under the equal protection clause because women's capacity to bear children is a significant biological difference between men and women.[36]

In *Planned Parenthood v. Casey*, the U.S. Supreme Court recognized equality-based arguments in favor of abortion access, though it still reaffirmed *Roe*'s privacy-based reasoning. The Court stated that the "ability of women to participate equally in the economic and social life of the Nation has been facilitated by their ability to control their reproductive lives."[37] In an article evaluating the constitutionality of restrictions on newly emerging prenatal testing techniques such as blood tests as well as the constitutionality of sex-selective abortion bans, legal scholar Jaime King argues for an individual autonomy-based approach.[38] Clearly, sex-selective abortion bans contravene women's rights to autonomy over their bodies.

On the other hand, bans on sex-selective abortion may seem consistent with equality-based arguments for abortion. A woman's right to equality does not appear to be jeopardized by being prevented from having a sex-selective abortion. However, if sex-selective abortion bans have the effect of negatively restricting abortion rights more broadly—and I argue in Chapter 6 that they do—then these bans do implicate women's equality rights. Thus, both liberty- and equality-based approaches to abortion dictate that sex-selective abortion bans burden reproductive rights.

Liberal feminists have been the most prolific feminist authors on sex-selective abortion in the United States. Yet, Catharine MacKinnon briefly discussed sex-selective abortion in a footnote in an article published in 1991. She argued that:

> [I]n a context of mass abortions of female fetuses, the pressures on women to destroy potential female offspring are tremendous and oppressive unless restrictions exist. While under conditions of sex inequality monitoring women's reasons for deciding to abort is worrying, the decision is not a free one, even absent governmental intervention, where a male life is valued and a female life is not.[39]

This quote suggests that she would favor restrictions on sex selection in a country like India. She would deviate from a universal approach to rights in the case of sex selection, but only because she believes that women in India are not able to freely exercise their reproductive rights anyway. Deviating from a universal application of rights requires her to declare a certain group of women as incapable of making freely informed decisions about their own bodies.

Indian Feminist Positions

In contrast to American liberal feminism, the Indian feminist response to sex-selective abortion was to push for legal regulations on reproductive rights. Indian feminists were troubled by the number of Indians aborting female fetuses and were disgusted by the publicly distributed advertisements for ultrasound services. These advertisements encouraged consumers to pay a small amount for a sonogram to detect the sex of the fetus so that they would save a larger amount in dowry by aborting a female fetus.[40]

The anti–sex selection law in India was adopted in 1994 as a result of feminist activism. The Indian law prohibits medical professionals from revealing the sex of the fetus to women; it does not directly prohibit abortion for sex-selective purposes.[41] In India, the right to abortion is not as contested as it is in the United States. Unlike in the United States where strong feminist activism surrounded abortion legalization, the Indian Parliament legalized abortion mainly for population control purposes. Nor is there today a strong movement in India to ban abortion. Consequently, feminists in India do not as cautiously guard the right to choose as do feminists in the United States. Thus, access to abortion is not generally at the center of Indian feminist activism.

Legislation in India prohibits medical professionals from revealing to the pregnant woman the future sex of her fetus. This anti–sex selection law appears to be a compromise—it sought to reduce the number of abortions of female fetuses while having the least impact on the right of a woman to terminate her pregnancy. Although there are some dissenters in India, there is no strong voice calling for the repeal of the existing bans on sex determination. Nevertheless, there is reason to question the Indian ban. Are those restrictions consistent with a woman's right to information about her body? How are the restrictions on sex-selective abortions impacting abortion rights more broadly? I discuss these questions in Chapters 5 and 6.

Sex Selection as a Procreative Liberty Right

While most liberal feminists object to bans on sex-selective abortion, they do not believe there should be an affirmative right to sex-select. American legal scholar John Robertson, however, takes a stronger position on sex selection, particularly pre-implantation sex selection. Robertson's notion of "procreative liberty" includes the right to select the sex of one's children.[42]

Starting from the position of the primacy of individual autonomy rights, he argues that "individuals should be free to use [reproductive] techniques or not as they choose, without governmental restriction, unless strong justifications for limiting them can be established."[43] In his book, he examines seven major reproductive technologies and does not find any justification to limit any of them. In respect to sex selection, he argues that "[e]ven gender selection might be acceptable [through PGD and IVF] because the expense and burdens of [the] practice make it unlikely that [PGD and IVF] would ever be so widespread as to alter societal sex ratios—a main concern with gender selection."[44]

In his more recent work, Robertson explicitly states that using PGD to achieve gender variety in a family should be permissible.[45] Guido Pennings points out that family balancing is an acceptable goal because "[t]he pleasure and happiness generated by the variety of having both boys and girls can be considerable."[46] He further argues that being a parent of children of both sexes brings different and more diverse experiences. For example, he writes, "the presence of siblings of the other sex might promote mutual understanding among children."[47] Some authors have argued that it is preferable for women to use sperm sorting and PGD rather than aborting female fetuses.[48] But only the very rich can afford IVF and PGD.

Other scholars have argued that a parent's right to reproductive liberty includes the ability to discriminate in the choice of their children, including selecting for traits that they prefer.[49] These scholars start with the presumption that in liberal democracies citizens should be free from government interference unless there is sufficient justification for state regulation.[50] Individuals who seek sex selection services tend to justify their position with libertarian notions of privacy.[51]

Many authors strongly oppose the procreative liberty approach to sex selection. One author believes that pre-implantation sex selection should be banned altogether because of the symbolic harm caused by parents who sex-select.[52] Another author suggests that pre-implantation sex selection devalues reproduction and parenting.[53] Yet another author argues that pre-implantation sex selection should be banned because it perpetuates gender stereotypes, is a slippery slope to designer babies, and misallocates medical resources.[54] Similarly, I do not support an affirmative right to sex-select. Instead, my approach would allow for restrictions on pre-implantation sex selection if it were being practiced by people in society in a way that was harmful to women and girls living in a particular society.

Other Feminist Positions on Sex Selection

Another feminist approach to sex selection suggests that people, particularly in societies where there is a strong desire for a boy child, should be allowed to sex-select for a boy in order to save unwanted girls from abuse. Christine Hicks argues that an unwanted girl child in places like India "will face [a] higher likelihood of abuse, infant death, starvation, sexual exploitation, human trafficking. . . . She is more likely to be sold into slavery for domestic exploitation. She is more likely to be abused and enslaved at every level, if she is born. She is more likely to be killed."[55] These predictions conflate the circumstances faced by all girls born into poverty with the circumstances of those girls who were specifically not desired by their parents. While these predictions may be true for girls who are born in dire poverty, they are not likely to materialize in middle-class families. Indeed, contrary to these predictions, one study has shown that infant mortality of girls in India did not increase when bans were placed on sex determination tests.[56] Though perhaps other discriminatory practices toward unwanted girls persist.

Religious-based Views on Sex Selection

A major religious-based movement in the United States strongly opposes abortion on the basis that it harms sentient beings. Though viewpoints in the movement fall along a spectrum, there is general agreement that aborting a fetus is wrong because it involves the killing of a life or a potential life.[57] People with this perspective support bans on sex-selective abortion because they support bans on all abortion. Many who espouse this viewpoint also believe that sex selection using reproductive technologies is wrong. The traditional Catholic perspective is that sperm sorting and PGD are problematic because they:

> entrust the life and identity of the embryo into the power of doctors and biologists and [establish] the domination of technology over the origin and destiny of the human person. Such a relationship of domination is itself contrary to the dignity and equality that must be common to parents and children.[58]

Even people who do not broadly oppose abortion argue that sex selection is problematic because it is like "playing God."[59] By this, people might mean that those who sex-select assert their arrogance by controlling things they should not.[60] However, one could argue that giving a sick child medicine is also like playing God. If the natural course of events were followed, then the nonmedicated child could have died. But no one objects to giving that child medicine on the grounds that giving medicine is like "playing God." Indeed, in some cases, the government would intervene if medication were not given to a dying child by his or her parents. But these two cases are not exactly alike—one involves using modern medicine to save a life while the other involves using medical technology to further a mere preference.

Advocates for sex-selective abortion prohibitions in the United States argue that the right at stake is not the right to be born, but the right of the fetus to be free from discrimination.[61] The problem with this position (among other things) is that neither the U.S. Constitution, international human rights, nor any other law that I am aware of recognizes a fetus's right to be free from discrimination.

Moreover, most international human rights treaties do not even recognize the right to life of the fetus. There is one notable exception—the American Convention of Human Rights (American Convention), whose signatories include many Latin and Central American countries that ban abortion altogether. The American Convention states that "[e]very person has the right to have his life respected. This right shall be protected by law and, in general, from the moment of conception."[62] But even this treaty does not indicate that a fetus has the right to be free from discrimination. Notably, the Inter-American Court of Human Rights (the body that interprets the American Convention) narrowed the application of this provision by finding that this provision does not preclude a country from providing legal access to abortion.[63]

Anti-abortion advocates might argue that fetal protection laws in the United States provide a basis for claiming that a fetus has a right to be free from discrimination. Those laws subject pregnant women to criminal penalties if they intentionally physically harm their fetuses. For example, a woman who is a drug addict would be criminally charged if the fetus was harmed from the drug use.[64] However, fetal protection laws do not restrict women from obtaining abortions. They protect fetuses to the extent that a woman (who otherwise wants to have a child) harms a fetus. Thus, they provide no basis for arguing that a woman who obtains a sex-selective abortion impinges on a fetus's right to be free from discrimination.

No court or other source of law that I am aware of has found that a fetus has the right to be free from discrimination. Indeed, in a concurring opinion, Justice Stevens has noted that "no Member of [the Supreme Court] has ever suggested that a fetus is a 'person' within the meaning of the Fourteenth Amendment," which would entitle the fetus to equal protection of the law.[65] Consequently, the fetus has no more of a legal right to be free from discrimination than it has a right to free exercise of religion. Recognizing a right of a fetus to be free from discrimination would grant full personhood status to the fetus and also open the door to a host of other reason-based abortion restrictions.

Eugenics Concerns

Another set of concerns about sex selection relates to eugenics. Sex selection is seen as a slippery slope to using of technology to create a "custom baby."[66] PGD is a technique whereby embryos are tested in a lab to determine whether or not they have certain traits. Selected embryos are then implanted in the uterus through in vitro fertilization (IVF).[67] PGD has been traditionally used for medical reasons such as testing the embryo for certain genetic defects, but it can be used for sex selection and has the potential to be used for nonmedical trait selection as well.[68]

Although in the United States there are no limitations on the use of PGD and IVF, an international treaty in Europe specifically addresses those techniques. The European Convention on Human Rights and Biomedicine of 1997 (Oviedo Convention) bans IVF for the purpose of choosing the sex of a child "except where serious hereditary sex related disease is to be avoided."[69] According to one commentator, the rationale behind this position is that choosing a child's sex turns the procreative process into a consumer experience and encourages the commodification of children.[70] Thus, the European perspective sees sex selection through the lens of eugenics—it is another form of (unacceptable) trait selection. Trait selection is problematic for a number of reasons, including the fact that certain traits would be discriminated against in favor of other traits, leading to a world of homogenous people.[71]

I disagree with the stance that other forms of trait selection would inevitably result if sex selection were permitted. It is possible to narrowly tailor the use of PGD and IVF for certain purposes while prohibiting it for other purposes. There may be other reasons to support bans on sex selection, but I do not think that the slippery-slope concern should be one of them. In this section, I have explained how my legal framework to sex selection builds upon and deviates from existing scholarly ethical and legal approaches. In the following section, I describe the international and comparative legal approaches to sex-selective abortion.

International and Comparative Laws

There is significant debate and confusion in United Nations documents and discussions about whether or not bans on sex-selective abortion are consistent with women's rights. Statements by the United Nations and other intergovernmental organizations simultaneously suggest that prohibiting sex-selective abortion impinges on women's rights, on the one hand, and that permitting it is discriminatory to women, on the other hand.

The mainstream perception in the United States is that most countries around the world explicitly prohibit sex-selective abortion. In an article covering the defeat of the federal sex-selective abortion ban in 2012, the *Washington Post* notes that "[s]everal nations, including Canada, the United Kingdom, Germany and France, ban sex-selective abortions."[72] However, none of these countries have adopted such restrictions.[73] They only restrict pre-implantation sex selection.

Proponents of sex-selective abortion bans in the United States also do their part to perpetuate this inaccurate view. Testimony during congressional hearings on an earlier version of the bill now pending in the U.S. Congress centered on the claim that a ban on sex-selective abortion was necessary to conform to international standards.[74] The preamble to that bill states "the United States may effectively function as a 'safe haven' for those who seek to have American physicians do what would otherwise be criminal in their home countries—a sex-selection abortion, most likely late-term."[75] However, only a few countries ban sex-selective abortion. Countries regulate sex selection in one of five different ways, all of which I describe in this section.

International Law and Policies: The Unresolved Tension Between Norms

Numerous bodies within the United Nations and other intergovernmental organizations have decried the practice of sex-selective abortion in India and other countries where a disproportionate number of female fetuses are aborted. Referred to as "gender-biased sex selection," sex-selective abortion was identified as a problem at the International Conference on Population and Development, which was held in 1994.[76]

The main legal hook for policy discussions on sex selection at the United Nations is the Convention on the Elimination of All Forms of Discrimination Against Women (CEDAW). CEDAW is the core women's rights treaty and has been ratified by all of the countries in the world except for a few, such as the United States.[77] Sex selection was not a widespread practice at the time the treaty was enacted in 1979. Thus, CEDAW offers no clear guidance on whether or not sex selection should be prohibited. Some treaty language has been used to support bans, while other treaty language suggests that such bans are not permissible.

One provision in CEDAW requires countries to "take all appropriate measures . . . [t]o modify the social and cultural patterns of conduct of men and women, with a view to achieving the elimination of prejudices and customary and all other practices which are based on the idea of the inferiority or the superiority of either of the sexes or on stereotyped roles for men and women."[78] But this language should not be interpreted so broadly as to require a country to enact laws prohibiting every practice that reflects prejudice or is based on the idea that boys are superior to girls.

Suppose a man thinks women are inferior to men and refuses to talk to them for that reason. This is a manifestation of gender discrimination, but few (if any) jurisdictions would force the man to talk to women. Forcing someone to change that private behavior seems to be going too far. Moreover, any law that would force the man to talk to women would contravene the man's right to talk (or not to talk) to whomever he wanted. Thus, not all practices that manifest gender discrimination are (or should be) prohibited.

Legal scholars Sherry Colb and Michael Dorf give an example along these lines in their recent book. They analogize sex-selective abortion to the sexual behavior of a racist person. They point out that if someone doesn't want to have sex with a person because of their race, then that is immoral and offensive, but not illegal (nor should it be).[79] They argue that even if aborting a fetus for sex-selective purposes is immoral and offensive, that does not mean it should be prohibited.

While the provision of CEDAW that calls for the broad elimination of discrimination suggests that sex-selective abortions should be prohibited, especially in countries where it is being used in a gender-biased manner, another section of CEDAW can be used to challenge any restrictions on sex-selective abortions. The introduction to the Convention (which is not binding) states that the "[c]onvention . . . affirms women's right to reproductive choice." Notably, it is the only human rights treaty to mention family planning. With the goal of pushing the U.S. Senate to ratify CEDAW, some have argued that CEDAW does not call for legalization of abortion.[80] But, its introduction suggests otherwise, and a number of other provisions suggest women should have access to family planning.[81]

Without any explicit treaty provision relating to the topic, much policy confusion has ensued at the international level on sex-selective abortion bans. The tension between restricting gender-biased abortion on the grounds that it is discriminatory, on the one hand, and a woman's right to access safe and legal abortion, on the other hand, plays out in an interagency statement issued by five intergovernmental agencies—including UN Women, Office of the High Commissioner for Human Rights, and the World Health Organization. It is one of the most authoritative documents on sex-selective abortion at the international level today.

The interagency statement frames sex-selective abortion as a form of gender discrimination. It states that "[i]mbalanced sex ratios are an unacceptable manifestation of gender discrimination against girls and women and a violation of their human rights."[82] A committee that monitors compliance with another treaty, the International Covenant on Civil and Political Rights, supports this position. In one of its general comments, the committee notes that "[t]he subordinate role of women in some countries is illustrated by the high incidence of pre-natal sex selection and abortion of female fetuses."[83]

On the other hand, the interagency statement also cautions that restrictions on sex-selective abortion, sex determination tests, and other reproductive technologies limit access to safe abortion. The interagency statement states that: "Restricting access to certain reproductive technologies in order to prevent an imbalanced male-to-female ratio in a given society should not result in the curtailing of the human rights of women."[84] This suggests that sex-selective abortion bans impinge on the human rights of women at some level. The recommendations, however, are silent on the question of whether states should adopt laws prohibiting sex-selective abortion and/or sex detection.

Other committees appointed by the United Nations to monitor a country's compliance with other treaties have also sent mixed messages about how to address sex selection. Some UN commities take the standard antidiscrimination approach. They believe that sex-selective abortions motivated by son preference are best addressed by changing people's attitudes. For example, the committee that monitors compliance with the International Covenant on Economic, Social and Cultural Rights recently urged Armenia to "[a]dopt measures to expedite the elimination of discrimination against women and girls, in particular addressing practices and social norms fueling son preference [and sex-selective abortion]."[85] Other bodies have explicitly expressed support for legal restrictions on sex selection. In reviewing India's compliance with the Convention on the Rights of the Child, the Committee on the Rights of the Child encourages India to "ensure the effective implementation of the Pre-conception and Pre-natal Diagnostic Techniques Act so as to prevent sex-selective abortions and strengthen regulatory mechanisms."[86]

Intergovernmental organizations do not clarify the line between permissible and impermissible restrictions on reproductive rights and permissible and impermissible enforcement measures. This is, in part, because the existing treaties do not provide clear guidance on how to address sex-selective abortion. In addition, there is likely disagreement among the UN state representatives, committee members, and staff on whether or not a country should adopt legal restrictions on sex-selective abortion. To make matters worse, UN agencies and committees have addressed sex selection only in countries where it is practiced widely, like India, but do not specify that their recommendations should not be used to justify bans in countries like the United States, Canada, or the United Kingdom.

This lack of contextual clarity in UN statements and documents allows these statements to be misappropriated by advocates for sex-selective abortion bans in the United States.[87] For example, in support of a ban, the federal bill banning sex-selective abortion cites several UN precedents that discuss sex-selective abortion and claims that those statements support a ban in the United States. The bill notes:

> [A]t the 2007 United Nation's Annual Meeting of the Commission on the Status of Women, 51st Session, the United States delegation spearheaded a resolution calling on countries to condemn sex-selective

> abortion, a policy directly contradictory to the permissiveness of current United States law, which places no restriction on the practice of sex-selection abortion. The United Nations Commission on the Status of Women has urged governments of all nations "to take necessary measures to prevent . . . prenatal sex selection."[88]

The UN interagency statement on sex-selective abortion, UN committee reports, and other UN policy documents do not provide clear guidelines to determine whether or not a country should adopt legal measures to curb sex-selective abortions. These documents also fail to address the situation in countries where immigrants are accused of practicing it widely. This lack of contextual specificity allows these statements to be misappropriated and misused. Next I discuss legislative approaches to sex-selective abortion in countries around the world.

National Laws: From Prohibition to Permission

Laws on sex selection around the world fall into one of five categories. First, some countries prohibit abortion altogether, except when it is necessary to save the life of the pregnant woman.[89] Clearly, in these countries sex-selective abortion would not be allowed since abortion for any reason is illegal (except in a very narrow set of cases).

Second, a few countries prohibit sex detection, but do not explicitly prohibit sex-selective abortion. India and Nepal are examples of such legal regimes.[90] The rationale for these laws is that if parents do not know the sex of the fetus, they cannot abort it selectively.

Third, despite popular perception very few countries explicitly prohibit sex-selective abortion. Only four countries in the world today have such laws: China,[91] Kosovo,[92] Nepal,[93] and Vietnam.[94] In addition, nine states in the United States prohibit sex-selective abortion. Despite such a prohibition being proposed every year since 2012, the U.S. Congress has not adopted national legislation to ban sex-selective abortion. Reacting to what they perceive to be a widespread practice among immigrants, other immigrant-receiving countries, such as the United Kingdom,[95] have also considered bans.

Fourth, a number of countries ban sex selection using pre-implantation technology.[96] For example, in the United Kingdom, the Human Fertilisation and Embryology Act of 2008 bans tests on embryos to determine their future sex if the purpose of the test is to permit parents to advance a preferred gender composition of their children.[97] The code of practice released pursuant to this act clarified that even sperm sorting should not be used for this purpose.[98]

Many European countries have signed an international convention agreeing to prohibit nonmedical pre-implantation sex selection.[99] Restrictions on pre-implantation sex selection in this treaty are generally motivated by eugenics concerns and the fear of commercialization of the reproductive processes.

The fifth category of legal responses to sex selection is to permit it. Sweden is perhaps the only country in the world that explicitly permits the termination of a pregnancy based on the sex of the fetus.[100] The issue in Sweden arose when a woman who had two girls sought an abortion because she did not want to have another daughter. The Swedish Board of Health and Welfare found that the woman should be able to obtain an abortion because denying it would be inconsistent with the right to an abortion and her pregnancy was within the legal time period.[101] In sum, despite popular perception, only a few countries around the world ban sex-selective abortion, and bans are in effect only in places where there are severe sex ratio imbalances.

Developing the insights about context from Chapter 1, I articulated a feminist framework in the section on "Reproductive Rights of Individual Women and Harm to Women and Girls in Society" to evaluate whether or not restrictions on sex-selective abortion promote women's equality. In the section on "Ethical and Legal Perspectives on Sex-Selective Abortion," I analyzed existing ethical and legal approaches to sex-selective abortion as well as pre-implantation sex selection. In this section, I summarized the international and comparative legal frameworks on sex-selective abortion. In the next section, I discuss the challenges to operationalizing the consequences-based feminist framework I propose and ways to address them.

Operationalizing a Transnational Feminist Legal Approach to Sex Selection

Feminists who take the universal approach to reproductive rights generally oppose limitations on reproductive choice. This view assumes that a woman's right to choose is indivisible: one either has it or one does not. Yet laws regularly reflect compromises between competing positions and rights. The laws of many countries, for example, place limitations on abortion in recognition of the state's interest in protecting the fetus. For example, women have full choice before a certain time period after conception and no choice after that time.[102]

In the section on "Reproductive Rights of Individual Women and Harm to Women and Girls in Society," I provided a rough sketch of a new feminist framework that can be used to assist feminists, advocates, and policymakers in determining whether or not a country should ban sex selection to promote women's rights. This legal test can be used across multiple country jurisdictions. It proposes different policy prescriptions based on the circumstances. In one context, a ban might protect women's rights, while in other contexts bans may undermine women's rights on the whole.

The feminist framework I propose gives primary importance to women's reproductive rights and views limitations on these rights as problematic unless they benefit women as a group in other ways. While the debate on abortion rights in the United States pits the right of a woman to her reproductive capacity against the right of a fetus to life, I call for a different framing in respect to sex-selective abortion. My proposal places women's rights on both sides of the equation. I argue that we must balance individual women's reproductive rights against the consequences to women and girls of widespread sex selection in any given society.

There are a number of challenges to operationalizing a test that relies on an assessment of the consequences of sex selection as practiced in any given society. Philosopher Jeremy Williams opposes consequentialist approaches to sex-selective abortion precisely for that reason. Williams is correct to point out that the right to choose is difficult to reconcile with bans on sex-selective abortions. He illustrates his point through the following hypotheticals, which he believes cannot be distinguished:

> Sasha is single and on a low wage. Faced with a lack of affordable childcare, and of other forms of support for lone parents, she decides that she cannot afford to have a child.[103]
>
> Belinda and her husband are considering having their first baby, which they believe they can afford, without compromising their careers or relationship, to which they are already deeply committed. Belinda is told, however, that there is a 25% chance that any child of hers will have a serious disability. She fears that the additional strain that this outcome would place upon her and her husband could destroy their marriage.[104]

> Parminder and her husband live under cultural conditions in which girls are much more costly to raise than boys. Females are widely discriminated against in the labour market, and so cannot contribute significantly to the family economy. A daughter will continue to be a financial drain on her family until such time as a husband can be found for her. And even if or when this happens, the parents will be expected to provide a substantial dowry. Under these conditions, Parminder believes that she cannot afford to have a daughter. However, a son would be an asset, and she wants to have one.[105]

There is a common thread in the reasons each of these women want to have an abortion. Giving birth to a child will have financial repercussions—Sasha will be pushed further into poverty, Belinda would have to expend more resources to care for a child with a disability, and Parminder's family will have to pay more to raise a girl. For Williams, if Sasha is permitted to obtain an abortion, there is no justification for denying Belinda or Parminder one as well.[106]

If we focus only on the individual situation of these women, then I agree that it is hard to justify why Sasha and Belinda should have the right to choose, but not Parminder. But if we expand our analysis to include the practices of many women in society and the consequences of those practices, then there would be reasons to justify limiting Parminder's behavior. There are so many women like Parminder who are aborting female fetuses. The consequences of the actions of many women negatively impact other women in society in different ways.

Williams also believes that it is impossible to determine whether or not society will be better off by prohibiting sex-selective abortions. He thinks that limitations on son preference–based abortion will lead to the birth of more unwanted girls. As a result, he concludes, "it is difficult to know whether a prohibition on sex selection would lead to an improved state of the world, in consequentialist terms."[107]

Unlike Williams, my concern here is not whether society will be worse off or better off if sex-selective abortion were banned. My concern is whether women as a whole will be better or worse off. Williams is correct that there are a number of challenges in assessing the consequences of the practice of sex selection in any given country. In this section, I discuss several challenges to operationalizing the transnational feminist framework and ways to address them.

1. *How do we assess the magnitude of sex selection in any given country?*

The best—but not perfect—tool to determine whether parents are preselecting the sex of their children is at-birth sex ratios. In the American convention, the at-birth sex ratio is defined as the number of boys for every one girl. Under this convention, the standard range of sex ratios across the world is 1.03 to 1.07, which means that without any parental intervention there would be 1 girl born for somewhere between 1.03 to 1.07 boys. If the sex ratio is above 1.07, then more boys are born than naturally expected and we assume that parents are sex-selecting in favor of boys. If the sex ratio is below 1.03, then fewer boys are born than naturally expected and we assume that parents are sex-selecting in favor of girls.

However, there are limitations to what sex ratios reveal about sex selection behavior. If an equal number of people select for boys and girls, then the sex ratio would appear normal and it would not reveal the sex-selective behavior. In addition, we cannot tell from the at-birth sex ratio what means parents have used to preselect the sex of the child. Some could be using preimplantation means to sex selection such as sperm sorting and PGD and IVF and others may be obtaining sex-selective abortions.

2. *How do we determine the consequences of an imbalanced sex ratio?*

Once it appears that the at-birth sex ratio is severely imbalanced in any given society, then it is important to ascertain the consequences of such an imbalance. An imbalanced at-birth sex ratio may not have any societal impact for several decades after it is observed. One result of a male-biased sex ratio is that some men who are seeking female partners to marry will not be able to succeed in their goal. This problem will only emerge when the generation that experienced at-birth sex ratio imbalances comes of age.

Even if at-birth sex ratios appeared skewed for a number of years, one approach would be to wait until the consequences of widespread sex selection are observable before adopting any policy responses to the practice.[108] Another approach would be to immediately adopt a policy response if sex ratio theories predict that women as a group will be negatively impacted by a male-skewed sex ratio. Below I evaluate the plethora of theories predicting the impact of sex ratios and argue that the predictions of one theory are more in line with recent empirical data.

Some economists, using a crude economic theory of supply and demand, have argued that sex selection in favor of boys will enhance the worth of girls. Gary Becker, a Nobel Prize–winning economist, for example, argued that if there were fewer women relative to men, their value would increase. He thought that parents might even receive a bride price and would educate their daughters better in societies where there were fewer women than men.[109] With boundless faith in the market as the fixer of all problems, Becker also believed that the market would eventually eliminate male-biased sex selection. Focusing specifically on India, another economist also argues that natural market forces will enhance the status of women since scarcity of women will lead to higher desirability and lower dowries.[110] We will see in Chapter 6 that some of these predictions have proven to be true (dowry rates have decreased in areas with a high male surplus), but that there are also negative consequences of a male-biased sex ratio (e.g., violence against women increases).

Marcia Guttentag, a psychologist, developed a more sophisticated theory about the consequences of imbalanced sex ratios. In a manuscript completed by her husband (Paul Secord) after she died, she argued that male-skewed sex ratios would have a mixed impact on women.[111] Guttentag and Secord concluded that in societies with male-skewed sex ratios, women would be greatly valued. Men would respect women more, but would also use their structural power to restrict women's economic and political roles, and to encourage them to take on traditional roles as mothers and homemakers. More women would be married, but the age of marriage would decrease. Women would have lower literacy rates and less education.[112] On the other hand, in societies with female-skewed sex ratios, they predicted that women would lose bargaining power because commitment would become less important and more men would marry later or remain single.[113] Thus, as noted above they predicted mixed results for women in societies with a male surplus.

South and Trent tested Guttentag and Secord's thesis using data from 117 countries.[114] They analyzed the association between sex ratios and the percentage of women ages 15 to 44 who were married or living in a consensual union, the average age at which women marry, the total fertility rate, the divorce rate, the illegitimacy rate, the female literacy rate, the female labor-force participation, and the female suicide rate.[115]

When they considered every country together, they found limited support for the associations that Guttentag and Second's theory would predict. However, when South and Trent examined wealthy countries and poor countries separately, they found more consistent results. The results for developed countries were more in line with Guttentag and Secord's theory than the results for less developed nations.[116] In developing countries, the effects of sex ratio were weak and often not in the direction Guttentag and Secord's theory would predict. The only statistically significant association they found supporting the theory was that an oversupply of men was associated with less workforce participation among women. In economically developed countries, a surplus of men was associated with higher marriage rates, a higher fertility rate, a younger age of marriage, and lower rates of female literacy.[117] In other words, Guttentag and Secord's predictions held true for more developed countries but not for less developed countries. The findings of the South and Trent study strongly suggest that the impact of a male surplus will depend on the context.[118]

Feminist scholar Mary Ann Warren emphasized context in her sex ratio theory. She believed that a shortage of women would have a negative impact on women in societies where they do not have economic control. On the other hand, she believed that a shortage of women will empower women in countries where there is more equality.[119] Mary Warren's prediction takes into account the varying levels of structural inequalities that exist between men and women across different societies and countries in our world today. Thus, she thought that a surplus of men may benefit women in some countries and harm women in other contexts depending on the underlying social structure in the country. In evaluating the consequences of sex-selective abortion in India in Chapter 6, I argue that Mary Warren's approach is most consistent with the empirical data from India today.

Even when research demonstrates that sex selection in favor of boys in a society has a negative impact on women or we rely on sex ratio theories to help predict the impact, another major question arises in applying the legal test I propose: When is the harm or negative consequence great enough to justify impinging on women's reproductive rights?[120]

3. *When are harms to women and girls great enough to call for restrictions on individual women's reproductive rights?*

Once we assess the harms that sex selection is causing to women generally, those harms should be weighed against the reproductive rights of individual women. The harms must be great enough to outweigh the burden that restrictions on sex selection place on the reproductive rights of women. American legal scholar Jaime King proposes a similar balancing test for adjudicating the constitutionality of reason-based abortion bans, including sex-selective abortion bans. She proposes that while a woman's interest in procreative liberty and sex equality takes priority, it can be limited if the relevant state interests are strong enough.[121] The Supreme Court of the United States also recently articulated a balancing approach to abortion access in *Whole Woman's Health*.[122]

There are several challenges in applying any balancing test. Justice Scalia characterized the balancing of competing interests as an illusion. "[T]he scale analogy is not really appropriate," he wrote, "since the interests on both sides are incommensurate. It is more like judging whether a particular line is longer than a particular rock is heavy."[123] By this Justice Scalia means that balancing rights sometimes involves comparing apples to oranges. Another challenge is how we assess the impact on women overall when some women appear to be harmed and others benefit. Yet another concern with a balancing framework is that the outcome is strongly influenced by the subjective views of the person applying the test.

Notwithstanding its inherent challenges, the weighing of competing interests is a common practice in many jurisdictions. It is the task of judges and policymakers to engage in this kind of analysis. The framing I propose is more appropriate than current-knee jerk reactions in policy discussions in migrant-receiving countries that call for abortion bans simply because they have negative consequences in other countries. My proposal gives feminists a tool for assessing sex-selective abortion bans from a women-centered perspective.

Conclusion

In this chapter, I have proposed an approach that can be utilized to evaluate sex-selective bans across multiple contexts from the perspective of women's equality. The competing rights at stake in bans on sex-selective abortion are women's reproductive rights, on the one hand, and the consequences of sex selection, on the other hand. In considering impact, policymakers should evaluate (among other things) the magnitude of the practice and the motives of the people who practice it. In Chapters 3 and 4, I provide background on sex-selective abortion bans in the United States from a legal, political, and empirical perspective. In Chapter 5, I describe how and why the practice of sex selection became widespread in India. In each country, I describe the magnitude of sex-selective abortions, the reasons for them, and the potential harms of the practice to women living in each country. In Chapter 6, I evaluate sex-selective abortion bans in the United States and India using the legal framework I developed in this chapter.

CHAPTER 3

The Politics of Sex-Selective Abortion Laws in the United States

Momentary national attention in the United States turned to sex selection when reality TV star Kim Kardashian and rap star Kanye West preselected the sex of their child using reproductive technology in June 2015.[1] They already had a girl and wanted to have a boy, so Kardashian had male embryos implanted in her uterus using in vitro fertilization (IVF).[2] It is perfectly legal for Kardashian and West to use this procedure to sex-select and there is no movement to ban sex selection using IVF. On the other hand, sex-selective abortion is currently prohibited in nine states and there is a movement underway to ban it in more states.[3]

When people in the U.S. think about sex-selective abortion, countries like India or China come to mind. Many people are aware that some women in India and other countries abort a fetus upon learning it is female with the intention of becoming pregnant again in the hopes of conceiving a male child.

Few people in the United States, however, are aware that bills to ban sex-selective abortion have spread like wildfire in state legislatures. Since 2009, the U.S. Congress and nearly half of all U.S. state legislatures have considered bills banning sex-selective abortion.[4] In 2012, the U.S. House of Representatives voted 246 to 168 for the Prenatal Non-Discrimination Act of 2012 ("PRENDA").[5] The bill had bipartisan support—20 Democrats joined 226 Republicans in voting for the bill.[6] In January 2015, Senator Vitter, a Republican senator from Louisiana, introduced a bill in the Senate that is virtually identical to the prior bills in Congress. In April 2016, the U.S. House of Representatives Judiciary Committee held a hearing on the 2016 version of PRENDA.[7] In January 2017, PRENDA was re-introduced in the U.S. House of Representatives.

Nine states currently have laws prohibiting sex-selective abortion.[8] Illinois became the first state to adopt a ban in 1985.[9] Pennsylvania followed suit in 1989.[10] A spate of bills were introduced to restrict sex-selective abortion in the 1990s, but none of them was adopted.[11] After a hiatus of decades, a 2008 article by Douglas Almond and Lena Edlund in the influential multidisciplinary science journal, *Proceedings of the National Academy of Sciences*, reignited legislative activity. The authors stated that they "document[ed] male-biased sex ratios among U.S.-born children to Chinese, Koreans and Asian Indians in the U.S." in the 2000 U.S. Census.[12]

It seemed that advocates for the bans had the proof they needed: Asian Americans were aborting female fetuses so they could have sons. However, as I explain in Chapter 4, that study and related studies have been misinterpreted in the popular media and political debates. I critique the popular discourse using a critical race lens. I also present original empirical data developed in collaboration with economists who used more recent U.S. Census data that leads to a different conclusion. New data suggests that few Asian Americans might be sex-selecting for both daughters and sons.

In this chapter, I map the actors in the sex-selective abortion debates: anti-abortion advocates, legislative representatives, legislatures, pro-choice voters, pro-choice organizations, and South Asian American organizations. As I argued in Chapter 1, anti-abortion advocates stereotype the behavior and motives of Asian Americans based on the practices of people living in Asia. I refer to this process as "decontextualization." Many pro-choice people and some pro-choice elected state legislative representatives have accepted these decontextualized arguments. Most mainstream pro-choice organizations and South Asian organizations have not made it their priority to lobby against bills banning sex-selective abortion. I explain why this might be occurring.

I use empirical methodologies to determine whether these bans are aimed at addressing the growing Asian immigration to the United States or are simply the result of a strong anti-abortion movement. I examine the voting records of the sex-selective abortion bills to determine whether or not pro-choice legislators support them. Finally, I examine the text of the sex-selective abortion bans and the text of its less popular cousin, race-selective abortion bans. While sex-selective abortion bans prohibit women from discriminating against their fetuses on the basis of sex, race-selective abortion bans are meant to stop women from discriminating against their fetuses on the basis of race. I explain why the logic of the race-selective abortion bills is flawed.

The Actors in the Movement to Ban Sex-Selective Abortion in the United States

This section explains how the anti-abortion movement seized the opportunity to limit abortion rights by adopting bans on sex-selective abortion and why some pro-choice Americans accept the framing advanced by anti-abortion groups. I also demonstrate that some legislative representatives who consistently vote against anti-abortion legislation voted in favor of sex-selective abortion bans.

Anti-Abortion Movement Campaigns for the Bans

In the U.S. Congress and state legislatures across the country, politicians who sponsor sex-selective abortion bans are at the forefront of the movement to make abortion illegal.[13] U.S. Representative Trent Franks (R-AZ), who sponsored sex-selective abortion bans in the U.S. Congress,[14] has stated, "I have made it one of my priorities in public office to fight for the end of abortion on demand."[15] U.S. Representative Chris Smith (R-NJ) is a vocal supporter of the federal bill that would ban sex-selective abortion. He also supports bills that would prohibit federal funding to groups like Planned Parenthood, which provide legal abortion services among other routine health care services.[16] Representative Smith has stated that "abortion is a serious, lethal violation of fundamental human rights" and that the "pro-life movement is not only on the side of compassion, justice, and inclusion," but also "the right side of responsible science and of history."[17] In the North Dakota and Texas state legislatures, sponsors of bans on sex-selective abortion also sponsored bills that prohibit abortion after the detection of a fetal heartbeat.[18]

Proponents of sex-selective abortion bans explicitly state that the laws are part of the effort to restrict access to abortion entirely. In 2008, Steven Mosher, head of the Population Research Institute (a leading anti-abortion group), stated, "I propose that we—the pro-life movement—adopt as our next goal the banning of sex- and race-selective abortion."[19] And in a 2008 article, an influential conservative thinker and law professor declared that the "key to eroding *Roe v. Wade* . . . is to pass a number of state or federal laws that restrict abortion rights in ways approved of by at least fifty percent of the public," such as "a ban on abortion for sex selection."[20]

Following this lead, anti-abortion groups have created model legislation to ban sex-selective abortion.[21] The toolkit created by Americans United for Life (AUL) starts with a discussion of the need for the ban, provides an overview of the global sex ratio crises, and contends that Asian American immigrants are undergoing sex-selective abortions much like people in other countries.[22] State-level advocates are using toolkits like this to design and propose bills in their states. For example, in 2012, the Missouri state legislature introduced a bill styled after AUL's model legislation that would prohibit abortions sought for sex-selective reasons or due to any genetic condition of the fetus.[23]

Pro-Choice Organizations: What Are They Doing?

Despite the fact that sex-selective abortion bans were the second most introduced anti-abortion legislation in 2012 and more than twenty-two state legislatures considered them in just six years, the most prominent reproductive justice organizations in the United States have not made challenging these bans a priority issue. Certainly, pro-choice organizations oppose the bans. Reacting to the federal anti–sex-selective abortion bill, Nancy Northup, the head of a leading reproductive rights organization, the Center for Reproductive Rights, notes: "While this bill's supporters have staunchly opposed many real measures to combat sex and race discrimination in the past, their equally vocal support for the most extreme anti-choice legislation makes it plain that this is just another thinly veiled attack on reproductive rights."[24]

Many racial and reproductive organizations came together to strategize against sex-selective abortion bans when they first emerged. In April 2009, Generations Ahead, the National Asian Pacific American Women's Forum (NAPAWF), SisterSong, and the Center for Reproductive Rights organized a daylong values clarification workshop on sex selection. After a discussion with many reproductive health, rights, and justice groups that participated, they took a position on sex selection that would both protect abortion rights and oppose gender discrimination.

In 2010, NAPAWF, Asian Communities for Reproductive Justice, and Generations Ahead released a toolkit called "Taking a Stand: Tools for Action on Sex Selection."[25] The introduction to the toolkit recognizes the complexity of the problem:

> The issue of sex selection challenges us to stand up for race and gender equality without undermining abortion rights and without perpetuating assumptions about sex and gender binaries. These proposals threaten to drive a painful wedge between reproductive and racial justice organizations, and pro-choice advocates. And in a world of assisted reproductive technologies that span from before conception through pregnancy itself, this issue requires us to consider implications of addressing sex selection both pre- and post-pregnancy.[26]

More recently, the organization working most extensively to combat misinformation about these bans is NAPAWF, a multi-issue group that advocates on behalf of Asian American and Pacific Islander women. NAPAWF has earned a number of victories in states where sex-selective abortion bans are introduced.

In 2014, I worked with Miriam Yeung, who was at that time the Executive Director of NAPAWF, and an interdisciplinary team of other people on a report containing original empirical data on at-birth sex ratios in the United States. Some of this data is included this book.[27] NAPAWF and other advocates disseminate our report to the state legislatures around the country that are considering adopting sex-selective abortion bans in an effort to give them accurate and current data. NAPAWF recently worked with the San Francisco City Council to help pass a resolution to declare sex-selective abortion bans racist.[28]

The 2014 report presented an empirical analysis of U.S. Census data from 2008 to 2012. We examined the number of boys to girls born to several groups within the Asian American community and found that the incidence of sex selection was low. To the extent it occurred, it was geared toward family balancing and not driven by an aversion to daughters.

When the bills were first introduced, the anti-abortion legislators and advocates used narrow empirical data from 1990 to argue that sex-selective abortion was widespread among Asian Americans. The pro-choice organizations responded by arguing that while sex selection is a problem, restricting sex-selective abortions was not the solution. However, the report we released changed the way organizations that lobbied against the bills talk about the issue. With new data and a better understanding of existing empirical studies, NAPAWF and other organizations argued that sex-selective abortions were, contrary to prior beliefs, not widespread. In any event, the new data refutes the view that there is widespread "son preference" in the Asian American community.

There are a host of possible explanations for why some mainstream reproductive justice organizations are reluctant to take a strong public stance against these bills. First, it may be that given the plethora of anti-abortion laws,[29] there simply may not be enough resources to prioritize lobbying against sex-selective abortion bans. Second, their voices may be muted because some pro-choice organizations and their leaders believe any sex selection (even in favor of girls) is sexist. To these feminists, sex selection assumes that one can choose the gender of one's child and denies the importance of society in gender identity formation.[30] Others may simply have moral objections to it. Indeed, Planned Parenthood has an explicit policy of denying abortions to women who seek it for sex-selective purposes.[31]

Third, it is possible that some pro-choice people do not oppose the bans because they accept the view that sex selection is widespread among immigrant communities and women are largely coerced into having these abortions. Finally, perhaps the lack of strong opposition to the bans may follow from the compartmentalization of nonprofit organizations—some organizations work exclusively on race issues and others on gender issues. Sex selection implicates both race and gender in the United States—as a result, it may fall through the organizational cracks.

South Asian American Organizations: Informed by the Practice in India

Sex-selective abortion bans are not on the radar of most South Asian American organizations other than NAPAWF, which is a pan–Asian American women's organization. If, as I posit here, sex-selective abortion bans are driven by an anti-abortion agenda that intentionally and unintentionally distorts facts about Asian Americans, then what explains why South Asian American organizations and South Asians generally are not actively working against them? This may be because their assumptions about the rate at which the practice occurs and the reasons for it may themselves be shaped by their understanding of the situation in India.

After the largest Indian American paper ran advertisements promoting sex determination tests and pre-implantation sex selection services, the owners of the paper abruptly pulled the ads. The chairman of Rediff.com India Ltd., the Indian company that had recently purchased the paper, noted:

> We all felt a little queasy. . . . We don't want to be remotely associated with anybody that discriminates for a boy child over a girl child. It's wrong to discriminate. You know, some years ago many of my friends marched through Delhi and Bombay to get the government to get rid of these tests.[32]

Many of the oldest South Asian organizations in the United States were domestic violence shelters or antiviolence advocacy groups such as Sakhi for South Asian Women. Dr. Das Dasgupta, founder of an organization that focuses on violence against South Asian women, noted that she worked with South Asian women who told her that their husbands harassed or abused them over giving birth to girls.[33] For leaders like Dr. Dasgupta, the natural response to allegations of sex-selective abortion in their communities is to work toward countering "son preference" rather than to challenge legislation aimed at stopping sex selection. Immigrants from India are informed by their understanding of how the practice is carried out in India; namely, that it is caused by a preference for boys, that it is widespread, and that it is harmful and illegal. Consequently, I argue that they approach sex-selective abortion bans in the United States with a decontextualized lens. Their views about whether or not the practice occurs in the United States, the motives for the practice, and its consequences are informed by what they know about the practice from India, why it occurs there, and what harms it causes in India.

Finally, like reproductive rights organizations, South Asian organizations that oppose the bans are placed in an awkward position. One activist told me that she does not want to take a position in opposition to the bans for fear that she will be perceived to be "pro–sex selection" if she does. It is difficult for an organization to formulate a message that conveys both opposition to the bans and opposition to the practice of sex selection.

Pro-Choice Americans: Restricting Abortion to Promote Women's Equality

Many people in the United States who otherwise support access to abortion are conflicted about how to react to sex-selective abortion bans. Women's equality is implicated both by its practice and prohibition. Aborting female fetuses on the basis of sexist intent affects women's equality. Prohibiting it restricts reproductive rights. Although many commentators have recognized sex-selective abortion bans as a ploy to limit abortion rights,[34] many pro-choice Americans support these limitations on the right to choose.

One person commenting on a story in the *Atlantic* on sex-selective abortion stated, "I lean pro-choice, but I doff my hat to the pro-life camp for this deft maneuver. They have demonstrated that it is logically impossible to be both 'pro-choice' and 'anti-discrimination.'"[35] This commenter has clearly accepted the powerful argument made by pro-life groups. However, I argue that the support from pro-choice people is based on a misunderstanding of the data on sex selection in the United States (which I discuss in the next chapter), a misunderstanding of the causes and complexities of sex selection in other countries, and by their failure to properly contextualize the practice when it occurs in the United States.

The prevailing narrative in the popular imagination is that sex selection is a part of a cycle of violence against women in India and China. Here, I examine this narrative primarily in regard to India. One example of this narrow portrayal is a film that has become popular among pro-choice groups: *It's a Girl: The Three Deadliest Words in the World*. The film was expensive to make—it was shot on location in India and China—yet it acknowledges no funding sources. The official biography of the film director did not list any of his prior films or any of his prior work experience. Only by searching for the ownership of the domain name of the film's website could one find that Evan Davis, the director of the film, worked for Harvest Media Ministry, a media company that makes anti-abortion and other videos for church groups.[36]

Evan Davis, the media director for Harvest Media Ministry, and Evan Grace Davis, the director of *It's a Girl*, have wholly separate personas on the Internet. On the website of Harvest Media, Evan Davis's biography proclaims that his "passion is to equip those who are called to bring the hope and light of Jesus Christ to the world through the provision of strategic media communication tools and storytelling methods."[37] Yet on his Facebook page that is associated with the film, he states under his religious views that "it's against my relationship to have a religion."[38]

Why go to such efforts to hide the fact that Evan Davis—aka Evan Grace Davis—worked for a company that creates videos on behalf of faith-based groups to promote their interpretations of the teachings of Jesus Christ?

Davis said there was no ulterior motive in his failure to disclose his affiliation with Harvest Media Ministry. He claimed that he no longer works for the organization, but Davis's biography is still on their website, and Shadowline Films (*It's a Girl*'s production company) and Harvest Media Ministry share the same address. Davis said that the two companies share "facilities and equipment," and that some of the funding sources for the movie are the ones he met through his work with Harvest Media.[39]

The problem is not that the movie is supported by anti-abortion groups, but that it distorts the realities of sex-selective abortion in other countries. Because the film's funding sources are so hidden and because of the general lack of American knowledge of the realities in India, pro-choice Americans may have accepted the narrative in the film without a critical eye. The only scenario presented in the film is one in which a woman is physically coerced into having a sex-selective abortion. To this end, the movie extensively covers the well-known story in India of Mitu Khurana, a woman who left her husband because he physically abused her after she refused to abort her female fetuses. Those who believe in the autonomy rights of women and those who believe in the right of the fetus agree: a woman should never be forced to have an abortion for sex-selective purposes or otherwise.

The film, however, fails to depict the most common cases in India: women who make the choice to abort a female fetus without physical violence or overt coercion. For example, poor women in villages in India have reported that they do not want to bring girls into the world—not because of any overt coercion, but because they do not want their daughters to go through the hardships they have faced as girls and women. Other women do not want to have multiple daughters and want to have at least one son to gain a higher status in their family.

Purporting to address sex-selective abortion in foreign countries, the film deceptively solicits donations for organizations that are working to ban sex-selective abortion in the United States. The website for the film encourages people to donate to Women's Rights Without Frontiers. The website of Women's Rights Without Frontiers makes no mention of the group's support for sex-selective abortion bans in the United States. It is only by searching other websites supporting state legislation to ban sex selection that one would find out that Women's Rights Without Frontiers is a coalition partner of ProtectOurGirls.com, a group that seeks to ban sex-selective abortion in the United States. Thinking that they are funding organizations that address sex-selective abortion in other countries, pro-choice Americans may have unwittingly contributed funding to organizations working to restrict reproductive rights in the United States.

Indeed, the movie was accepted by and received acclaim from pro-choice feminists in the United States. It was widely screened by pro-choice groups across America, including the New Jersey Chapter of the National Organization for Women and feminist groups on university campuses. It was an official selection for the Amnesty International Film Festival in 2012 and appeared in the movie review section of *Ms.* magazine.

Another explanation for the film's popularity among pro-choice groups is because the framing of Asian cultures as antiwomen fits comfortably with some feminist views. In 1999, Susan Moller Okin, a well-known liberal feminist political philosopher, wrote an essay entitled "Is Multiculturalism Bad for Women?"[40] As Leti Volpp points out, Okin's answer is clear: Yes, it is. In her essay, Okin lists many practices and ways in which minority and immigrant cultures are repressive to women: "French schoolchildren wearing headscarves, African immigrant polygamous marriages, female clitoridectomy in immigrant communities, Hmong marriage by capture, parent-child suicide by Japanese and Chinese immigrants, and 'wife murder by immigrants from Asian and Middle Eastern countries whose wives have either committed adultery or treated their husbands in a servile way.' "[41]

Leti Volpp's critique of Susan Okin's perception of nonwhite peoples is very relevant to understanding the discourse on sex-selective abortion in the United States today. Volpp, a law professor at Berkeley, points out:

> To assert that these cases reveal a tension between multi-culturalism and feminism is not only to rely upon a caricature of the culture of immigrant communities and communities of color, but also to posit very specific and problematic versions of feminism and of multiculturalism. These discussions assume a feminism that replicates the colonialist feminism of a century ago. In the colonialist paradigm, native women were completely passive subjects of a native male subordination that grossly exceeded that experienced by women in the West. Colonialist feminism emerged, in this account, in order to uplift the suffering women of the "East." This brand of feminism was used to justify colonization as part of a civilizing process, along with the rule of law, education, and Christianity.[42]

Informed by this understanding of Asian people, some (otherwise pro-choice) Americans are primed to accept the anti-abortion framing that paints Asian cultures as backward and repressive to women.

With the belief that most cases of sex-selective abortion involve violence in India and that such violence is part of the "culture" of Asian people, it is natural for people to assume that people from Asia will carry their violent cultural practices with them to the United States and will replicate them there. But as I elaborate in the in-depth discussion on India in Chapter 5, the coercion narrative is overstated—not all women in India are physically coerced to abort female fetuses. Moreover, explanations that rely on culture fail to account for the social and economic context in which sex selection occurs. Even if culture (to some extent) is transportable to another country by an immigrant, context is not.

Do Pro-Choice Legislators Vote for Bans?

Abortion is an issue that generally splits across party lines in the United States. It is obvious why an elected representative who opposes legal abortion rights would vote in favor of restrictions on sex-selective abortion. But do pro-choice legislators also vote for them? I examined the voting records of the six state legislatures that have passed bans from 2011 to 2014. I excluded the other two states that have previously banned sex-selective abortion—Illinois and Pennsylvania—from this analysis because the politics surrounding those laws were very different from that of the recent legislative movement. Those bans were passed in the 1980s and, as discussed further in Chapter 4, the rhetoric surrounding those bans did not involve the narrative that the practice was widespread among Asian immigrants.

An analysis of voting records in the six states that have enacted sex-selective abortion bans from 2011 to 2014 shows that votes on those laws closely follow party lines. There is obviously overwhelming support from Republican legislators. On average, 92% of Republican legislators voted in favor of the bans in the Houses of Representatives and Senates in these six states. However, Democrats also voted for the bans. Approximately 10% of Democrats voted for the bans in Arizona, Kansas, North Carolina, and North Dakota. Table 1 lists the voting records of the six state legislatures (broken down by House of Representatives and Senate of each state) that have passed the laws from 2011 to 2014.[43]

North Carolina was the only state where no Democrat voted for the sex-selective abortion ban. In Oklahoma and South Dakota, the bans achieved meaningful support from Democrats. In Oklahoma, nearly 90% of Democrats in both the House and Senate voted for the ban; in South Dakota, approximately 40% of Democrats in the House and 70% of Democrats in the Senate voted to ban sex-selective abortions. These two states are home to the most restrictive abortion laws in the United States.[44] In both states,

Table 1. Votes on Sex-Selective Abortion Bans by Political Party (from 2011 to 2014)

	Arizona (2011)		*Kansas (2013)*		*N. Carolina (2013)*		*N. Dakota (2013)*		*Oklahoma (2010)*		*S. Dakota (2014)*	
	H	S	H	S	H	S	H	S	H	S	H	S
Republicans (Total)	40	21	92	32	76	33	71	33	62	26	52	28
% voted for ban	95	100	92	88	97	97	83	73	97	92	98	89
% voted against ban	5	0	5	6	1	3	14	18	0	0	0	11
Democrats (Total)	20	9	33	8	43	17	23	14	39	22	18	7
No. of Democrats who voted for ban	2	0	5	0	0	0	5	3	35	19	7	5
% voted for ban	10	0	15	0	0	0	22	21	90	86	39	71
% voted against ban	80	51	76	100	93	70	74	64	3	9	56	29

Sources: For the votes on H.B. 2442, 50th Leg., 1st Reg. Sess. (Ariz. 2011); H.B. 2253, 2013 Leg., Reg. Sess. (Kan. 2013); S.B. 353, 2013 Gen. Assemb., Reg. Sess. (N.C. 2013); and H.B. 1305, 63d Leg. Assemb., Reg. Sess. (N.D. 2013), *see* Vote Smart, http://votesmart.org/ (last visited Apr. 21, 2014). For the vote on S.B. 1890, 52d Leg., 2d Reg. Sess. (Okla. 2010), *see* Bill Information for SB 1890 (2009–2010), Oklahoma State Legislature (Apr. 5, 2010), http://www.oklegislature.gov/BillInfo.aspx?Bill=SB1890&Session=1000. For the vote on H.B. 1162, 89th Leg., Reg. Sess. (S.D. 2014), *see* House Bill 1162, South Dakota State Legislature (Mar. 31, 2014), http://legis.sd.gov/Legislative_Session/Bills/RollCall.aspx?Vote=16245&Session=20. Numbers have been rounded.

laws that restrict access to abortion consistently receive bipartisan support.[45] Accordingly, as measured in 2011, 96% of counties in Oklahoma[46] and 98% of counties in South Dakota[47] were without abortion providers.

While the Republican Party is traditionally associated with an anti-abortion stance and the Democratic Party with the pro-choice position, we cannot assume that just because a state legislator runs as a Democrat that she supports legal abortion rights. Indeed, according to Democrats for Life, an organization of pro-life Democrats, there were eight Democrats in the South Dakota legislature and seven in the Oklahoma legislature that are pro-life as of October 2013.[48]

To determine whether the Democrats who voted for the bans in each state that passed the bans are pro-life or pro-choice, I examined their prior voting records on anti-abortion legislation. In particular, I examined how these Democrats voted on bills requiring doctors to get admitting privileges at nearby hospitals, requiring doctors to inform their patient of a fetal heartbeat, and requiring mandatory ultrasounds. I found that a total of 47 Democrats who voted for the sex-selective abortion bans otherwise consistently voted in favor of legislation to restrict abortion access. This is not surprising.

What is surprising is that nineteen Democrats (mostly in Oklahoma) who voted for the sex-selective abortion bans consistently voted *against* bills aimed at restricting access to abortion. I assumed that Democrats who consistently vote against bills limiting access to abortion were pro-choice (except for their votes in favor of the sex-selective abortion bans). Approximately 25% of Democrats in state legislatures who voted for anti–sex-selective abortion laws opposed all other restrictions on abortion access. Except for two pro-choice Democrats (one in Arizona and one in South Dakota), all of the pro-choice Democrats who voted for the anti–sex selection bill were in Oklahoma.

For each Democrat that voted in favor of the sex-selective abortion bans adopted in Arizona, Kansas, North Dakota, Oklahoma, and South Dakota, Table 2 places them in one of the following four categories: (1) consistently votes for bills to limit abortion access, (2) consistently votes against bills to limit abortion access, (3) has a mixed voting record (sometimes votes for and sometimes votes against limiting abortion access), and (4) has only voted on one anti-abortion bill (other than the ban on sex-selective abortion).

Thus, in Oklahoma, the first state to ban sex-selective abortion, Democratic state legislators who are otherwise in support of the legal right to abortion voted for the bans. In the states that adopted the bans after Oklahoma, at

Table 2. Prior Voting Records of Democrats Who Voted for Sex-Selective Abortion Bans

	Consistently Votes for Bills Limiting Abortion Access	*Consistently Votes Against Bills Limiting Abortion Access*	*Mixed Voting Record*	*Limited Voting Record*
Arizona	1	1	0	0
Kansas	5	0	0	0
North Dakota	5	0	1	2
Oklahoma	28	17	8	1
South Dakota	8	1	0	3
Total	47	19	9	6

Source: Vote Smart, Just the Facts, www.votesmart.org.

Note: The numbers are totals for both houses of each state's legislatures.

most only one pro-choice Democrat voted in favor of the ban. It may be that since Oklahoma adopted the law, pro-choice legislators have become more informed about these bills.

In March 2016, the Indiana legislature passed a sex-selective abortion ban. Vice President Mike Pence, governor of Indiana at the time, signed the bill into law.[49] In the bill's final House and Senate votes, no Democrat in either Indiana house voted for the ban.[50] This may be because Democrats have become more educated about the bans[51] or it may be because the sex-selective abortion bans in the state legislation were part of other restrictions, including race-selective and disability-selective abortion bans. Disability-selective abortion bans prohibit a woman from obtaining an abortion even if the fetus has a genetic anomaly such as Down syndrome. But it is possible that some Democrats would have voted for bans on sex-selective abortion if this ban was introduced separately from race-selective and disability-selective abortion bans.

In this section, I mapped the actors in the movement to ban sex-selective abortion. Sparked by data misrepresented to be broader than it truly was, pro-life advocates played on information about sex-selective abortion among people in other countries to push for bans in the United States. The reason for widespread sex-selective abortion, they argued, was because Asian cultures are misogynist—Asian men do not want daughters and physically coerce their wives into aborting female fetuses.

Pro-choice legislators in Oklahoma appeared to buy this narrative and voted for the bans in large numbers. Additionally, many people in the United States that otherwise support legal access to abortion appear to be in support of legal restrictions. Some accept the decontextualized arguments and the "coercion" narrative. Mainstream pro-choice organizations do see these bans as a "wedge issue" and a ploy to gain support among pro-choice people, but avoid vocal campaigns against them. The most notable exception is the American Civil Liberties Union's (ACLU) suit against Arizona brought on behalf of NAPAWF and the National Association for the Advancement of Colored People. Even that suit does not directly challenge the constitutionality of the bans. Leaders in the South Asian community are also reluctant to advocate against the bans—some fear appearing to be "pro–sex selection" and others are informed by their own understanding of the horrors of the practice in India.

In the following section, I test another possible hypothesis for the spread of anti–sex-selective abortion bills. Asian Americans are the fastest growing Asian group in the United States. Their population growth patterns vary by states. I consider whether Asian American immigration growth is associated with the introduction of bans.

Sex-Selective Abortion Bans and the Growth of Asian American Immigration

Anti-abortion advocates have lobbied for the introduction and passage of the bans on sex-selective abortion. In their rhetoric, they do not mention the restriction on abortion as a goal. Instead they argue that it is needed to stop Asian immigrants from discriminating against female fetuses. Indeed, proponents of the bans have referred to the growth of Asian immigration as a justification for the bans.[52] For example, Don Hagger, a Republican state representative in South Dakota, stated:

> Let me tell you, our population in South Dakota is a lot more diverse than it ever was. There are cultures that look at a sex-selection abortion as being culturally okay. And I will suggest to you that we are embracing individuals from some of those cultures in this country, or in this state. And I think that's a good thing that we invite them to come, but I think it's also important that we send a message that this is a state that values life, regardless of its sex.[53]

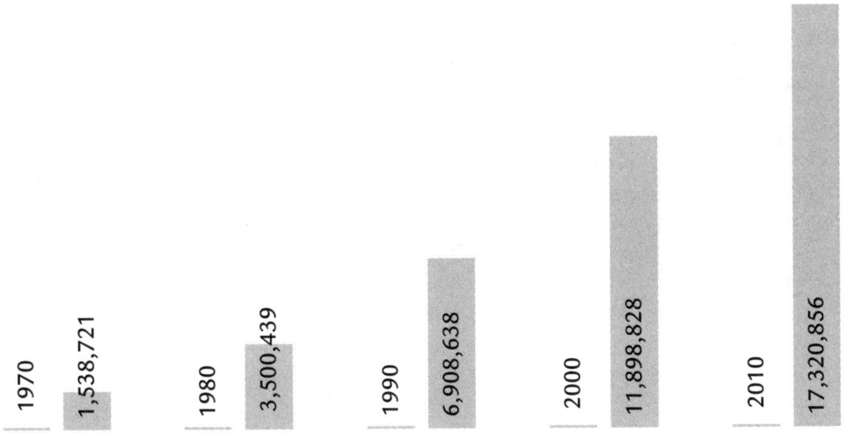

Figure 1. Growth of Asian Population in the United States.
Source: 2010 U.S. Census.

Don Hagger's perception of the growth of Asian immigration is accurate. The number of Asian Americans has nearly doubled every decade since 1970, as depicted in Figure 1. In 2012, the Asian American population was the fastest-growing racial group in the country.[54] According to the U.S. Census Bureau, while the U.S. Hispanic population grew by 2.2% in 2012, the Asian population grew by 2.9%.[55] Among the 17,329,586 million Asian Americans in the United States, 3,183,063 are of Indian descent and 4,010,114 are of Chinese descent.[56] In other words, nearly 42% of all Asian Americans trace their heritage (through one or both parents) to India or China. The growth rate of Asian Americans has varied dramatically by state. From 2000 to 2010, the Asian population in Nevada grew more than 116% whereas in Rhode Island it grew by only 30%.[57]

Since sex-selective abortion bans target the (assumed) practices of Asians in America, one would expect that states with the highest Asian population growth rates are more likely to consider such bills than states with lower growth rates of Asian Americans. State legislatures in 21 states have considered but failed to pass bans on sex-selective abortion as of 2014 (see Table 3). In 2016, the Washington state legislature also considered but rejected the ban.[58]

I examined the Asian immigration growth rates from the 2000 U.S. Census to the 2010 U.S. Census in each state that has considered and/or passed sex-selective abortion bans from 2009 to 2014. I found that, since 2009,

Table 3. States That Have Considered But Not Passed Anti–Sex-Selection Abortion Laws (up to 2014)

State	*Year(s) Considered by State Legislature*
California	2014
Colorado	2013
Florida	2012, 2013
Georgia	2010
Iowa	2013, 2014
Idaho	2010
Indiana	2013
Massachusetts	2012, 2013
Michigan	2009, 2010, 2012
Minnesota	2009, 2010
Missouri	2012, 2013, 2014
Mississippi	2009, 2010, 2014
New Jersey	2009, 2010, 2011, 2012
New York	2011, 2012, 2013, 2014
Ohio	2012
Oregon	2013, 2014
Rhode Island	2011, 2012, 2013, 2014
Texas	2013
Virginia	2013, 2014
Wisconsin	2013, 2014
West Virginia	2009, 2010, 2011, 2012, 2013, 2014

nearly 70% of the states where the Asian population grew by more than 70% from 2000 to 2010 considered and/or adopted laws to ban sex-selective abortion. On the other hand, 51% of the states where the Asian population grew less than 70% considered and/or adopted sex-selective abortion bans.[59] This variation, however, is not statistically significant. Thus, looking only at Asian immigration growth rates does not explain why sex-selective bans are booming in state legislatures.

I tested another reason behind the emergence of these bills: anti-abortion sentiments among state legislators in the United States. The fight against abortion now occurs in state legislatures where numerous abortion restrictions have been proposed over the last decade. I used a state's passage of anti-abortion laws as a proxy for the general climate in the state legislature regarding abortion rights. In order to asses a state legislature's view of abortion rights, I separated state legislatures into two categories: (1) those that, as of 2012, had passed abortion-restricting laws (a) requiring women seeking abortions to submit to ultrasounds, (b) allowing health care providers to refuse to perform abortions if they find them morally objectionable, (c) declaring that life begins "at the moment of conception," (d) defunding Planned Parenthood by limiting funds to the organization, and/or (e) outlawing abortions after 20 weeks' gestation; and (2) states that had not passed any such laws as of 2012.[60]

Twenty-four state legislatures fell in category (1) and 24 states were included in category (2). It should be noted that I have not identified whether there was a change in the elected members of state legislatures from the time that the sex-selective abortion ban was introduced and when the other anti-abortion measures were introduced. I assumed that the general climate regarding abortion remained relatively constant in these state legislatures between 2009 and 2014 (the time period during which the sex-selective abortion bills that are part of this study were considered and/or adopted).

Of the states that had adopted other anti-abortion laws as of 2012, nearly 70% of them have also passed and/or considered bills on sex-selective abortion since 2009. Conversely, only 44% of the states that had not adopted other anti-abortion laws as of 2012 have considered and/or adopted sex-selective abortion bans. There is a statistically significant association with a state legislature's adoption of other abortion restrictions and the introduction or adoption of sex-selective abortion bans.[61]

Of the states that had not adopted other anti-abortion laws, only 37% of the states with low Asian immigration rates considered and/or passed the laws and 67% of states with high Asian immigration rates considered and/or passed the laws. There is a statistically significant association between Asian immigration growth rates and consideration of sex-selective abortion bans in state legislatures that do not have a record of passing anti-abortion laws.[62]

On the other hand, in states that had other anti-abortion laws in place by 2012, I found that 68% of the states that had low Asian immigration growth considered and/or passed the bans, while 71% of high Asian immigration growth states considered and/or passed the bans. This means that in state legislatures that passed other anti-abortion laws, the level of Asian immigration into the state is not associated with whether or not they considered the bans.[63]

Thus, for state legislatures that have strong anti-abortion sentiments, the growth of immigration of Asian Americans into their states does not appear to be a strong motivating factor. It does seem relevant for state legislatures that do not have a recent record of adopting anti-abortion legislation. This analysis suggests that Asian immigration is relevant in introducing and adopting bills, but only in state legislatures that are not otherwise hostile to legal abortion access. In states that have a recent history of passing anti-abortion legislation, anti–sex selective abortion bills seem to be introduced regardless of the growth patterns of Asian immigration.

Sex-Selective and Race-Selective Abortion Bills: A Textual Analysis

When they first began to be introduced in 2009, sex-selective abortion bills also contained restrictions on race-selective abortion. Sex-selective abortion laws are textually flawed because they address the alleged behavior of Asian American women, but punish acts of the medical professionals. I demonstrate below that they are not likely to prevent sex selection in the United States and instead will lead to other negative consequences. The consequences are further discussed in Chapter 6. The logic of race-selective abortion bans is even more absurd—they assume that minority women racially discriminate against their own fetuses.

Challenges to Enforcing Sex-Selective Abortion Bans

Anti–sex-selective abortion bills aim to prevent sex-selective abortion, but they do not punish the seeker of the sex-selective abortion. Instead, the bills penalize medical professionals who perform a sex-selective abortion. Leaving aside the question about how a medical professional could (or even should attempt to) accurately determine the actual reasons why a woman is seeking an abortion, the logic of the bills is inherently flawed. The bills permit other forms of nonabortion sex selection, and they do not allow for any exceptions for genetic conditions.

Flawed Logic: Separating the Mens Rea and Actus Reus

Advocates argue that sex-selective abortion bills are meant to address the sexist behavior of Asian Americans who abort female fetuses. But women who are seeking sex-selective abortions are not penalized. To avoid any ambiguity, a few statutes explicitly state that abortion-seekers cannot be charged.[64] Instead, the bills punish medical professionals who knowingly perform a sex-selective abortion. The professionals are subject to civil penalties such as fines[65] and may also face criminal penalties.[66] The anti-abortion movement has consistently argued that abortion providers and not abortion-seekers should be punished.

For most crimes, the accused must be shown to have both the requisite *mens rea* (the guilty mind or some level of criminal intent)[67] and the *actus reus* (the criminal act or conduct).[68] The anti–sex-selective abortion bills target the acts committed by medical professionals (i.e., performing the abortion) but are concerned about the state of mind of the abortion-seeker (i.e., discriminating against the fetus). Thus, the bills are looking at the state of mind (*mens rea*) of the abortion-seeker (i.e., does she have a sexist intent?) and the act (*actus reus*) of the medical professional (i.e., did he perform the abortion?).

It does not make sense to punish a person for doing something based on someone else's state of mind. The statutes address this disjunction between the intent and act by holding the medical professional liable *only* if she had knowledge that the abortion-seeker wanted an abortion for sex-selective reasons (the *mens rea*) and having that knowledge she still performed the abortion (the *actus reus*). The logic—punishing a medical professional for someone else's sexist intent—is flawed.

Sonu Bedi, a professor at Dartmouth College, offers another critique of the statutes. He argues that sex-selective abortions should not be illegal because they are "thought crimes."[69] He points out that these laws are fashioned like "hate crimes" in the sense that the motivation (or the bias in the mind of the person who commits the act) matters. But unlike hate crimes, the underlying act of obtaining an abortion is not illegal. If a man hits a woman because she is African American, the assault is already a criminal offense and his racist motivation escalates the criminal penalties. In the case of sex-selective abortions, abortion during pre-viability is otherwise legal in the United States. But the wrong motivation behind the abortion (discrimination against the fetus) transforms the act from something that is not otherwise punishable to something that *is* punishable. According to Bedi, this renders it a "thought crime."

Loopholes in the Bills: Sperm-Sorting and Pre-Implantation Genetic Diagnosis (PGD)

The supporters of the bans claim that they are needed to prevent Asian American parents from sex-selecting in favor of sons. However, these laws will not prevent that. They do not prohibit people from using pre-implantation methods of sex selection, two of which are widely available in the United States—sperm sorting and PGD. As mentioned in Chapter 1, sperm sorting is the process of separating sperm based on whether each spermatozoa bears an X- or Y-chromosome. Artificial insemination is then used to inseminate the uterus with the sperm that will result in a child of the desired sex. PGD involves testing a fertilized egg that has been conceived through IVF to determine its future sex and implanting the fertilized egg into the uterus. Thus, anti–sex-selective abortion laws do not prevent all sex selection.

No Exceptions for Genetic Conditions

None of the states that have adopted bans except for two—Illinois and Oklahoma—permit abortions for sex-linked disorders.[70] A sex-linked disorder is a disorder that is caused by or linked to genes located in sex chromosomes.[71] One example of such a disorder is hemophilia, which is caused by a defect in the X-chromosome. In some cases, a woman may not want to carry a male or female fetus to term because she will give birth to a child with a debilitative condition. Even when state statutes do not make exceptions for sex-linked disorders, a woman seeking an abortion in that state because her fetus has a sex-linked disorder could avoid liability under the statute by arguing that she is not seeking it solely on the basis of the sex of the fetus but because of a genetic condition.

Race-Selective Abortion Bans: Borrowing from the Logic of Sex-Selective Abortion Bans

Although race-selective abortion bans were initially introduced in the same bills as sex-selective abortion bans, they have not gained much support in state legislatures. As a result, recent anti–sex-selective abortion bills have dropped the race-selective language altogether. For example, although the

U.S. congressional bills of 2012 and 2013 included a race-selective abortion ban, the 2015 bill does not. However, the 2016 version of the bill includes race-selective abortion bans.[72]

At this time, Arizona and Indiana[73] are the only states in the United States that have adopted a law to prohibit race-selective abortion; eight other states and the U.S. Congress have considered and rejected the bans.[74] In those bills, a race-selective abortion is defined as "an abortion performed for purposes of eliminating an unborn child because the child or a parent of the child is of an undesired race."[75] The 2013 bill introduced in the U.S. Congress explains the rationale for race-selective abortion bans:

> A thorough review of the history of the American population control movement and its close affiliation with the American Eugenics Society reveals a history of targeting certain racial or ethnic groups for "family planning." This history likely contributes to the current statistic that a Black baby is five times as likely to be aborted as a White baby, often in a federally subsidized clinic.[76]

Race-selective abortion bans are designed to rectify what has long been a belief of the anti-abortion movement (as well as some African American groups and leaders): abortion providers target African Americans for abortion services in an attempt to reduce the number of African Americans that are born.

Under Arizona's law, a medical professional is liable if he performs an abortion on a woman if he has knowledge that it is for race-selective purposes. The legislative history of the Arizona statute demonstrates the rationale for the law. First, legislators argue that data suggests that more African American women have abortions than Caucasian American women. A senator discussing the Arizona bill contends, "African American babies are now aborted at five times the rate of White babies to the point that nearly 50 percent of Black babies are aborted."[77]

Second, legislators claim that there is a conspiracy among abortion providers to eliminate minority races. A senator in the Arizona state senate stated that "[t]he great majority of abortion clinics were purposely located in minority neighborhoods by founders of Planned Parenthood. More than 70 percent of abortion clinics are still located in minority neighborhoods today."[78] Another senator explained that in 2008 some abortion providers were "exposed as having agreed to accept funds from persons who expressly requested that their donations be used to reduce the African American population."[79] Catherine

Davis, on behalf of the National Black Pro-Life Coalition and testifying in the subcommittee hearing held in April 2016 in the U.S. House of Representatives, argued that a federal ban on race-selective abortion was needed to "hold organizations like Planned Parenthood accountable."[80] Thus, the argument is that a race-selective abortion ban will prevent black fetuses from being destroyed.

The text of the race-selective abortion ban was crafted to mirror the language of the sex-selective abortion ban. However, this analogy becomes absurd when the actors with the purported racist and sexist intent are brought into the picture. Proponents of sex-selective abortion bans argue that Asian Americans discriminate against the sex of their fetuses and this causes a disproportionate number of abortions of female fetuses. They further incorrectly argue that there are massive numbers of "missing women" in the United States. They then apply the same logic to race and argue that race discrimination causes a disproportionate number of minority fetuses to be aborted.

In the case of sex-selective abortion bans, proponents argue that the sexist beliefs of Asian American parents cause them to obtain the abortions. But supporters of race-selective abortion bans believe that it is the racist views of abortion providers that cause a disproportionate number of abortions among minority communities. Yet, the text of the bill prohibits medical professionals from performing an abortion if the patient is seeking it on the basis of "color or race of the child, or the race of a parent of that child."[81] Even if anti-abortion groups are right that abortion providers target minority women for abortions, it makes little sense to say that minority women obtain abortions because they object to the race of their own fetuses. But race-selection abortion statutes rest on exactly that assumption.

Some legislators have explicitly stated that African American woman are racist toward their own race. Arizona Rep. Steve Montenegro, for example, "insisted that some abortions are performed because a mother does not want a . . . minority baby."[82] The statute raises many issues, including how one defines "race," whether a fetus has a "race," and the assumption that only nonwhite fetuses have a "race." The statute also rests on the questionable assumption that an African American woman would racially discriminate against her own African American fetus. On the other hand, in the context of sex-selective abortion bans, it is conceivable that a woman would want to abort a fetus because of its sex and then get pregnant again and hope for a fetus of a different sex.

The only scenario in which race-selective bans make some sense is if a nonminority woman conceives a child with a minority man and wants to abort because of race discrimination against the fetus. But those situations are likely rare, and moreover, advocates for race-selective abortion bills do not claim that the bill was designed to address that scenario. The ACLU, on behalf of the National Association for the Advancement of Colored People and NAPAWF, filed a lawsuit challenging the Arizona law on the basis of the Equal Protection Clause in the U.S. Constitution. The complaint states:

> The [race-selective abortion ban] demeans, stigmatizes, and discriminates against Black women who decide to end a pregnancy. The legislative history of the Act demonstrates that it is based on the false premise that, unlike a woman of another race, a Black woman making a personal, private, and constitutionally protected medical decision about whether and when to have a child is motivated by racial animus towards her embryo or fetus, towards Black children, and/or towards the Black community as a whole.[83]

The ACLU, however, does not argue that sex-selective or race-selective abortion bans violate a woman's right to abortion as protected under *Roe v. Wade* and its progeny; rather, they argue that the race-selective abortion ban treats African American women differently than non–African American women. The argument rests on the legislative history and intent of the statute, but not on its text. The statute is facially neutral—it applies to all women, not just African American women. The Federal District Court for the District of Arizona rejected their petition since it was not brought by the people whose rights were burdened by the statute.[84] The Federal Court of Appeals for the Ninth Circuit upheld the dismissal.[85] Planned Parenthood's suit against Indiana, on the other hand, recently enjoyed more success when the Federal District Court Judge for the Southern District of Indiana granted a preliminary injunction against the state's enforcement of disability-selection, sex-selection, and race-selection bans.[86]

Groups that support the legal right to abortion do not disagree with the statistics offered by anti-abortion advocates. The Guttmacher Institute, for example, notes that "the abortion rate for black women is almost five times that for white women."[87] Latina woman have abortions at twice the rate of white women. But advocates do not agree on the reasons for the disproportionate rates of abortion along racial lines. The Guttmacher Institute argues that the disproportionately high rates of abortion among African American and Latina women is because they have more unintended pregnancies due to the lack of access to and failure to use contraception.[88] One thing is clear, however: the disproportionate rate of abortions among minority communities in the United States is an important concern in need of investigation, discussion, and solutions and race-selective abortion bans do not do that.

Conclusion

Bans on sex-selective abortion are spreading like wildfire in American states. Proponents of these bans argue that Asian Americans are aborting female fetuses just like people who live in India and China. Even though the behavior of Asian Americans is targeted by the bans, I found that whether or not a state considers a bill banning sex-selective abortion is not associated with the growth of Asian American immigration in states that have a record of passing restrictions on abortion access. It should be no surprise that the anti-abortion movement is pushing for sex-selective abortion bans. What is surprising is that pro-choice legislators are voting for them.

While these bills were the second most often introduced anti-abortion legislation in U.S. state legislatures in 2012, other than some notable exceptions, pro-choice organizations struggled to present a coherent and forceful opposition to them. This reaction could be because many feminists view the practice of sex selection (whether in favor of a boy or a girl) to be sexist, believe the coercion narrative about sex-selective abortion put forth by anti-abortion groups, accept the misrepresentation of empirical data about the extent of sex selection, and/or do not have the resources to fight the bans given the plethora of other anti-abortion bills being introduced in state legislatures.

In the next chapter, I focus in greater detail on the empirical data on sex-selective abortion practices in the United States and demonstrate how the data was misrepresented by anti-abortion advocates as well as the media. I also present an empirical analysis of sex ratios that tells a different story than the prevailing narrative. Few Asian Americans sex-select. While some Asian Americans may be motivated by a desire to have at least one son, most Asian Americans that do sex-select likely desire gender variety in their families.

CHAPTER 4

Sex Selection in the United States: From Gender-Biased Sex Selection to Family Balancing

Quantitative data sparked the explosion of sex-selective abortion bans across the United States. Bills were introduced in state legislatures in 2009, the year after Douglas Almond and Lena Edlund, economics professors at Columbia University, published a well-publicized study suggesting that Asian Americans[1] sex-select. They looked at the ratio of boys to girls born to Chinese, Indian, and Korean parents and compared it to the ratio of boys to girls born to Caucasian Americans in the 2000 U.S. Census. Appearing in a well-regarded academic journal, the two-page article's findings were very narrow—that some Asian Americans might be practicing male-biased sex selection after they already had given birth to girl children.

The media, and advocates for sex-selective abortion bans, however, greatly exaggerated and misrepresented Almond and Edlund's findings. The study was used to perpetuate the view that a great majority of Asian Americans abort female fetuses because of "son preference." Other commentators reversed the causation—they argued that the study's findings were evidence that there is a "son preference" among Asian Americans. Pro-choice people and advocates did not challenge this portrayal. Instead, at the time the article was released, they consistently argued that restrictions on abortion were not the answer, but that sexism among Asian Americans was what needed to be changed. By this response, they accepted the view that Asian Americans favor sons. Only after we reexamined the U.S. Census and published our data did this narrative begin to change.

There is a general perception that data does not lie. But the problem is not with Almond and Edlund's data; it is with the interpretation of their data. Indeed, both the design and interpretation of results of empirical studies reflect social biases. Tufuku Zuberi and Eduardo Bonilla-Silva made this point in their pathbreaking work *White Logic, White Methods*.[2] They define "White Logic" as "a context in which White supremacy has defined the techniques and process of reasoning about social facts"[3] and "White Methods" as "practical tools used to manufacture empirical data and analysis to support the racial stratification in society."[4]

Zuberi and Bonilla-Silva argue that many empirical studies about race are flawed because the studies see race as an "unalterable characteristic" when in reality it is a social construction. Zuberi points out that researchers sometimes compare race across time and space, but in doing so they fail to recognize that these definitions change over space and time.[5] Studies on race that ignore these concepts are flawed in their design.

The authors also argue that "[e]mpirical results may be a way to understand what is happening; however, these same data tell us very little about why it happens."[6] They further argue that "[d]ata do not tell us a story. We use data to craft a story that comports with our understanding of the world. If we begin with a racially biased view of the word, then we will end with a racially biased view of what the data have to say."[7] Thus, while numbers may be objective, interpretations of them are not.

Using the lens of race, Zuberi and Bonilla-Silva critiqued the methodology used by sociologists. Their book is an anthology with twenty chapters devoted to analyzing existing research from this lens and proposing new research that is conscious of race bias. The critiques in the book are equally applicable to statistical research done by economists and scholars in other disciplines as well as sociologists. I use several insights presented in the anthology to critique research on sex ratios among Asian Americans in this chapter.

A related nascent field in the legal academy and social sciences known as "e-CRT" has recently emerged. Those writing in this field use empirical methods with a critical race theory (CRT) lens.[8] Important contributors to this movement include Professors Osagie Obasogie, Joan Williams, and Mario Barnes.[9] In her 2012 presidential address at the Law and Society conference, Professor Laura Gomez called for increased engagement between social scientists and critical race theorists to use empirical methods to study questions about race.[10] The University of California, Irvine Law Review held the first symposium on the topic.[11] Along this vein, I collaborated with economists to conduct research on sex ratios among Asian Americans. Our findings, contrary to the prevailing view, suggest that Asian Americans want gender-balanced families.

In the section "Critiquing Empirical Studies on Sex Ratios of Asian Americans," I critique the assumptions and interpretations made in the key academic empirical studies on sex selection among Asian Americans. I then demonstrate in "Data and Its Misrepresentation Spurs Legislative Activity" how anti-abortion advocates and the media (mis)interpreted and in some cases intentionally misrepresented the data. The section "New U.S. Data on the Sex Selection among Asian Americans: Son Preference or Family Balancing" presents data from a more recent U.S. Census that suggests that (very few) Asian Americans may be using pre-implantation or post-implantation methods to sex-select in favor of both boys and girls. In the section "Survey Data Suggests the Majority of Asian American People Prefer Gender-Balanced Families," I present survey data on the preferences of parents for the sex of their children. Finally, in "New Data and the Debates on Sex-Selective Abortion Bans," I discuss the implications of our new findings.

Critiquing Empirical Studies on Sex Ratios of Asian Americans

Douglas Almond and Lena Edlund, economics professors at Columbia University, wrote the first academic study to suggest that Asian Americans sex-select. Their two-page article entitled "Son-Biased Sex Ratios in the 2000 United States Census" was published in a well-regarded multidisciplinary scientific journal. The authors determined the ratio of boys to girls in children born to parents who both identified themselves as Chinese, Indian, or Korean. They then compared this to the ratio of boys to girls born to Caucasian Americans. As depicted in Figure 2, they found that the first child born to Chinese, Indian, and Korean parents was just as likely to be a male as the first child born to Caucasian families.

The sex ratio of both groups was 1.05 for their firstborn child. Because the sex ratios of these Asian American groups were the same as the sex ratios of both Caucasian Americans as well as what the authors considered to be the biologically normal sex ratio (1.05), the economists concluded that these Asian American groups did not sex-select when they had their first child. The data they used was a 5% representative sample of the 2000 U.S. Census that is made publicly available by the U.S. government.

They then examined the births in those families who continued to have children. In families that had a girl as their first child, the sex ratio for the second births was 1.17 among Chinese, Indian, and Korean parents. The sex ratio of the third child for these parents who had two prior girl children was 1.51. But note that, in their sample, there are only 324 children born to parents identifying as Chinese, Korean, or Indian American and who have two prior girl children. The sex ratio at the second and third birth was deemed to be abnormal because it deviated from the sex ratio of Caucasian American families at this level, which was again 1.05.[12]

One year after Almond and Edlund's study was published, Jason Abrevaya, a professor in the economics department at the University of Texas, published his own findings on the matter.[13] Abrevaya reports that he thinks there were "2,000 'missing girls' in the United States between 1991 and 2004."[14] That comes out to about 150 per year during that time period.

In 2011, James Egan, with his coauthors, published an important work on Asian American sex ratios using data from the National Center for Health Statistics (NCHS). That data contains birth records for every birth in the United States, but it does not record the sex of the prior children a woman has had. Egan and his coauthors estimate that there were 1000 missing girls per year across the entire United States from 1983 to 2002.[15]

Both estimates of "missing girls" represent a small fraction of the total Asian American population in the United States, which, according to the latest U.S. Census, is more than 17 million people.[16] I am not suggesting that even one abortion for purposes of sex selection is morally acceptable or appropriate. I do not support the practice. I provided the number of missing women to demonstrate that the practice did not occur widely among Asian Americans, unlike what was represented in the popular media and by proponents of the bans.

Abrevaya's data set is much richer than that of both Almond and Edlund and Egan and his coauthors. Abrevaya uses (1) the publicly available 5% sample of the U.S. Census that was also used by Almond and Edlund, (2) the publicly available data from the National Center for Health Statistics (1971–2004), and (3) data from 1970 to 2005 he obtained from the California Department of Health Services (CDHS).[17] Linking personally identifiable information from California to publicly available information, he was able to determine the sexes of the prior children born to every mother who gave birth in California during the time period in question.[18]

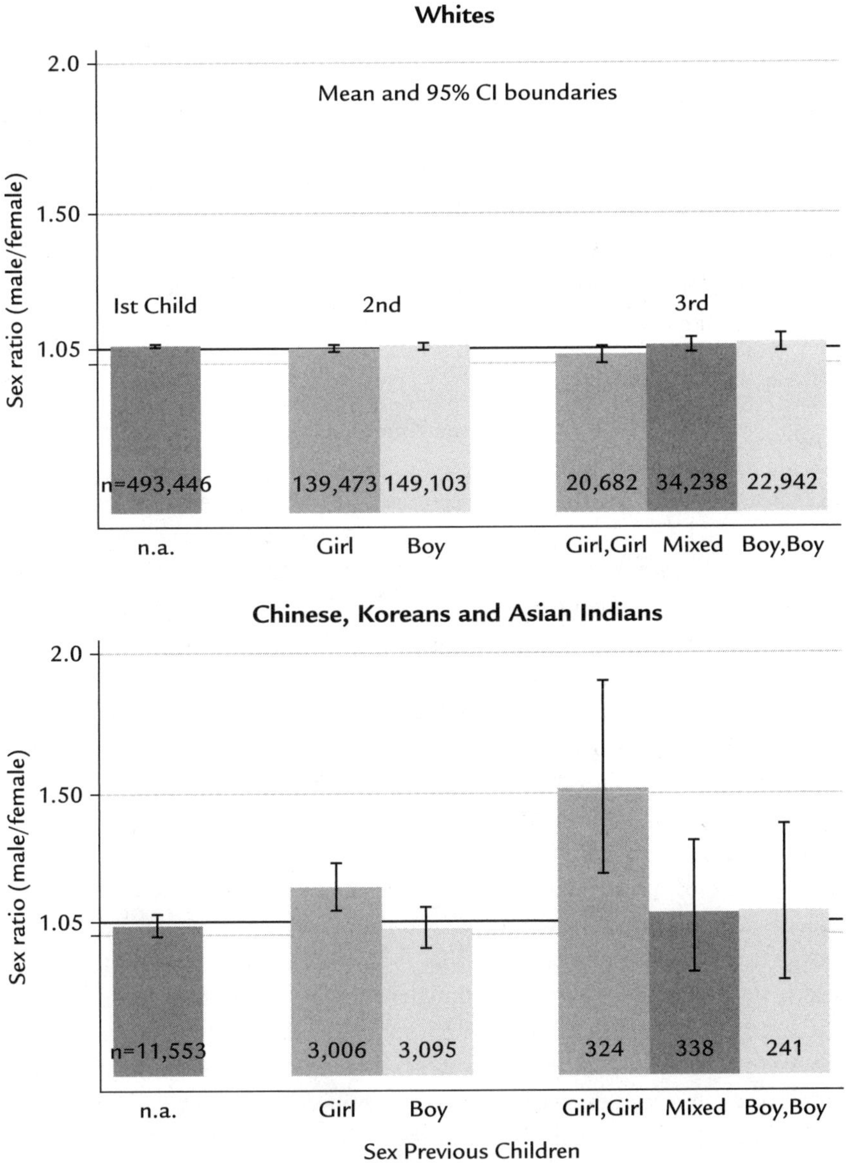

Figure 2. Sex Ratio by Parity and Sex of Previous Children.

Source: Douglas Almond and Lena Edlund, *Son-biased Sex Ratios in 2000 United States Census,* 105 Proc. Nat'l Acad. Sci. 5681,5681, fig. 1 (2008).

Below I examine those three studies from a critical race theory perspective. I explain why it is problematic to use the biological patterns of Caucasian Americans as the baseline or "control group" in making judgments about the behavior of Asian Americans. I demonstrate how a carefully researched quantitative article made careless comparisons between Asian Americans and Asians. Finally, I argue that when data supports an interpretation that is contrary to popular perception, some researchers minimize or ignore that data rather than further exploring it and using it to challenge the dominant narrative of "son preference" among Asian Americans and lack of "son preference" among Caucasian Americans.

Whites as the Control Group

In each of these studies, the authors demonstrate that Asian American sex ratios are abnormal by comparing them with Caucasian American sex ratios. Caucasian Americans are the baseline and any deviance from that baseline is deemed to occur through human manipulation. Abrevaya states that he uses the Caucasian sample "as a 'control' for comparison with Chinese, Indian and Korean samples since there is likely to be minimal [sex] selection among [Caucasians]."[19]

It is not clear why he assumes that Caucasian Americans do not sex-select. Pre-implantation means of sex selection are readily available in the United States and have been for decades. Indeed, a survey of opinions indicates that Caucasian Americans (like Asian Americans) are more likely to want a boy as their first child than a girl.[20]

Instead of assuming that there is no sex selection among Caucasian Americans and therefore the sex ratios of their births can be used as a control, it would be more appropriate to say that even if Caucasian Americans do sex-select, we are not likely to observe that behavior by examining their sex ratios because their population is so large that small deviations in behavior (unlike for Asian Americans) are less likely to skew the sex ratios of the entire group. Unlike the other studies, Egan and his coauthors articulate precisely this logic. They state that "[w]e assumed that if there were any gender selection in the control [Caucasian] population it was minimal or was minimal or neutral, in its effect on sex ratios."[21] But even this logic raises questions of its own; for example, why aren't the sex ratios of African Americans used as a control?

Using Caucasian Americans as a baseline is not just problematic because it assumes their behavior is the "norm" and any deviation from it is abnormal, but also because it may lead to inaccurate conclusions. According to some studies, sex ratios vary by racial group, even when parents are not using abortion or other means to sex-select.[22] Evidence of the disciplinary silos within which research on sex selection is conducted, is that the empirical studies by Almond and Edlund and Abrevaya, who are all economists, do not mention this scientific research.[23]

On the other hand, Egan and his coauthors, who are based in medical schools, do highlight this research. Figure 3, reproduced from their article, depicts sex ratios by race. It appears that African Americans' sex ratios are less male-skewed than those of Caucasian Americans, even in the absence of parental intervention. They note that "maternal demographics, environmental factors and healthcare could still account, at least in part, for observed race and nationality differences."[24] A more robust study would control for all of these other possible reasons for variations in sex ratios such as maternal age, prenatal care, and race, rather than assume that when the sex ratio of a group deviates from Caucasian American sex ratios, it means that the group is sex-selecting.

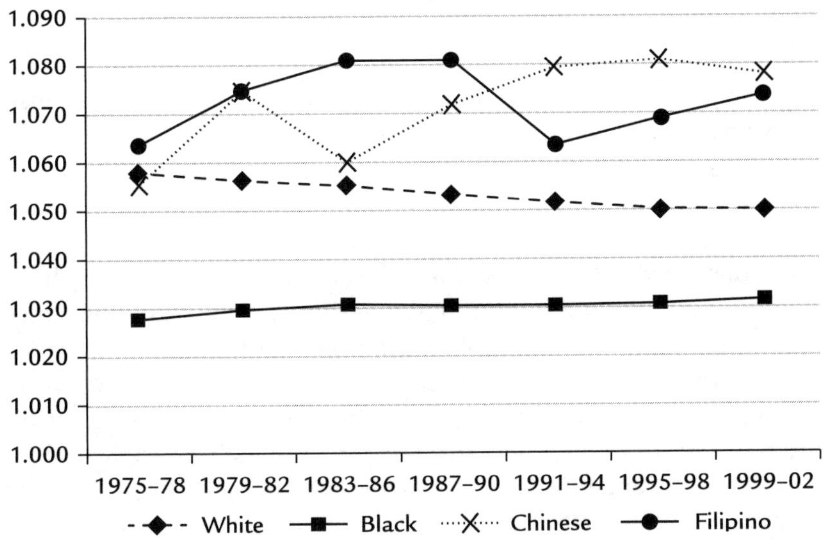

Figure 3. Male to Female Sex Ratios at Birth in the United States in 4-Year Intervals from 1975 to 2002 by Selected Races.

Source: Egan et al., *Distortions of Sex Ratios at Birth in the United States: Evidence for Prenatal Gender Selection,* 31 Prenat. Diagn. 560, 561, fig. 1 (2011).

Recognizing that sex ratios are not constant across countries and races (even absent any parental intervention), the United Nations Population Fund suggests that normal sex ratios fall within a range: 1.03 to 1.07 males for every female.[25] In quantitative sex ratio research, it would be more appropriate to use the "standard range" as a baseline rather than view one race as the "norm." If researchers measured sex selection using the standard range, the range of deviations in sex ratios of Asian Americans from the "norm" would be even more muted.

Natural sex ratios are always male-biased. In other words, ever since births were recorded by sex, more boys have been born than girls. Some scientists suggest this is an evolutionary response to the fact that male infants have a lower survival rate than female infants and the fact that men tend to die before women.[26] A recent study challenges the conventional wisdom that more boys are conceived than girls. The study suggests, on the other hand, that an equal number of boys and girls are conceived. The reason that fewer girls are naturally born than boys is because female embryos and fetuses are more likely to be spontaneously aborted.[27]

Comparing Apples to Oranges: Sex Ratios of Asian Americans and Sex Ratios of Asians

Almond and Edlund lump together the sex ratios of people living in the United States who trace their origin to three different countries—China, Korea, and India. These countries differ in terms of language, government policies, religion, history, and much more. The authors then compare this conglomerated sex ratio (which I refer to in this section as the "Asian American sex ratio" for the sake of brevity) with the sex ratios of the people who live in India, China, and Korea. From the numerical comparisons (which I discuss below), they conclude that the sex ratios of Chinese, Indians, and Koreans in the United States "echo patterns in corresponding Asian countries" and further state that "the magnitude of the deviations . . . for second and third children [of Chinese, Indian, and Korean Americans] is comparable to that documented for India, China and South Korea."[28] These specific statements have been cited by the media and legislative advocates to conclude that sex selection is widespread among Asian Americans. But the inference Almond and Edlund make from the data is problematic for a host of reasons.

Almond and Edlund's analysis found that the sex ratio of the third child of Chinese, Indian, and Korean Americans is 1.51 (i.e., the number of male children born for every female child). They then argue that this figure is similar to the sex ratio in India. They point out that "[a]s a comparison, for India, the corresponding figure was found to be 1.39:1."[29] They are correct that the third births of Asian Americans and Indians seem to have a very similar sex ratio (1.51 for Asian Americans and 1.39 for Indians). But this comparison is misleading because it is only half the picture. The full picture comes from comparing the second births of Asian Americans with the second births of Indians. The sex ratio for second births of Asian Americans is 1.17 when parents have previously had a girl.[30] On the other hand, the sex ratio for the second birth of Indians is 1.32 when parents have previously had a girl.[31] Thus, the sex ratio of Indians at the second birth is far more male-skewed than that of Asian Americans. A significant amount of sex selection occurs at the second birth in India when there is one prior girl child, but sex selection is rarer in the United States at the second birth in the three Asian American communities. This is why it is inaccurate to say that the overall magnitude of sex selection in India is the same as among Asian Americans.

The conclusion they draw from the comparison of the Asian Americans sex ratios to the sex ratio in China is also inaccurate. They point out that that the overall sex ratio in China is 2.25:1.[32] But this sex ratio is significantly greater than the sex ratio for Asian Americans that they articulated. Consequently, unlike what Almond and Edlund state, the magnitude of sex selection was hardly the same among Asian Americans as that of people living in China and India at the time they published their article. It was far more male-skewed in India and China.

The comparison to Asian American sex ratios and the sex ratio in Korea is inaccurate for another reason—it was actually balanced in Korea at the time of their article (and continues to be).[33] Korea is often cited as a sex ratio success story in Asia for eradicating sex selection.[34] Yet, while ratios were balanced in Korea, the ratios among Korean Americans (when combined with Indian and Chinese Americans) were male-skewed.

Later studies, though they received less media attention, made a point of stating that the magnitude of sex selection among people living in Asia and among Asian Americans was not the same. For example, Egan and his coauthors correctly point out that sex ratios in the United States were "lower than some of the values reported for the same populations in their native countries"[35] and as a result the "magnitude of prenatal sex selection in the United States is not on the scale of [that] seen in China and other Asian countries where it results in major sex ratio imbalances."[36]

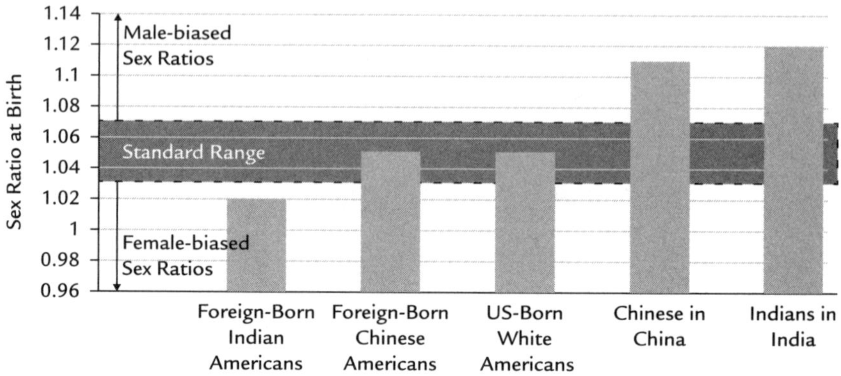

Figure 4. Comparison of Sex Ratios in India and China with Foreign-Born Indian, Chinese, and Caucasian Americans.

Source: Sital Kalantry & Miriam Yeung, *Replacing Myths with Facts: Sex-Selective Abortion Laws in the United States,* University of Chicago Law School International Human Rights Clinic, National Asian Pacific Women's Forum, Advancing New Standards for Reproductive Justice (2014), available at https://ihrclinic.uchicago.edu/page/replacing-myths-facts-sex-selective-abortion-laws-united-states.

Rather than compare sex ratios at birth parities, a more accurate comparison would compare the overall sex ratio of the entire populations of countries. Figure 4 depicts recent sex ratios at birth of people living in India, China, and among foreign-born Indian and Chinese Americans. The sex ratios in China and India are very male-biased when compared to the standard range. However, they are not male-biased for Chinese and Indian Americans (when all of their births are taken into account). Quite remarkably, foreign-born Indians actually have more girls than they have boys. Yet, this data is rarely found in empirical studies or media reports. This data contradicts the dominant norm of "son preference" and its corollary, "daughter aversion." When phenomena are quantified, they become easy to compare across countries, but making such comparisons without providing the full context can lead to dangerous conclusions.

Confirmation Bias and Unexplored Pathways

Zuberi and Bonilla-Silva argued that researchers design and interpret studies to confirm what they already believe about race. This confirmation bias rings true for sex ratio research. Data that confirms the dominant narrative is highlighted and data inconsistent with it is ignored. The dominant narrative is that Asians have a preference for sons, this preference manifests itself in abortions of female fetuses, and the "culture" of people living in Asia is the same as that of people who live in the United States who trace their roots to Asia.

Findings outside of this narrative are not adequately addressed. In both Almond and Edlund and Abrevaya's study, female-skewed sex ratios are observed among Asian Americans. Almond and Edlund's data, represented in Figure 2, shows that the when Chinese, Indian, and Korean parents had one boy, the sex ratio of the next child was female-biased. To be sure, the deviation is very slight toward females, but Almond and Edlund do not address it at all in their discussion.

As observed in Abrevaya's study, in the 1970s people of Chinese descent appear to have had more girls at their third and fourth births than their first two births. Abrevaya relegates a discussion about this to a footnote where he states: "[s]trangely, there is a very low likelihood of boy births among third/fourth Chinese births in the early and mid 1970s."[37]

The reason for this, he assumes, is because "this period predates the availability of ultrasound technology and, therefore, is likely not related to gender selection."[38] The reality is that ultrasounds as well as other technology for sex determination (such as amniocentesis tests) were available in the 1970s.[39] One interpretation of female-biased sex ratios among Chinese Americans is that there is no "son preference" among that community, but that observation is never made.

Similarly, when data about Caucasian Americans does not fit societal perceptions, it is ignored or discredited. For example, Abrevaya finds that the sex ratios of Caucasian Americans are male-skewed. He states that "[w]hite mothers . . . are slightly more likely to give birth to sons after their daughters are born." Yet he concludes that "[w]hile it is conceivable that these effects are the result of gender selection, the lack of systematic evidence for [Caucasian] mothers would make such a conclusion unwarranted."[40] He also found that for Caucasian births, there is a small positive association (.14 percentage points) between a first-born girl and a terminated pregnancy between the first and second birth. But he did not interpret this variation to indicate that sex selection might occur among Caucasian Americans even though it was statistically significant.[41]

The country with the highest male-skewed sex ratio in the world is Liechtenstein, a small country in Western Europe.[42] However, researchers are not flooding to Liechtenstein to study why this is happening. Sex ratios in African countries are significantly female-skewed,[43] and as noted above there is also a slight female-skew of sex ratios among African Americans, but this phenomenon has not been studied. While anecdotal evidence prevails that Caucasian Americans use IVF and PGD to select for girls in the United States, little research is conducted about this. All of these interesting research questions are mostly ignored because there is no dominant narrative that suggests that African Americans or Caucasian Americans want to have boy children. As mentioned above, data is just numbers, but it is the conclusions drawn from the data that reflect society's biases. In the next section, I discuss how the media and legislative advocates further misrepresented these studies to confirm and advance an inaccurate narrative about Asian Americans.

Data and Its Misrepresentation Spurs Legislative Activity

Almond and Edlund's 2008 findings were widely covered in the media.[44] The same day they were published in the *Proceedings of the National Academy of Sciences*, an influential multidisciplinary science journal, National Public Radio aired an interview with Professor Almond. When asked to provide an explanation of their findings, Professor Almond states:

> To us, given the context that in certain Asian countries there's a traditional preference for sons, that desire of sons is being exercised not only in Asia but in the United States, and that the technologies for prenatal sex determination, there's now evidence that those are being used to generate male birth.[45]

He assumes that all Asian countries have a "traditional preference for sons" and that the same preference exists among Asian Americans and is being used to abort female fetuses. His interpretation is that "son preference" causes sex selection.

Other media stories claimed that the data proved that "son preference" was a widely held view among Asian Americans. For example, the title of the *International Herald Tribune* article about the study was "U.S. Asians Show Bias for Boys." These stories cited demographers who claimed that the statistical deviation in sex ratios in Asian American families shows that there is a "preference for male children."[46]

Accepting Almond and Edlund's claims about the magnitude of the practice, William Saletan, a science writer for *Slate* and author of a book on abortion politics, writes, "[s]ex selection of this magnitude has previously been documented in China, South Korea, and India, but not in the United States."[47] He was concerned that the 1.51 sex ratio in the studies meant that sex selection was widespread. Perhaps realizing that their data was being misinterpreted, the authors told several reporters by email that "[w]e should emphasize that our paper does not imply that sex selection is practiced by all or even most Asian-Americans."[48] Nonetheless, even pro-choice organizations appeared to initially understand the data to be evidence of sexist attitudes among a large number of Asian Americans. In a fact sheet about sex-selective and race-selective abortion, NARAL Pro-Choice America states that "[t]hough domestic data are conflicting, some reports indicate members of certain communities in the United States maintain a preference for sons over daughters."[49]

At best what Almond and Edlund's findings tell us is that very few Asian Americans intervene to have a boy child when they already have one or two girl children. These families did not intervene when they had their first child. Another very plausible interpretation of Almond and Edlund's findings that gained no currency was that some Asian American people were sex-selecting to ensure that they had at least one boy child without having to have more than three children. Instead, the media took the misleading conclusions in the study to mean that a large portion of Asian Americans abort female fetuses, therefore finding that the practice demonstrates that Asian Americans prefer male children.

Studies about sex ratios of Asian immigrant populations are also exaggerated in other migrant-receiving countries. For example, one newspaper article about a recent study[50] on sex-selective abortions of Indian-born women living in Canada is entitled "Sex-Selective Abortion May Be Driving Boy Boom Among Indian-Born Moms in Canada: Study."[51] Meanwhile, the authors of the study themselves told reporters that their study demonstrates that 235 sex-selective abortions occurred per year from 1993 to 2012, although they do not mention that number in their article because perhaps it minimizes the importance of the findings.[52]

The anti-abortion movement quickly recognized that the narrative emerging from Almond and Edlund's findings would have great appeal to pro-choice people who are deeply concerned about women's equality. Shortly after Almond and Edlund's article was released, Steven Mosher, a leading anti-abortion figure, proposed that the movement "adopt as our next goal the banning of sex- and race-selective abortion."[53] This is part of a larger strategy to chip away at abortion rights through state-level restrictions.[54]

It was only after Almond and Edlund's article was published that legislation began to be introduced in great numbers in state legislatures to prohibit sex-selective abortion. In 2009, five state legislatures considered (and rejected) sex-selective abortion bans that year. Undeterred, anti-abortion legislators continued to introduce these bills. In 2010, eight state legislatures considered the bans, and only one of them passed it. In 2011, five state legislatures considered the ban and one of them adopted the law. Legislative activity heated up in 2012, when nine states considered the bill, and in 2013, when 16 states considered the bill and three passed it.[55] In 2016, Indiana joined the ranks of the states that have banned sex-selective abortion, but an injunction currently blocks that statute from taking effect.[56]

Almond and Edlund's study features prominently in the bills. For example, the text of the bill introduced in Florida states:

> In a March 2008 report published in the Proceedings of the National Academy of Sciences, Columbia University economists Douglas Almond and Lena Edlund examined the sex ratio of United States born children and found "evidence of sex selection, most likely at the prenatal stage." The data revealed obvious "son preference" in the form of unnatural sex-ratio imbalances within certain segments of the United States population, primarily those segments tracing their ethnic or cultural origins to countries where sex-selection abortion is prevalent.[57]

The states that had passed bans prior to Almond and Edlund's article had done so three decades before. In 1985, the Illinois legislature adopted a provision relating to sex-selective abortion[58] and Pennsylvania banned it in 1989.[59] In both Illinois and Pennsylvania anti-abortion advocates introduced the bans as part of a larger overhaul of the states' abortion laws in light of U.S. Supreme Court decisions.[60]

In reviewing the transcripts of the Illinois Senate and House of Representatives discussions of the bill, I found no mention of global sex ratio trends or the fact that sex-selective abortion was practiced in other countries.[61] Similarly, during the deliberations on the Pennsylvania bill, no supporters of the bill mentioned the situation in other countries or the global sex ratio, and there was no discussion of the behavior of Asians living in the United States.[62]

Instead, the focus of the legislative discourse was broadly on the behavior of all Americans. The main sponsor of the bill, Representative Stephen Friend, cited a *New York Times* poll that indicated that 20% of the medical geneticists interviewed for the poll counseled for sex-selective abortions. He contended that even if no sex-selective abortions "are performed [in the United States] and that poll is wrong, then this legislation prohibiting it does no harm whatsoever."[63]

In testimony submitted to a congressional hearing on the 1989 Abortion Control Act, the Pennsylvania Pro-Life Federation cited anecdotes from newspapers to show that some women (but not specifically Asian American women) in the United States have obtained sex-selective abortions. The group admitted that "[a]lthough no one knows exactly how many sex selection abortions have been performed in the U.S., there are indications that the demand for sex testing are [*sic*] on the increase."[64] The testimony, however, made no reference to the situation in any other country.[65] Senator Karen Ritter, an opponent of the bill, was the only person to mention sex selection in other countries, but only to distinguish the situation from the United States: "This is a terrible practice in other countries like India and China, but we do not do it here."[66]

The absence of a discussion about sex-selective abortion in other countries in the legislative histories of the Pennsylvania and Illinois bills was not because this practice was not occurring abroad at that time. Indeed, Nicholas Kristof reported in the *New York Times* in 1993, "China manufactured its first ultrasound machine in 1979 and by the end of the 1980s it was making 10,000 annually and importing more than 2,000 each year. One Chinese demographer estimates that 100,000 ultrasound scanners were in place around the country by 1990."[67] According to Kristof, sex-selective abortion had become common in China by 1993, and presumably the ultrasound machines were being used to detect the sex of the fetus.[68]

After the Illinois and Pennsylvania bans were passed, a spate of bills was introduced to restrict sex-selective abortion in the 1990s.[69] After Pennsylvania became the second state to enact a law banning sex-selective abortions, no other state enacted a ban until 2010, when Oklahoma passed the anti–sex-selective statute two years after Almond and Edlund's article was published. In stark contrast to the legislative history of the 1980s bans, bills introduced since 2009 are replete with references to the practices of people living in Asia. It is only when a small number of Asian Americans seemed to be having boys, likely not by chance, as their second and third child did people start to look to the behavior of people in Asia for an explanation. They just assumed that "culture" is the driver.

Members of the U.S. Congress and representatives in state legislatures misrepresented the implications of Almond and Edlund's findings even more than the media. The data about relatively few people is used to suggest that all Asian Americans abort female fetuses. Additionally, the data of other researcher's findings don't always agree; Abrevaya finds only 150 missing girls per year, whereas Egan and his coauthors claim 1000 missing per year. In any event, the trend toward male-biased sex ratios peaked in the mid-1990s and all saw it decrease after that.[70]

Nevertheless, in testimony before the South Dakota House of Representatives, the Vice President of the South Dakota Right to Life states: "You cannot explain the male to female demographics that are occurring in birth ratios in some ethnic groups here in the United States, and *this is widespread*, unless you account for sex-selective abortion."[71]

In a hearing before a U.S. Congressional Committee, Steven W. Mosher, President of the Population Research Institute, went even further and directly accused thousands of Asian Americans of aborting female fetuses:

> While it is difficult to say with any exactitude how many sex-selection abortions take place in the U.S. each year, the number is not trivial. . . . [W]e are talking about communities consisting of 3.9 million Chinese Americans, 2.8 million . . . Asian Indians, [and] 1.6 million Korean Americans[.] [T]he highly skewed sex ratios found in census surveys suggest among these groups alone, that tens of thousands of unborn girls have been eliminated, for no other reason than they are considered by some to be the wrong sex.[72]

By citing the entire Asian American population in the United States, he is suggesting that a significant number of them are aborting female fetuses.

Another study often cited in the legislative debates is Sunita Puri's qualitative study. Unlike the quantitative studies, Puri's study does not claim to be representative of Asian women, but it also presumed to represent all Asian American women. In discussing Puri's study, the preamble of the Prenatal Non-Discrimination Act (PRENDA) states:

> Sex-selection abortions are often coerced, and therefore, the opposite of "choice." Researchers at the University of California at Berkeley

> and the University of California at San Francisco completed a study of Indian-American women who had undergone sex-selection abortions in the United States. The study found that sex-selection abortions are often the product of violent coercion. . . .
>
> Forty percent of the women had terminated prior pregnancies when they learned that the unborn child was female. Of the women who discovered they were pregnant with a girl during the interview period, 89 percent underwent a sex-selection abortion. Among those that did not abort their unborn daughters, 100 percent expressed ambivalence about prior sex-selection abortions. Further, 100 percent cited physical and psychological trauma from the past abortions as reasons for not seeking another. Most tragically, 100 percent expressed guilt, shame and sadness over their inability to "save" the daughters they had aborted.[73]

Despite the extensive discussion of Puri's study and reference to data from the study, the one piece of crucial information absent in the federal bill is the fact that only 65 women were interviewed for the study. Moreover, the interviewed women were all known to be seeking sex selection services.

Additionally, sex ratios are inaccurately used as conclusive evidence of the abortion of female-fetuses. For example, U.S. Representative Trent Franks (R-AZ) submitted an article in a congressional hearing record, which claimed: "[w]hat is causing the skewed ratio: abortion. If the male number in the sex ratio is above 106, it means that couples are having abortions when they find out the mother is carrying a girl."[74] The reality is that even if the sex ratios prove that some parents are intervening, no one knows for sure what method of sex selection families are using simply by examining the sex ratios.

Selective abortions of female fetuses are only one cause of imbalanced sex ratios.[75] People can sex-select through artificial insemination, whereby only sperm that will produce the desired sex are allowed to fertilize the egg. This process is known as sperm sorting.[76] Another method of sex selection involves removing eggs from a woman and fertilizing them outside of the body using a procedure called in vitro fertilization (IVF).[77] One or two cells are removed from the embryo three days after fertilization, and the sex of the embryo is determined through chromosomal analysis of the removed cells using PGD.[78] Only the embryos of the desired sex are implanted in the uterus. These sex selection procedures are legally available in the United States and, indeed, fertility clinics actively promote their availability.[79] Three of the four states with the largest Asian populations in the United States—California, New York, and Texas[80]—also have the most fertility clinics in the country.[81] The possibility that pre-implantation sex selection is the reason for the male-skewed sex ratios is never part of the discussion.

Anecdotal evidence from the *New York Times* suggests that Asians were using preconception technologies to achieve the desired sex of the child as early as 2001. The *New York Times* reported on a controversy that erupted when some providers published advertisements in an Indian American newspaper targeting its readership for sex selection services. One of the doctors who placed the advertisement noted, "[j]ust from my own patient population, I'm seeing an increase in those kinds of patients. That's why I started advertising in *India Abroad*."[82] Dr. Masood Khatamee, the Executive Director of the Fertility Research Foundation, stated that he advertised in the Indian immigrant newspaper "because he had seen an increase in the number of Indian clients coming to him for gender selection or, as he put it, 'family balancing.'"[83] In Sunita Puri's study, 14 out of the 65 women (more than 20%) that she interviewed used some form of preconception sex selection. Thus, abortion is not the only procedure leading to modest male-skewed sex ratios in the United States. Yet that point is absent from the media and legislative discussions about the sex-selective abortion bans.

New U.S. Data on Sex Selection among Asian Americans: Son Preference or Family Balancing?

Miriam Yeung and I directed a project team of researchers, advocates, and students that culminated in a report published in 2014 by the University of Chicago Law School International Human Rights Clinic (which I directed at the time), National Asian Pacific Women's Forum, and Advancing New Standards in Reproductive Health (ANSIRH).[84] We wanted to update the data on the sex ratio of Asian Americans because the existing studies relied on data that was decades old. The data used in Almond and Edlund's study is from the U.S. Census of 2000. The most recent data used in Egan's study is from 2002. Abrevaya's newest data is from 2005. We also wanted to examine multiple unexplored questions such as the sex ratio at the third birth parity of Asian Americans when they have two prior boy children?

Arindam Nandi, an economist at the Center for Disease Dynamics, Economics and Policy, and Alexander Persaud, a PhD candidate in economics at the University of Michigan, analyzed more recent demographic data in the

United States. The Coase-Sandor Institute at the University of Chicago Law School did a replication study to confirm the results.[85]

Persaud and Nandi analyzed household data in the American Community Survey (ACS) during the period from 2008 to 2012 to determine male-to-female ratios of the children of Chinese, Indians, and Koreans. We used the same methodology as Almond and Edlund, and to confirm that our methodology was in line with theirs, we reanalyzed the data they used. Our replication of Almond and Edlund's analysis of the 2000 U.S. Census found substantially the same sex ratios that they reported. We restricted our study to the same Asian American groups they used and also determined the sex ratios of Caucasian Americans. By replicating their study, we are not suggesting we validate their survey design or methods. Given that their study made a significant contribution to the field and to the political landscape, we thought it was important to apply the same methodology to more recent Census data.

We used the 2012 five-year pooled sample of ACS data from the Integrated Public Use Microdata Series (IPUMS).[86] The ACS is an ongoing statistical study conducted by the U.S. Census Bureau that collects demographic information of U.S. residents. It is a repeated cross section that covers roughly three million addresses per year all across the country. Crucially, the ACS includes data on household size and composition, as well as nativity and age, which are key components of our analysis. We restricted our sample to parents who are in at least one of the following categories:

1. Both parents are Caucasian (reference group)
2. Both parents are Asian Indian
3. Both parents are Korean
4. Both parents are Chinese

Parents from multiple racial or ethnic groups are excluded. Only two-parent households where one parent is identified as the head of the household are included. In calculating the sex ratios of groups across all births, households that were included had the following characteristics:

1. No children were born outside the United States (to avoid picking up the effects of other countries' policies, e.g., China's one-child policy);
2. No children are stepchildren or adopted children; and
3. All children are 12 years of age or younger.

Additionally, in calculating first, second, and third birth parities, we excluded twins from our analysis.

We calculated sex ratios at birth parities one, two and three, with birth parities two and three subdivided into groups based on the sex of the previous child or children. In total, there are six birth-parity groups: first birth, second birth after girl, second birth after boy, third birth after two boys, third birth after two girls, and third birth after a mix of a girl and boy (any order). All ratios use household weights because the unit of analysis is a household-child.

Sex Ratios of Children of Asian Americans and U.S.-Born Caucasian Americans in the 2008–2012 ACS Data

Figure 5 reports the sex ratios of Chinese, Indian, and Korean children and U.S.-born Caucasian children at three birth parities in the ACS data from 2008 to 2012. Like Almond and Edlund, we found that the sex ratios of Asian Americans (1.33) are more male-skewed when they have two prior girls than the sex ratio of Caucasian Americans (1.04). The ratio in our recent data is less male-skewed than what was found in Almond and Edlund's research. What is surprising is that we found that when Asian Americans have had two prior boys, the sex ratio of the third child (.89) is far more female-skewed than it is for U.S.-born Caucasian Americans (1.07). Almond and Edlund did not observe this result.

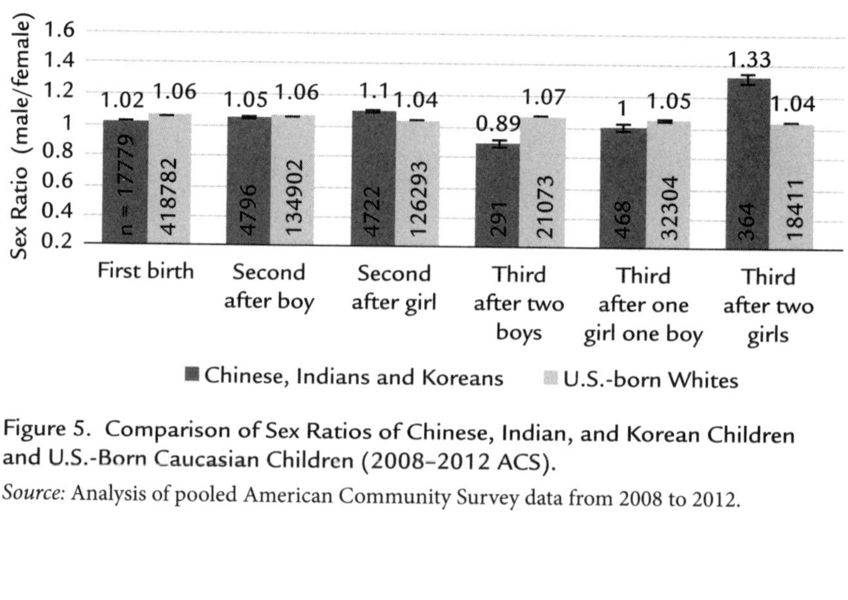

Figure 5. Comparison of Sex Ratios of Chinese, Indian, and Korean Children and U.S.-Born Caucasian Children (2008–2012 ACS).

Source: Analysis of pooled American Community Survey data from 2008 to 2012.

We also wanted to examine what this means for the overall sex ratio of Asian Americans. If the magnitude of the sex selection among Asian Americans is as great as it is among people in parts of Asia, then we would also expect to see a male-skewed sex ratio across all births of Asian Americans. However, we found that the overall sex ratio of Chinese, Indian, and Korean children, taking all births in eligible families into account, is 1.04 (Figure 6). U.S.-born Caucasians, by contrast, have a higher overall sex ratio of 1.05 for the same period (Figure 6).

In disaggregating the Asian American groups, we find that Chinese and Koreans have a sex ratio almost identical to that of U.S.-born Caucasians—1.06 and 1.05, respectively (Figure 6). Indians have an overall sex ratio of 1.02—both lower than U.S.-born Caucasians and lower than the standard range of 1.03–1.07 (Figure 6). What this means is that when we look at sex ratios across all births, Asian Americans (when aggregated and disaggregated) have sex ratios that are well within the standard range of sex ratios. This suggests that no parental intervention has occurred. The only group that is outside of the standard range is Indian Americans, and the sex ratio of their children is actually female-skewed. This is in stark contrast to the sex ratios in India and China.

To summarize, we found that sex ratios of Asian Americans have changed since Almond and Edlund's study and other studies were published. Indeed, prior empirical studies had also observed a change in sex ratios over time.

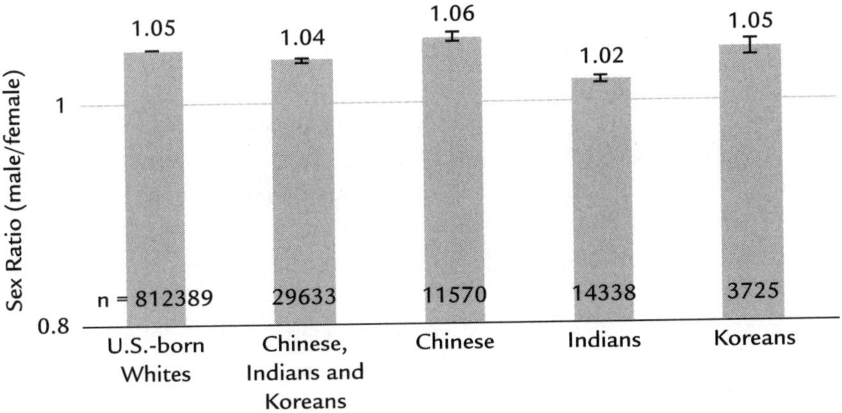

Figure 6. Comparison of Overall Sex Ratios of U.S.-Born Caucasian Children and Chinese, Indian, and Korean Children (as a group and each separately) (2008–2012 ACS).

Source: Analysis of pooled American Community Survey data from 2008 to 2012.

Almond and Edlund found male-skewed sex ratios in the 2000 U.S. Census, but not in the 1990 U.S. Census.[87] Both Egan and his coauthors and Abrevaya saw a spike from 1990 to 1994 toward more male-skewed sex ratios and a decrease thereafter.[88] In light of these variations over time, Egan suggests that "[m]ore data are needed to evaluate these temporal trends."[89]

Our analysis of new Census data confirms that sex ratios among Asians in the United States are rapidly changing over time. Like Almond and Edlund, we found that when Chinese, Korean, and Indian parents have two girls, the sex ratio of the third child shows a male-bias (1.33). However, unlike Almond and Edlund's study, which analyzed data from 2000, we found that in more recent data the sex ratio of the third children of Chinese, Korean, and Indian parents is female-biased after they have had two boys (0.89). This suggests that a very small number of Chinese, Korean, and Indian families are taking measures to ensure that they have both boy children and girl children in their families.

Additionally, we find that the overall sex ratios of Chinese, Indians, and Koreans, taking all births of eligible parents into account, are not male-biased. This is true for the group and for each ethnicity separately. I interpret this data to mean that, to the extent Asian Americans are sex-selecting, so few of them are doing it that it does not impact their overall sex ratios.

Survey Data Suggests the Majority of Asian American People Prefer Gender-Balanced Families

Sex ratio research has limitations. Even where researchers find imbalanced sex ratios, those ratios do not tell us the motivations for people's behavior. Researchers who conclude that a group of people prefer sons based on male-skewed sex ratios in that group are filtering the data through their understanding about that group of people. Although researchers conclude that Asian Americans prefer sons based simply on the sex ratios, the reality is that researchers cannot be certain of the attitudes or beliefs of Asian Americans by examining only sex ratios nor should they make broad conclusions about the attitudes of all Asian Americans based on the behavior of a few.

To explain what motivates the behavior of Asian Americans, I included two questions in an annual national survey conducted by the Cornell Survey

Research Institute (Cornell SRI). The survey is of adult residents age 18 and over who are residents of the continental United States. The survey sample consists of both cellular and landline exchanges in the continental United States. The sample selection procedure ensures that every household with a phone has an equal chance to be contacted, and, once contacted, every adult in the household has an equal chance of being included in the study. People were asked to identify White or Caucasian, Black or African American, American Indian, Asian or Pacific Islander, or other race. In total, 1000 households were surveyed. By way of comparison, the most recent Gallup Poll survey on gender preferences surveyed 1020 people nationally using a similar methodology.[90]

The following questions relating to gender preferences of children were included in the poll:

Suppose you could have only one child:

1. Would you prefer to have a boy?
2. Would you prefer to have a girl?
3. I do not have a preference for the sex of the child.
4. I do not want any children.

Suppose you could have only two children:

1. Would you prefer to have two boys?
2. Would you prefer to have two girls?
3. Would you prefer to have one girl and one boy?
4. I do not have a preference for the sex of the children.
5. I do not want any children.

Consistently across each racial and ethnic group, more respondents said they would prefer to have a son than a daughter if they could have only one child as can be observed in Table 4. This result is consistent with Gallup poll surveys that have asked the respondents the sex of the child they would want if they could only have one child. The Gallup poll, however, does not break down their results by race or ethnic group.[91] In the Cornell SRI poll, only 18.8% of the Asian Americans surveyed said they would want to have a boy if they could only have one child. Similarly, 16.8% of Caucasian Americans said they would want a boy if they could have only one child. On the other hand, a significantly greater percentage of Native Americans (28.6%) and African

Table 4. Results of Poll of Continental U.S. Residents on Gender Preferences by Race and Ethnicity

	Caucasian Americans	*Asian Americans*	*African Americans*	*Native Americans*	*Other*
If you could have only one child:					
Boy Only	16.8%	18.8%	32.7%	28.6%	19.0%
Girl Only	11.2%	10.4%	15.0%	8.2%	4.8%
Don't Care	66.1%	66.7%	47.8%	59.2%	66.7%
Don't Want Children	5.9%	4.2%	4.4%	4.1%	9.5%
If you could have only two children:					
Only Boys	5.0%	6.3%	8.0%	18.4%	0.0%
Only Girls	2.7%	6.3%	6.2%	2.0%	0.0%
One Boy/ One Girl	49.4%	60.4%	58.4%	44.9%	52.4%
Don't Care	38.2%	25.0%	24.8%	34.7%	42.9%
Don't Want Children	4.7%	2.1%	2.7%	0.0%	4.8%
Total Respondents	**768**	**48**	**113**	**49**	**21**

Source: Poll conducted by the Cornell Survey Research Institute Poll 2015.

Americans (32.7%) indicated they would want a boy if they could have a boy. Across all groups, fewer numbers wanted to have a girl if they could have only one child. Thus, when asked about their attitudes, Asian Americans do not manifest a greater preference for sons than any other racial group in the United States.

When the respondents are told they can have two children, 5% of Caucasian Americans want two boys and 2.7% want only girls. If this disparity were observed among Asian Americans, some might see this as proof of "son preference," but few would interpret this to mean "son preference" among Caucasian Americans. Contrary to the dominant narrative of "son preference" among Asian Americans, 6.3% of Asian Americans want only boys and an equal percentage—6.3%—want only girls when they are told they can have only two children.

Another interesting result is that 60.4% of Asian Americans want to have one boy and one girl if they could have only two children. The desire for gender balance is greater among Asian Americans than any other group. Approximately 58% of African Americans desire a gender-balanced family, whereas only 49.4% of Caucasian American desire a gender-balanced family. Still, a quarter of the Asian Americans surveyed stated that they have no preference for the gender balance of their families. These results are consistent with another poll conducted by the Cornell Survey Research Institute in 2015 among New York State residents only, the state with the second largest Asian American population.[92]

Just because someone responds to a poll to express a preference for something, does not mean that he or she will undertake actions in light of that preference. In other words, just because someone says they want to have both a boy and a girl in their family if they could only have two children, does not mean they will sex-select. Yet, the survey results combined with an analysis of our recent Census data on sex ratios suggest that a small number of Asian Americans who have two children are intervening to ensure that their third child is of the sex not represented among their prior two children. This sex selection may be by sperm sorting and IUI or a combination of IVF and PGD or aborting after a blood test or sonogram. Having provided my interpretation of new data as well as a critique of the interpretation of the old data, in the next section, I discuss the implications of our new findings and the implications of those findings for the political conversation on sex-selective abortion bans in the United States.

To be sure, the new research on sex ratios shows that more families who have two girl children appear to be selecting than families that have two boy children. Even in light of our new data, there are likely a few Asian Americans who select in favor of boys because they hold sexist views about girls and women. Perhaps those families desire to have at least one boy to carry on their family name, to cremate them when they die so that their souls are freed from rebirth, or to support them in old age. Yet, these (albeit sexist) reasons are different from the reasons that people in India abort female fetuses. In Chapter 6, I elaborate the point that the practice of selecting in favor of a boy carries a different meaning in the United States than in India.

New Data and the Debates on Sex-Selective Abortion Bans

The new data on sex ratios I presented above and the survey on preferences for family composition suggests that a very small fraction of Asian Americans that have three children have intervened to ensure that the third child is of a different sex than their prior children. They do so because they want to have families that have at least one girl and at least one boy.

People who oppose legal abortion will be unmoved by this data and its interpretation. Even if they accepted that there are only one hundred Asian Americans who sex-select and a smaller portion of them that abort female fetuses, they would still push for the bans. For them, one abortion is too many.

When Almond and Edlund's article was released in 2008, pro-choice groups generally responded by claiming that the solution to sex-selective abortions among Asian Americans is not to adopt legal prohibitions, but to change attitudes and inequality in society. This response tacitly accepts that Asian Americans abort female fetuses because of a culturally ingrained misogyny.

The new demographic and survey data and interpretations may change the perceptions of pro-choice voters and pro-choice legislators who currently support these bans. Once the justifications for the bans are disconnected from stereotypes about motives and behavior of immigrants, anti–sex-selective abortion bills are less likely to gain momentum.

The political debates in the United States are asking the wrong questions, fueled mainly by inaccurate interpretations of old Census data research. The discussion as it stands now is whether we should adopt bans to stop a widespread practice motivated by discrimination. Instead, the question legislative representatives should ask is whether they should pass laws prohibiting behavior that few people engage in (e.g., abortions motivated by a desire to have a certain gender composition in one's family). The bans are particularly troubling because they create a number of other concerns, such as profiling Asian American women. I discuss other implications of the bans in greater detail in Chapter 6.

Conclusion

The anti-abortion movement seized upon a study by economics professors Almond and Edlund to start a nationwide campaign to limit access to abortion. The study made narrow findings that were misinterpreted by the media and misrepresented by some advocates. In this chapter, I have critiqued quantitative studies on sex ratios from the perspective of critical race theory. Together with my coauthors, we examined new demographic data from many different perspectives. We not only looked at the at-birth sex ratios of

Asian Americans after they have two boy children, but we also focused on the at-birth sex ratio of their third child after they have had two girl-children.

Our new empirical research tells a different story about Asian American reproductive patterns. We interpret the data to suggest that by and large, Asian Americans desire both boy children and girl children. A few Asian families who have three children may have intervened to achieve balanced families. Survey data of people's attitudes about the sex of their children also shows that Asian Americans are more likely to desire balanced families than Caucasian Americans. Despite popular perception, the practice of sex selection among Asian Americans is very different from the behavior of Asian people in Asia. The next chapter presents a detailed case study of the causes and consequences of sex-selective abortion in India.

CHAPTER 5

Sex-Selective Abortion in India: Magnitude, Causes, and Responses

I have argued that in evaluating bans on cross-border practices, policymakers, feminists, and advocates inappropriately draw assumptions about the practice based on how it is undertaken in the country where the practice first emerged. In the discussions about sex-selective abortion in the United States, comparisons to the situation in India abound. Anti-abortion advocates, media reporters, and some pro-choice people inaccurately assume that the magnitude of sex-selective abortion among Indian American is similar to what it is among Indians. In the section "The Sex Ratio Crisis Emerges in India" in this chapter, I provide a historical overview of sex ratios in India and I describe the extent of the practice there today. The popular perception in the United States is that Indian Americans widely sex-select and do so for the same reason as some do in India—a cultural preference for boys. In Chapter 4, I argued that the practice is not widespread among Indians in the United States. In "Causes of Sex-Selective Abortion" in this chapter, I explain that the factors that contribute to sex selection in India are specific to the context of India and are not present in the United States. The popular perception in the United States that most women in India who obtain such abortions are coerced is inaccurate.

Feminists in India pushed for a legal response to sex-selective abortion—a ban on sex determination tests in India. Decades after the ban, the sex ratio crisis persists. In the section "Ban on Sex Determination and Its Impact," I describe the Indian legal response to sex-selective abortion, its impact, and its unintended consequences. My comparative and in-depth study of sex-selective abortion in India injects accurate information into the discussions about sex-selective bans in the United States. I then compare and distinguish the societal factors in India and context that contribute to the practice of sex-selective abortion from the context in the United States. In evaluating whether or not cross-border practices violate women's human rights, policymakers and others should endeavor to obtain accurate information about the magnitude, causes, and consequences of the practice in the foreign country.

The Sex Ratio Crisis Emerges in India

In the 1970s, amniocentesis tests were introduced in India. They were designed to test for fetal abnormalities, but they could also be used to identify the future sex of a fetus. Amniocentesis involves withdrawing amniotic fluids and then testing it in a lab. This procedure can be conducted during or after the fifteenth week of gestation.[1]

The All India Institute of Medical Sciences, the country's most prestigious medical school, was the first to offer this test at its government teaching hospital. Other government hospitals soon followed suit. These government hospitals began to use the tests to identify the sex of the fetus and would offer an abortion if the sex was not what the mother desired.[2] The doctors performing the sex-selective abortions justified the procedures on population control grounds. Population control is even more crucial in India today than it was in the 1970s. India has only 2.5% of the world's land and yet 17% of the world's people reside there.[3] The population density of India is 377.7 inhabitants per square kilometer, while China's is 142.9 and the United States's is 31.85.[4] In the 1970s, American foundations actively supported population control efforts in India, including sex-selective abortions.[5]

The use of amniocenteses for purposes of sex determination was banned in government hospitals in 1978, but private clinics emerged to fill the growing demand.[6] Since amniocenteses involved the removal of amniotic fluid and a laboratory for the testing, the tests were mostly available in cities and only affordable for middle-class or rich people. Shortly thereafter, a new technology was introduced in India that offered a relatively inexpensive method and that did not require access to expensive laboratories—ultrasound machines. Ultrasound machines create sonograms, which are visual representations of the fetus. The anatomy of the fetus is developed around eighteen weeks of gestation such that a trained professional would be able to detect the future sex of the fetus. However, medical professionals are not always able to accurately identify the developing genitals, particularly if the fetus is not in an appropriate physical position to allow for such a determination.[7]

By the mid-1980s, many clinics in the capital city of New Delhi offered prenatal ultrasound exams.[8] With a growing middle class and increasing access to ultrasound machines, more abortions occurred and the sex ratio became further male-skewed.[9] General Electric, an American company, was an important supplier of ultrasound machines in India.[10]

Quantifying "Missing Women"

Amartya Sen drew attention to the maltreatment of women when he coined the phrase "missing women." In 1990, Sen postulated that more than 100 million women were missing in the world due to disparate treatment and other social inequalities.[11] Unlike the modern sex ratio studies that use Caucasian sex ratios as a baseline, he used the sex ratio of sub-Saharan Africa as a baseline to determine the number of "missing women" in India.[12] His methodology was not perfect, however, because it fails to account for issues such as biological differences in sex ratios among races, differing fertility and mortality rates, and gender-specific migration.[13]

Sen's work created a genre of studies that estimate the number of "missing women." Economists have debated the appropriate formula for calculating this number. Although Sen's original use of the phrase captured multiple forms of women's inequality, today the concept of "missing women" has been reduced to quantifying the number of female fetuses that have been aborted.[14]

Used in its narrow sense, estimates of the number of "missing women" in India today vary widely. In the 1980s, estimates ranged from 100,000 to 220,000 missing women annually. In each year since 2000, it is estimated that there are 300,000 to 700,000 missing women.[15] Large variations in estimates are due to different assumptions about what constitutes the "normal" sex ratio, different mortality adjustments, and the use of different sources of data. Some studies use the Indian census, others use the National Family Health Survey, and still others use the Sample Registration System.[16]

Most commentators blame imbalanced child sex ratios on the selective abortion of female fetuses. But abortion may not be the only reason for these imbalances. The Guttmacher Institute notes that ultrasounds can only reliably determine a fetus's future sex during the second trimester of pregnancy and later. Yet only 10–15% of all abortions are performed after the first trimester in India.[17] Some argue that a portion of the male-skew in sex ratios can be explained by the relative improvement over time in the life chances of men and boys.[18] Another author cites poverty and malnutrition as factors that cause female fetuses to be disproportionately and spontaneously aborted.[19]

It is important to point out that the convention in the United States is to define sex ratio as the number of boys for every one girl. Using this measure, the standard range of sex ratios across the world is between 1.03 and 1.07. This means that without any parental intervention, for 1 girl born anywhere between 1.03 to 1.07 boys should also be born. On the other hand, in India, sex ratios are calculated as the number of females for every 1000 males. Under the Indian convention, a normal sex ratio would be anywhere between 930 and 970 women to 1000 men. Many authors, though, believe that the normal sex ratio should be 950 females to 1000 males. These authors assume that any deviations from 950 means that some parents are sex-selecting. While I used the American convention for describing sex ratios in earlier chapters, I adopt the Indian convention in this chapter.

The existence of a large surplus of males due to sex selection was discovered by accident when the Indian government created a new category of measurement in the Indian census—the number and gender of children between 0 to 6 years of age. This category was not created to measure sex selection, but to measure literacy rates and schooling.[20] The category captured both the greater number of female fetuses that are aborted as well as girls that die due to malnutrition and other factors. Although sex ratio at birth would be a more accurate predictor of the approximate number of sex-selective abortions, that measure is not used in studies since many births are never registered in India.

The child sex ratio dropped from 927 in the 2001 Census to 914 in the 2011 Census. Yet as the child sex ratio became more male-skewed, the sex ratio of the entire population became more balanced. It rose from 934 in the 2001 Census to 944 in the 2011 Census. Figure 7 depicts the sex ratio of the total population and the child sex ratio since 1951 in India.

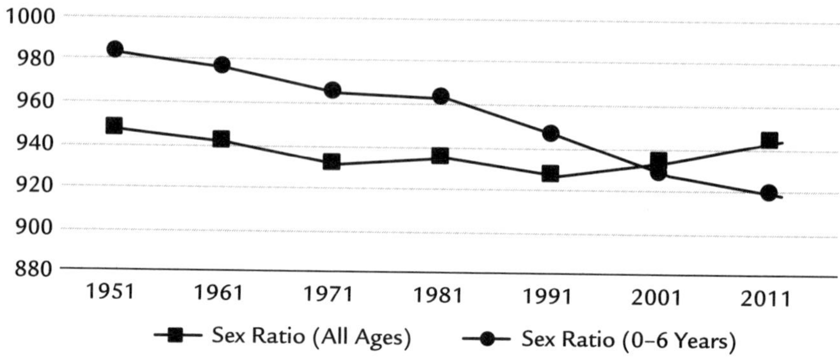

Figure 7. Total Population and Child Sex Ratios in India from 1951 to 2011.
Source: Indian Census and Mary John, Sex Ratios and Gender Biased Sex Selection History, Debates and Future Directions 28 (2014).

Regional Variation in Sex Ratios

The sex-selective abortion debates in the United States treat India as one homogenous entity where sex selection prevails throughout all parts of the country. However, the reality is that there is great regional variation in sex ratios among the Indian states and territories. According to the 2011 Indian Census, 10 states or territories had child sex ratios at or above 950 and 19 states had child sex ratios above 930. The state of Haryana has the lowest child sex ratio at 830. A state on the higher end of the spectrum is Arunachal Pradesh, where the sex ratio is 972. Figure 8 is a histogram showing the distribution of child sex ratios in the Indian states and territories.

The child sex ratios in the states and territories have changed over the course of 10 years. Figure 9 illustrates the changes in sex ratios from the 2001 to the 2011 Census. Child sex ratios improved in eight states, but none of those states reached 950 except for Mizoram and Andaman & Nicobar Islands (which already had sex ratios above 950 in the 2001 Census). The largest decrease in the child sex ratio was seen in Jammu & Kashmir (it decreased by 82), and the largest increase occurred in Punjab (it increased by 48). From this overview of the extent of sex selection in India, it is obvious that the magnitude of the practice in the United States among Indian Americans is very different from the magnitude of the practice among Indians. In the section that follows, I examine a survey of the literature and in-country research in India, and I give an overview of the factors commonly cited for why some women in India abort female fetuses.

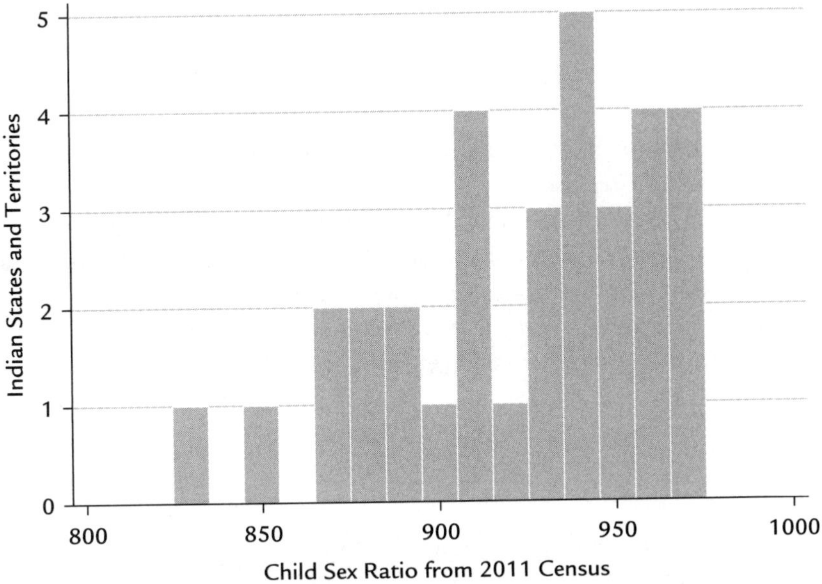

Figure 8. Child Sex Ratios in Indian States and Territories.

Source: Indian Census Bureau, available at http://censusindia.gov.in.

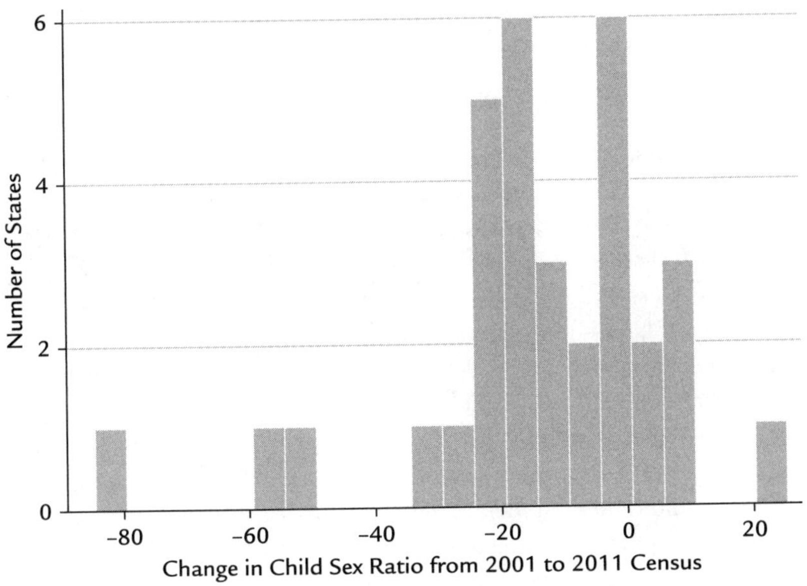

Figure 9. Changes in Child Sex Ratios in Indian States and Territories (2001 to 2011).

Source: Indian Census Bureau, available at http://censusindia.gov.in.

Causes of Sex-Selective Abortion

The British colonialists believed that female infanticide was ingrained in Indian culture. Yet many historians have demonstrated that Britain's economic policies toward its colonial subjects were in part responsible for an increase in infanticide. Commentators in India today cite "son preference" as shorthand for numerous structural reasons that lead people to desire to have at least one son. While many social institutions encourage parents to have boys and discourage them from having girls, the explanation for the spread of sex-selective abortion involves an evolving economy. Pushed by government policies and changing modes of production, families started to have fewer children. These factors, together with the availability of ultrasound machines in the 1980s and 1990s, are reasons for the spread of the practice. The prevailing view is that while there is "son preference," there is also "daughter aversion." A survey of women's attitudes and sex ratio studies, however, indicates that most people are comfortable with having a girl. What they want is at least one boy to carry the family name and to fulfill a Hindu religious sacrament, among other things.

British Blame Culture for Female Infanticide

Early British writers were the first to claim that some Indians killed their newly born female children. They came to this conclusion when they observed the dearth of women in the upper castes. J.P. Grant, Officiating Secretary to the Government of India, described what he understood to be its causes. He noted, "one [cause] is a religious one, founded on the peculiar [tenets] or considerations of caste; the other is a pecuniary one arising out of the habitual expenditure of large sums upon marriage ceremonies."[21]

The prevailing view was that the landed class, the Rajputs, killed daughters in an attempt to consolidate power and because of their adherence to hypergamy, which requires women to marry up in caste. Because the Rajputs were the highest classes, their daughters had no one to marry. It was believed that they would rather kill their daughters than live with the shame of having unmarried daughters.[22] Despite the existence of the practice, the British were unable to find support for it in Hindu texts. On the contrary, the *Brahma Bywant Purana* states that thc killing of a fetus is criminal, as is the killing of a woman or a female child.[23]

In 1870, in an effort to stop the practice, the British passed the Female Infanticide Act. It was later repealed in 1906 even though the practice had not subsided.[24] Talwar Oldenburg postulates that it was repealed because the British did not want to be seen as intruding upon local customs at a time of great economic crises and political instability.[25]

According to Vishwanath, while it may have been true that the British learned of infanticide in 1789 when they observed fewer women in public, the pressures of British economic policies in India could have also spread the practice across the country. By the time the British started to count the number of females and males in the population, the policies were already in effect.[26] Supporting this view, Talwar Oldenburg concludes that British colonial rule caused more infanticide to occur when it drove up the price of land and forced many people into debt.[27] The British also replaced the positive norms in place about women's rights to property by codifying customary law, which excluded those norms.[28] Talwar Oldenburg further argues that the British incorrectly linked dowry to infanticide in an effort to use it, and other practices thought to be contrary to women's rights, as a "cover" for colonizing.[29]

Mara Hvistendahl's recent book on sex selection points out that at the time the British had "discovered" infanticide in India, it was also occurring in England. In 1864, infant deaths accounted for 61% of all child murder cases in England.[30] In the Middle Ages, several European cultures believed that life did not begin until days or even weeks after birth and parents would kill unwanted infants shortly after birth.[31] Though by the nineteenth century most considered infanticide morally unacceptable, many continued to kill babies in secret, especially in England.[32]

Despite these occurrences of infanticide, the practice was not seen as part of British "culture." Distinguishing European infanticide from Indian infanticide, British historian John William Kaye states: "[i]n this Christian country, it is to be feared that the dark crime of infanticide is painfully on the increase. . . . Still it is only a crime—incidental, exceptional. In some parts of India it has been, for many generations, a *custom*."[33]

This is a classic example of how foreign people are defined by their "culture" while the dominant group avoids the stigma. For the dominant group, the same practices are seen as aberrations and not manifestations of its culture. This also occurs in the discourse around sex-selective abortion in the United States.

Decades after the English Crown assumed control of India from the East India Company in 1858, the colonial government conducted its first survey of the Indian people. They found in the state of Gujarat that there were 954 females for every 1000 males.[34] In Rajasthan, the sex ratio was 905, while in Punjab it was 832.[35] In the 1921 Census, the British classified Indian castes into those that killed daughters and those that did not, effectively codifying the view that infanticide was a custom among some castes.[36]

In an article based on his PhD thesis submitted to the Princeton Economics Department, Pravin Visaria concluded that sex ratios became dramatically more male-skewed from colonization until the 1960s. He believed that female mortality was the cause.[37] In the 1901 Indian Census the sex ratio was 961, in 1951 it was down to 946, and in 1971 the number had fallen to 930 women for every 1000 men.[38]

Hvistendahl points out that "[t]oday the logic put forth two hundred years ago by British imperialists in India is applied to sex selective abortion. If you have investigated Asia's gender imbalance, chances are you learned that cultural traditions are to blame."[39] Just as "son preference" culture is used to explain sex-selective abortion in India today, generations ago the British firmly blamed Indian culture for female infanticide. This blame was as unjustified then as it is today. Many scholars have pointed out that killing female infants was not sanctioned by or an inherent part of Indian culture. Rather, it was tied to a host of economic factors, including economic changes imposed by Britain's own policies. Next I discuss the reasons for sex-selective abortion in modern India today.

Explanations for Sex-Selective Abortion

Many commentators in India cite "son preference" as a cause of sex-selective abortion. Many factors are often cited as evidence for "son preference." The tradition of patrilocal residence, where a couple settles into the husband's family's home, is seen as a driver for the desire to have a son and not a daughter. In some communities in India, a daughter is thought to be *paraya dhan* (someone else's wealth). Even where a daughter works outside of the home, if she is married her parents will be reluctant to accept any money from her. On the other hand, sons are the breadwinners for a family. Traditionally parents rely on their sons to provide financial support during old age, given the general lack of a pension system in India.[40] Under the Indian Code of Criminal Procedure, however, a father or mother could sue his or her son or daughter for maintenance.[41] Wealthier families desire sons because they do not want to share their wealth with daughters; that wealth would be transferred to another family.

Dowry is another explanation for sex selection within primarily Hindu communities. Although dowry is prohibited under the Dowry Prohibition Act of 1961, the practice continues today.[42] A dowry is a payment of money—sometimes very large sums—that a woman's parents have to pay to the groom's family when their daughter gets married. For poor parents, having to provide a dowry when a daughter marries can be a significant financial burden.

While dowry may not be as much of a burden for wealthier families, these parents may desire sons in order to perpetuate their family name and to keep their money within the family. A Hindu religious tradition is also often used to explain a desire by Hindus to have a son. Many Hindus believe that only sons should light the funeral pyre of their parents and that *moksha* (liberation from the cycle of rebirth and reincarnation) is only possible through their sons.[43]

Another demand-side factor is the low status of women, which occurs, among other reasons, because women lack opportunities for paid work, their unpaid work is not valued, and they generally do not own property. Although inheritance laws have been reformed, a daughter is often expected to give up her rights to her parents' property in favor of her brothers.[44] An Indian government agency has pointed out that, in India, women own just 10.9% of the land.[45] Even when women have a right on paper to inherit property, their right gets subverted in a variety of ways. Members of their natal family will persuade or coerce them into relinquishing their share of the family property.[46] These social institutions and customs are frequently distilled into this equation: Girls are economic liabilities to a family, whereas boys are economic assets.

However, the discourse on sex-selective abortion in the legislative halls in the United States conflates sex-selective abortion with domestic violence. Some suggest that the abortion itself is part of a cycle of violence against girls and women that begins with violence against the female fetus. Others have argued that all or most women who obtain sex-selective abortions are physically forced to do so by their husbands or other family members. This view is not only prevalent in the legislative and popular discussions in the United States, it also has currency in the popular media in India.

In the famous premier episode of the now popular Indian talk show *Satyamev Jayate*, hosted by a Bollywood star, sex-selective abortion was discussed only in the context of physical coercion.[47] Some Indian academic studies also view sex selection through the lens of violence against women. For example, Kumkum Sangari situates sex selection within the continuum of domestic violence faced by women in India.[48]

While there is no doubt that women may be forced to obtain abortions by physical coercion or demands by their family members for a male heir, women do often obtain them without coercion. Mary John points out that there is little correlation between domestic violence and adverse child sex ratios—the state of Kerala has the most reported cases of domestic violence according to the National Crime Records Bureau, but also has a female-skewed sex ratio.[49] There is physical violence associated with sex selection in some cases,[50] but it is important to note that this has not been proven in many or most cases.

Most of the factors I cited to explain a culture of "son preference" are actually social norms that are embedded in societal institutions. Dowry, sons as caretakers in old age, and inheritance practices are examples. These social norms were traditionally reflected in the legal institutions. It is only in the last fifty years that many sexist practices have been prohibited, but they are still prevalent. Parents' decisions about the gender composition of their families are made within and influenced by these social norms. These societal norms and institutions are generally not present in the United States, even among Indian Americans. Dowry is not known to be practiced among the Indian American community nor is there evidence of a patrilocal family structure. In addition, better support for the elderly by U.S. government institutions reduces the desire to have a boy child for economic support.

Anti-abortion advocates claim that sex-selective abortion is part of the culture of Indian Americans. It is further assumed that immigrants bring these cultural views with them when they migrate. But none of the factors that tilt the equation in favor of the boy child in India exist in the United States except possibly the religious explanation. That is, some Indians living in the United States may believe that only a male heir should perform the final rites of passage for them when they die.

Beyond a Culture of "Son Preference": Economic Factors and Individual Motives

In explaining why sex-selective abortion is widespread in parts of India, commentators often attribute sex selection to culture. But the reality is more complicated than that. The cultural explanation crowds out other factors that have led to a desire for families to have fewer children. In the past, families could have just continued having children until they had a boy, but changes in the modes of production and governmental policies have contributed to a decline in fertility rates.[51] The United Nations Population Division estimated that the fertility rate in India in the 1950s was 5.9 children per woman. This number was not as high as in many other developing countries at the time where the average was often seven children or more.[52] By 2009, fertility in India had declined to 2.6 children per woman, less than half the rate of the early 1950s. There are a host of reasons for the desire for smaller families.

Some argue that as agrarian modes of production become less prevalent (where the labor of children might have been important), people have fewer children.[53] In urban areas, increasing prices and the cost of living influence people to have smaller families.[54] Another reason for the reduction in family size has to do with governmental policies. While people are aware of China's one-child policy (which it recently announced it will change),[55] few are aware of the coercive policies adopted by Indian state governments to enforce a two-child norm model. In pursuit of the goal of smaller families, certain states have adopted laws barring people with more than two children from holding posts in local governing bodies. Currently, the two-child norm is a part of the population policies in Uttar Pradesh, Madhya Pradesh, Rajasthan, and Maharashtra.[56] However, some states have begun to repeal laws that coerce people to have no more than two children.[57]

The Indian Supreme Court has found that the two-child norm in the Haryana Panchayati Raj Act of 1994 did not violate the Indian Constitution. The Court held that the "disqualification on the right to contest an election by having more than two living children does not contravene any fundamental right nor does it cross the limits of reasonability. Rather it is a disqualification conceptually devised in the national interest."[58] Thus, according to the Indian Supreme Court, a person's right to have children can be restricted in favor of the larger societal goal of population control.

Another factor that has led to the increase in sex-selective abortion is economic growth propelled by a change in India's economic policies. India's economy opened its doors to foreign investment in 1991 in a major economic overhaul. This new era was called "liberalization." Prior to that transformation, India's economic policies were driven by Prime Minister Jawaharlal Nehru's vision of socialism. As a result of economic liberalization, foreign capital arrived in India and the middle class grew, which was productive for both the consumers of goods and the workers in these newly established businesses. Some have noted that with more money in the hands of the middle class, they could pay for sex determination tests.[59] Others point out that liberalization created an increased demand for dowries and lavish weddings because of newly available consumer products.[60] This further contributed to a desire to have a boy child to garner dowries and made it more expensive to have a girl child.

Much research on "son preference" makes assumptions about behavior on the basis of macro-trends instead of focusing on the individual level.[61] But surveys and accounts of women's views defy the simplistic view of "son preference" as the cause of sex selection. Some women say they do not want to have daughters because girls face a lot of adversity in society. One woman asks, "[w]hat do you want us to do with our daughters? Why should we let them live? So that they can suffer like we do?"[62] I also saw this reasoning firsthand when I worked with women from poor communities outside of New Delhi. Several women stated that once a daughter is married, she is no longer able to return to her parents' family and must suffer the abuse of her in-laws.

One study of women's attitudes, conducted by the Lawyers Collective, included a survey of 168 households across New Delhi.[63] The top reason women cited for wanting boy children is that they carry the family name (26%), and the second most cited reason was that boy children are necessary to perform death rites for Hindus (17%).[64] An overwhelming majority of women (79%) said that two would be the ideal number of children.[65] When asked about what they thought would be the ideal sex of the first child, a surprising 71% said that it did not matter. For only 11% of women was a male desired as the first child; 18% said that they preferred a female first child.[66] Additionally, 60% of the respondents said one female child was ideal.[67] Another study of opinions in other districts in north India with some of the lowest child sex ratios found that when asked how many children one ought to have, they responded, "one boy and one girl."[68] Taken together, it appears that for the women surveyed, the ideal family is two children and the great majority of women are agnostic about whether the first child should be a boy or a girl.

Nonetheless, how people respond to a survey is not necessarily consistent with what they will do in reality. Yet, there is some consistency with the survey results and actual birth patterns in India. In analyzing a survey of more than

1 million households in India conducted in 1998, Prabhat Jha and his coauthors found that the sex ratio for the first child is 871 females to 1000 males (recall that the standard range is considered to be from 930 to 970 females for every 1000 males).[69] But in the second birth parity for parents with no prior son, the sex ratio was 759 per 1000 males; and the ratio decreased in the third birth parity to 719 per 1000 males for parents with no prior sons.[70] These results suggest that many fewer parents are intervening at the time they have their first child than when they have their second or third child.

In Jha's study, it can be further observed that a very small number of parents with one or two boy children may actually be selecting for girls. Jha's study finds that the sex ratio of the second child of mothers who have one prior boy is 1102 females per 1000 males, and the sex ratio of the third child of mothers who have two prior boys is 1176.[71] These sex ratios are slightly female-skewed (they are above the standard range of 930–970 females to 1000 males). Even if some parents who have boy-children are intervening to have girl children, the proportion of parents who undertake female-biased sex selection is much lower than the proportion of parents with girl children who undertake male-biased sex selection. This is what leads to the male-skewed sex ratio.

The Lawyers Collective survey found that nearly 80% of women were indifferent to whether their first child was a girl or boy. Indeed, there is much more intervention by parents at the second birth than the first birth. The sex ratio studies deviate from the survey in the sense that while 60% of the women thought one girl child was ideal, people are not intervening unnaturally in such great numbers to ensure that they have a girl child.

Many believe that an aversion to daughters is the opposite side of the same coin as "son preference." But if "daughter aversion" were widespread among Indians, then we would see many more parents abort female fetuses at first birth than they do. Instead, it is in the second birth parity where the male-skew is much worse for those with prior girl children, and the male-skew worsens further at the third birth parity for parents with two prior girl children. We also see some evidence for marginal female-biased sex selection. It may not be that parents do not want a daughter—it may be that they instead want at least one son and are indifferent to the sex of the other children they have. The survey of attitudes supports this conclusion, and a qualitative study by Tulsi Patel confirms this view. She concludes, "female foeticide is not approved and/or practised for the first female foetus."[72]

Many commentators presume a culture of "son preference" is the reason for sex-selective abortion, but few studies examine people's individual experiences. These experiences are varied, and people may have different motivations for engaging in sex selection. At least from the account of some women who engage in the practice, they are not doing so out of a hatred of or aversion for daughters. Rather, their intent seems to be compassion. They feel compassion for the girls who are born into an unequal society where violence is prevalent. Nor is sex selection caused by hatred or animus toward the fetus. It is instead the fear of raising a daughter in a society of inequality and violence toward girls and women. Others may simply want to balance their families—they want to have children of both genders.

Does this mean the practice is not problematic? No. It is still wrong. But this more nuanced analysis allows us to formulate more sophisticated responses. The decision seems less problematic if it is seen as resulting from a desire of families to have fewer children while at the same time ensuring they have at least one boy child. The desire for the boy child stems from social institutions and economic pressures—as well as religion-based practices—that tilt the scale in favor of boys. Most parents do not have a hatred for daughters or "daughter aversion." The problem, then, is not as much with individual motives but with the social institutions that shape the desire to have a boy child as well as the consequences of the practice. In the next section, I describe the response of feminists in India when sex selection began to occur more widely and the impact of the legal ban on sex determination and its unintended consequences.

Ban on Sex Determination and Its Impact

The central government of India prohibited medical professionals from revealing the future sex of the fetus to parents in 1994 after decades of intense lobbying by women's organizations. These organizations were disgusted by the sexist ads for sex determination tests, about the structural inequalities in society that contributed to the practice, and about the potential consequences. Even after amendments were made to the law to make it stronger, many commentators believed that the law was a dismal failure. Sex ratios continued to become more male-skewed after the law was enacted. However, while the law did not prevent all or most sex-selective abortions, there likely would have been even more had the law not been enacted. The law that sought to prevent only sex-selective abortion now appears to have had a wider and unintended impact on abortion access more generally.

The Ban on Sex Determination

In the 1980s, offensive advertisements promoting sex determination tests were commonly visible in India. One such advertisement stated, "Pay 500 rupees now and save 50,000 [in dowry] later."[73] In the state of Haryana, the sex ratio dipped as low as 879 women per 1000 men.[74] In response, feminists lobbied for a ban on sex determination tests.

Unlike in the United States where the anti-abortion movement pushes to ban sex-selective abortion, in India it was the women's movement that agitated for restrictions on sex selection. A voice from this movement, Vibhuti Patel, notes, "from 1976 onwards, the woman's movement in India has consistently campaigned to create public opinion against this form of femicide so that Indian women don't become endangered species within the next 50 years."[75]

In 1982, a group of women's organizations organized a protest meeting to demand a complete ban on sex determination tests.[76] In Mumbai, a group called the Forum Against Sex Determination and Sex Pre-Selection was created in 1985.[77] These groups were explicit in their goal—they did not want to place restrictions on abortion access, but instead demanded that medical professionals be prohibited from telling patients the sex of a fetus.[78] The state government of Maharashtra, where Mumbai is located, passed legislation to ban sex determination tests in 1988 before any national legislation was adopted.[79]

Six years later, in 1994, the government of India enacted the Pre-Natal Diagnostic Techniques (Regulation and Prevention of Misuse) Act (PDNT). This act, which came into effect in 1996, prohibited the use of techniques (such as ultrasounds and amniocentesis) to determine the sex of the fetus after conception. However, neither the national nor state governments took the necessary measures to enforce the PDNT.

Consequently, advocates brought a petition to the Supreme Court of India using a mechanism called public interest litigation. This mechanism allows people without standing to bring cases relating to societal-level problems directly to the Indian Supreme Court.[80] In September 2000, the Center for Enquiry into Health and Allied Themes (CEHAT), Mahila Sarvangeen Utkarsh Mandal (MASUM), and Sabu George argued to the Indian Supreme Court that the government had failed to implement the PDNT.[81] The petitioners asked, among other things, that appropriate authorities be appointed at the state and district levels to monitor compliance with the PDNT.

The Court issued an interim order with very specific directions to the central government and state governments to facilitate implementation of the

PDNT.[82] It is not uncommon for the Indian Supreme Court to maintain jurisdiction over a case and require the executive branch to provide the court with reports and updates regarding compliance with court orders. In 2003, the Indian Supreme Court finally issued an opinion in the case. It declared sex-selective abortion "immoral" and "unethical" and consolidated the various directives it had issued in its prior orders.[83]

The law adopted in 1994 had only addressed post-implantation methods of sex selection, but with technology rapidly evolving in India, methods of pre-implantation sex selection became available on the market. Indeed, India continues to be a site for "medical tourism" where foreigners travel to India to obtain medical procedures, including in vitro fertilization (IVF), at a fraction of the cost in their home countries.[84]

In 2002, the Indian Parliament recognized this gap and responded to the Indian Supreme Court orders.[85] It amended the PDNT, changing its title to "The Pre-Conception and Pre-Natal Diagnostic Techniques (Prohibition of Sex Selection) Act" (PCPNDT). [86] In addition to other things, the PCPNDT increases the penalties and other regulations targeted at clinics.[87] Other minor amendments to the PCPNDT were made in 2011. Even though the amendments were meant in part to address advancements in sex determination technology, the reality is that most people are not likely to use IVF for sex selection purposes because it is too expensive. In 2012 wages in India averaged $215 per month,[88] and IVF, together with a test to determine the sex of an embryo, costs $5500.[89]

Medical personnel and individuals who violate the PCPNDT are subject to criminal penalties and fines. Every clinic that uses diagnostic tests that can also be used for sex determination must register them.[90] Each local jurisdiction must appoint a local officer (called the Appropriate Authority) to monitor compliance with the PCPNDT.[91] The PCPNDT further requires all clinics, centers, and laboratories to maintain records of all prenatal diagnostic tests they conduct in order to monitor their use. Additionally, the PCPNDT prohibits anyone from selling ultrasound machines to unregistered clinics or laboratories.[92] Further, the PCPNDT prohibits any kind of advertising of preconception or prenatal sex determination.[93] Interestingly, the PCPNDT incorporates the idea that sex-selective abortions are coercive—there is a rebuttable presumption in the law that a "pregnant woman was compelled by her husband or any other relative . . . to undergo prenatal diagnostic technique."[94]

The PCPNDT does not ban the abortion of female fetuses, but, by limiting information about the sex of the fetus, its objective is to prevent sex-selective abortions.[95] The PCPNDT is silent about what happens if the sex has been determined in violation of the law. While the mother would be subject to certain penalties for violating the PCPNDT, a pregnant woman who obtained a sex determination test in contravention of the PCPNDT could still legally obtain an abortion under the Medical Termination of Pregnancy Act of 1971 (MTP).[96]

On the other hand, Indira Jaising, a prominent feminist lawyer, takes the position that sex-selective abortions are banned under the MTP because they are not specifically enumerated.[97] Despite no explicit language banning such abortions, the MTP is interpreted as allowing for broad abortion access.[98] Under the MTP, abortions are available where medical professionals believe, among other things, that the continuance of the pregnancy would cause "grave injury to her physical or mental health."[99] An explanation to the MTP states that contraception failure for married women is presumed to be a grave injury,[100] which suggests that the exceptions were meant to be interpreted broadly.

Impact of the Ban

Despite the enactment of a ban on sex determination, many claim it has had little impact. The proof usually cited for the lack of implementation is that national sex ratios have only gotten more male-skewed since the adoption of the law. A variety of explanations have been offered for why the PCPNDT has not been effective. First, commentators note that it is inherently difficult to enforce. Ultrasounds are not completely banned, and, on the contrary, they are now a common part of prenatal care practices. It is difficult to prevent medical professionals from conveying the sex of fetuses in the privacy of their patient rooms. Indeed, medical professionals who convey the sex of the fetus do so in coded terms. Regulating ultrasounds is like regulating the misuse of prescription medication. In the United States, prescription medication is legally available for certain purposes but is often used for prohibited purposes.

The sex ratio crisis began with the spread of ultrasound technology in India. The PCPNDT was meant to regulate the use of ultrasound (and other methods) for sex determination. Despite the fact that the PCPNDT prohibits medical professionals from disclosing to a woman or her family members the sex of her fetus, there are many who will offer this service in violation of the law. A robust black market for sex determination and sex-selective abortions has developed. It is very profitable for medical professionals and even nonprofessionals to provide these in-demand services with very low startup costs consisting solely of the cost of a mobile ultrasound machine. Activists who work for nonprofit organizations have told me that illegal ultrasound operators bring portable ultrasound machines to local villages for sex detection purposes. They sometimes also misidentify the sex of the fetus, causing women to abort male fetuses. Others believe that medical professionals have a strong lobby and have made a "mockery of the law."[101]

While the profit motive is strong, many medical professionals actually justify their actions on moral grounds. The Lawyers Collective survey of 52 gynecologists in the New Delhi area (all of whom were women) found that 27% of them stated that a woman has the right to choose the sex of her child. Thirty-seven percent even said that if the sex of a woman's fetus is female, she has the right to abort. Many gynecologists believed it was normal and acceptable for women to want to balance their families. One respondent lamented that only the poor are subject to the PCPNDT while the rich can circumvent it. Another gynecologist openly admitted that "she herself goes by her 'discretion' and feels that women and their families should have the right to design their family."[102] Another respondent stated, "if after 2 daughters, the 3rd is terminated, what is wrong with it? Everyone has a right to design her family."[103]

These comments made by doctors suggest that they disagree in principle with the ban on sex determination tests and think that it inhibits women from exercising their right to family balance. Knowing that their responses could subject them to scrutiny, few doctors would likely have admitted to providing sex selection services in violation of the law. But they clearly think it is morally acceptable and desirable for families who have only one or two girl children to know the sex of their fetuses and to act upon that knowledge to abort female fetuses.

The Lawyers Collective also conducted a survey of registered owners of ultrasound machines in the New Delhi area and found that while 48% of the owners were clearly in favor of the ban, 28% said that the record-keeping requirement of the ban was too burdensome and that doctors were unnecessarily harassed.[104] Clearly, this is not a representative sample of all owners of ultrasounds; those owners conducting illegal operations are unlikely to ever register. Moreover, those owners that are flouting the law might not respond to the survey. Thus, if one-third of the ultrasound owners who responded to the survey view the PCPNDT as cumbersome and unnecessary, many more medical professionals likely take that view. Both of these surveys reveal the difficulties in enforcing the PCPDNT—some medical professionals think it is ethical to violate the law when women have one or two prior girls, and some believe the law is cumbersome.

Second, the implementation mechanisms for the PCPNDT are inherently weak. The PCPNDT does not provide for the involvement of the police in monitoring compliance with the law. It instead relies on officers appointed by the state.[105] The enforcement of the law is an additional task placed in the hands of bureaucrats who often fail to devote adequate time and resources to implementing the law.[106]

Third, many observe a general lack of political will to enforce the law. There have not been many convictions against medical professionals for violations of the PCPNDT.[107] Since 1994, when the sex determination ban was first adopted, there have only been 206 convictions.[108]

Finally, Indira Jaising and Asmita Basu point out that the text of the PCPNDT is confusing and should be amended. They note that the law is not clear on what providers are covered. Although "genetic counseling centers" fall within the ambit of the PCPNDT, by "[n]ot having defined 'genetics' or 'genetic counseling' " the PCPNDT "makes the definition of 'genetic counseling center' meaningless."[109] Therefore, gynecologists may believe they are not covered by the PCPNDT because they do not provide "genetic counseling."[110] The reason for this lack of clarity is because the PCPNDT was originally designed in 1994 to address amniocentesis tests, but now ultrasounds are used in routine prenatal care for purposes other than genetic testing. Today ultrasound machines are the main conduit of sex detection.

Despite the general lackluster implementation of the PCPNDT, there are well-known examples of local officials who zealously enforce the law. For example, a district collector from Hyderabad, Arvind Kumar, is noted for ensuring regular and effective monitoring of the PCPNDT. As a result, the city of Hyderabad showed a marked improvement in its child sex ratio as compared to neighboring districts.[111] Ad hoc private efforts for enforcement have also been made. For example, pregnant women working for a nonprofit organization ask to know the sex of their fetuses and when medical professionals reveal it to them, the medical professionals are reported to the authorities.[112]

General Electric (GE), a corporation that makes ultrasound machines and sells them in India, also made efforts to aid the implementation of the PCPNDT. In recognition of the fact that their ultrasound machines were being used to illegally detect and convey the sex of a fetus, they implemented a stringent sales review process, including regular auditing, rigorous sales screening, and tracking of ultrasound machine sales. All ultrasound machines were also labeled with a visible sticker stating that the law prohibits female feticide and sex-selective abortions. In addition to standard contract terms stating that illegal use of the ultrasound technology is prohibited, all contracts specified that the machines should not be used to determine and communicate the sex of the fetus to patients. GE also implemented a training program for its sales personnel so that they could instruct end users about the ramifications of using the technology in violation of the PCPNDT. Additionally, sales personnel were advised to terminate any sales discussions or contracts if they become suspicious that the customer would misuse the technology in violation of the law.[113]

While it is true that sex ratios have only gotten more male-skewed since the introduction of the ban on sex determination, one study suggests that sex ratios might have been even more male-skewed were it not for the ban. Six years before a ban was adopted by the central government, the state of Maharashtra acted to ban it. Arindam Nandi and Anil Deolalikar compared the sex ratios in Maharashtra after it adopted a state ban to the sex ratios in neighboring states. Through a difference-in-difference analysis, the economists conclude that the sex ratio in Maharashtra, although it got worse after adoption of the ban on sex determination, was better than the sex ratios in neighboring states. Thus, had Maharashtra not banned sex determination, the sex ratio in that state would have been even more male-skewed.[114] This demonstrates that the ban had at least some impact (it prevented some sex-selective abortions) even though it was not successful in preventing all (or even most) of them. Nonetheless, no one will argue that the PCPNDT has achieved the goal of prohibiting sex selection altogether.

Unintended Consequence of the Ban: Restricting Abortion Access

Unlike in the United States, abortion rights were never at the forefront of the women's agenda in India. Abortion, in India, is not a constitutional right.[115]

In the 1960s, population control policies took center stage, and the ability of women to obtain abortions was seen as a way to curb population growth. An act of Parliament, the Medical Termination of Pregnancy Act (MTP), legalized abortion in 1971. Prior to the MTP, the Indian Penal Code penalized the causing of a miscarriage, where both medical providers and abortion-seekers were subject to criminal liability.[116]

There is no strong anti-abortion movement in India, and abortion is not generally considered morally problematic from a Hindu perspective. Despite this, as part of the campaign to end sex selection in India, terminology like "murder" and "female foeticide" was employed to raise awareness about the problem. The imagery used to support campaigns against sex-selective abortions resembled the images in the anti-abortion movement's messages in the United States. For example, pictures would depict a fetus in a woman's womb or suspended in space suffering violent attacks.[117] Even if it was not the intent of the advocates, those pictures convey the message that sex-selective abortion is wrong because of the harm it does to a fetus and not because the practice is sexist. Recently, the state of Maharashtra even proposed to amend the Indian Penal Code to treat "female feticide" as murder.[118] Feminist organizations strongly opposed this amendment.

There is increasing awareness among advocates who campaign to end sex selection that they should clarify that their goal is not to end access to all abortion services. For example, a United Nations Population Fund report cautions advocates against using words such as "female feticide." It states:

> Personhood is attained after birth; a foetus does not have independent life until born. The terminology of "female foeticide," though commonly used, is misplaced in its emphasis on "killing of a foetus." Use of such terminology undermines the MTP Act and wrongly equates every legal abortion with killing. It is also detrimental to women's access to safe abortion, further adding to the stigma and misconception that abortion is illegal.[119]

Many groups now work toward addressing underlying inequality in society rather than focusing on abortion.[120]

Nevertheless, the enforcement of laws and policies to counter sex selection has inadvertently led to restrictions on nonselective abortions. The 2011 Census results in India revealed the most skewed child sex ratio to date.[121] As a result, some state and district authorities imposed regulations on abortion providers and chemists.[122] In 2012, a study was conducted in 215 chemist shops in Maharashtra to explore the effect of the new regulations on the availability of medical abortion. Results showed that medical abortion drugs were available in only 10% of chemist shops, 32% of shops had never stocked these drugs, and 58% reported that they stopped stocking the drugs after the government began enforcing the new regulations. The most commonly reported reasons for not stocking the drugs were the increased burden of the documentation needed to dispense them (91%) and threats from a drug inspector or some other authority about stocking them (56%).[123] The study further found that some providers stopped offering legal abortion services, especially in the second trimester.[124]

Another study found that doctors are refusing to perform most second-trimester abortions. For example, one gynecologist states that:

> Most of us have stopped doing second-trimester abortions, because it can make trouble if this has been done for sex selection. . . . You do second-trimester abortions only if the woman is unmarried. If the patient does not want any more children, if she is interested in making an appointment for a sterilization, then we do a second-trimester abortion. Not for temporary contraception.[125]

Doctors presume that any married woman seeking an abortion after twelve weeks of conception is doing so because the sex of the fetus is female.

Despite this hesitation, there may still be symbolic reasons to have a ban in place—there are probably fewer sex-selective abortions than there would otherwise be. Additionally, a ban conveys a strong message that the society and government oppose the practice. Indeed, even at the time they were pushing for it, activists knew that the ban might not work to stop sex selection, but by criminalizing it, they thought that the government would send a strong message against the practice. The existence of a prohibition on sex selection also encourages organizations and government entities to work on changing the underlying structural inequalities that contribute to parents' desire to have at least one son.[126] In interviews with parents in rural parts of North India with the lowest child sex ratio even decades after the ban was adopted, some parents refused to practice sex selection and proudly pointed to their daughters.[127]

Conclusion and the Way Forward

Despite the enactment of legislation aimed at curbing sex-selective abortion, the child sex ratio in India has become more skewed over time. The narrative used to explain the male surplus is one where culture meets technology. Part of the cultural story is that families want to have only boys and not girls. This story leaves out factors like changes in fertility patterns, and changes in modes of production. It also overemphasizes "daughter aversion" as the driver for sex selection.

Discussions rarely seek to determine the motives and perspectives of women. When people do focus on the family unit, it is presumed that women are violently forced to obtain abortions. The coercion narrative is largely dismissed by authors in India, but it remains part of the popular imagination in the United States. For some women in India, sex selection is a way to gain status in their family and society and to limit the number of children they give birth to.

Others argue that the individual motivations of parents are reprehensible. Families want sons and do not want daughters. "Daughter aversion" is less of a driving factor than people assume. Examining survey and birth parity data, it appears that the families that sex-select do so both to have fewer children and to ensure they have at least one son. The practice is not by and large driven by "daughter aversion."

There is a near universal view in India that sex selection in favor of boys is problematic and that the government should make efforts to stop it. But there are dissenting voices. From a feminist perspective, Nivedita Menon recently questioned whether restrictions on sex determination and abortion are consistent with a woman's right to privacy, autonomy, and reproductive rights in general.[128] Another view, to which few openly admit, comes from a population control perspective and holds that sex-selective abortion should not be curbed because it helps control overpopulation.[129]

Those who believe that sex-selective abortions should be prevented propose solutions in line with a supply and demand framing. Solutions to limit the supply of illegal services involve better enforcement of the PCPNDT.[130] The view is that if people do not have access to ultrasounds, then they will not be able to identify the sex of the fetus. Solutions to reduce the demand for sex-selective abortions involve improving women's status. In this vein, structural changes are called for, such as access to more (and better quality) education, access to property through inheritance, and the ability to engage in and obtain meaningful employment opportunities.[131] Others argue that women's status will improve with the enforcement of laws against dowry and violence.[132] Aside from changes in laws and policies, commentators support programs aimed at changing people's mindsets so that they value girls more. An example of such a program involves celebrating the birth of a baby girl by sending a marching band and distributing sweets to neighbors, a practice normally done only when a son is born.[133]

In an effort to stop women from obtaining sex-selective abortions, some local officials track pregnant women and require people to register pregnancies.[134] In one village in Punjab, monitoring involved using information technology and other coercive methods.[135] Other tactics include holding "mourning" ceremonies in front of the home of families that are suspected, often without any proof, to have obtained sex-selective abortions.[136] There were a number of suicides as a result of these informal, coercive methods.[137]

Many feminists have objected to these types of methods. The primary concern is that pregnant women not seeking sex-selective abortions are also being targeted. Indeed, those are precisely the type of programs American anti-abortion groups also help to fund.[138] But even if there is a way to know that a woman is at risk of having a sex-selective abortion (say, because she has one or two prior daughters), these tactics are still problematic because they are disparately applied to poor women and violate women's privacy rights and bodily integrity.

Other efforts by local governments include programs that pay a certain amount of money to families with daughters. The first such policy was introduced by the state of Tamil Nadu, which paid parents when a daughter was born and then gave more money at various stages of schooling until she turned 21.[139] The program in New Delhi is known as the Ladli Scheme.[140] In another state, the government pays families $11.20 a month for a girl in school—but only if her mother gets sterilized after having one daughter.[141]

Feminists have expressed great concern about these programs on a host of grounds. Many argue that government programs pledging to give money to a woman at the time of her marriage reinforces the idea of dowry; and indeed, these transfers are being used by parents to pay dowry costs. In Northwest India, these programs are often referred to as "dahej" (dowry) schemes by some community members.[142] Others oppose these programs because they do nothing to target the underlying patriarchal structures and inequality that lead parents to sex-select in the first place. Some critics think that the programs are underinclusive because the eligibility requirements are too demanding.[143] Additionally, the programs, to the extent they work, do nothing to change the behavior of middle-class and rich people.

It will be nearly impossible for the government of India to stop illegal ultrasound providers from giving women information about the sex of the fetus. There have been successful raids by police who are tipped off by pregnant women who pretend to seek sex determination tests and when the providers give that information, they inform the police. But these are few and far between. New methods of sex detection, such as blood tests, are also on the horizon that could make regulation even more difficult. A pregnant woman can prick her finger and send a sample of her blood to a lab for analysis, and the results are very reliable as early as seven weeks of gestation.[144]

With increasing acceptance of women's employment outside of the home and increasing opportunity for some women, men will no longer be seen as the only source of care for their parents in old age. This phenomenon and other social norms that lead to parents desiring to have at least one male child will change. But changing economic and social inequality is a long-term process. In the short-term, I suspect that child sex ratios are not likely to become more balanced in the next few decades. In the next chapter, I discuss the grave consequences for women and girls in India of imbalanced sex ratios that are manifesting themselves in parts of India and evaluate laws against sex-selective abortion from the transnational feminist framework.

CHAPTER 6

Transnational Legal Feminist Approach to Sex-Selective Abortion Bans in the United States and India

Bans on sex-selective abortion that are being passed in the United States are reason-based restrictions on a woman's right to choose. They prohibit sex-selective abortion during both pre-viability and post-viability. No woman should abort a fetus on the basis of its future sex, and only a few women in the United States probably do. On the other hand, in some countries, a sizable number of women select in favor of boys.

In Chapter 2, I articulated a woman-centered perspective to evaluate bans on sex-selective abortion. Under this balancing test, prohibitions on sex determination tests or sex-selective abortion can be justified if there is significant evidence that the practice is widespread in the society and that as a result of the practice there is evidence of significant negative consequences for women and girls as a whole in that society. If, on the other hand, sex selection is not widely practiced, then adopting such a ban does no more than restrict reproductive rights without any benefits for women and girls in society.

The prior three chapters provided an in-depth look at anti–sex-selection laws and practice in the United States and India, which have both adopted some form of a ban on sex selection. In both countries, advocates have justified bans from a feminist perspective. According to advocates, prohibitions on sex selection prevent sex discrimination. In this chapter, I evaluate these claims using the feminist perspective I developed in Chapter 2. In applying this framework, I draw upon the features of the transnational legal approach I articulated in Chapter 1. I conclude that U.S. states and the federal government should not adopt bans as they burden reproductive rights and do not fix any problems. Moreover, the U.S. Supreme Court should find that the bans are unconstitutional.

Evaluating Bans on Sex Selection in India

Sex selection became widespread in the 1980s and 1990s in India with the advent and distribution of ultrasound machines. Sonograms were being used to detect the sex of the fetus. To prevent this practice, the government of India enacted the Pre-Natal Diagnostic Techniques (Regulation and Prevention of Misuse) Act (PDNT) in 1994. This act prohibited the use of ultrasounds and amniocentesis to determine the sex of the fetus after conception. In 2002, responding to the Indian Supreme Court orders,[1] the Indian Parliament amended the PDNT, changing its title to "The Pre-Conception and Pre-Natal Diagnostic Techniques (Prohibition of Sex Selection) Act" (PCPNDT).[2] The PCPNDT (among other things) increases the penalties and imposes further regulations upon clinics.[3] Below I examine how the ban burdens reproductive rights and the consequences of the practice.

Does the PCPNDT Burden the Reproductive Rights of Women?

The PCPNDT prohibits medical professionals in India from telling any woman the sex of her fetus. Medical personnel and individuals who violate the PCPNDT are subject to criminal penalties and fines. Although the law was carefully crafted not to restrict abortion directly, the PCPNDT denies women information about their bodies and calls into question the reasons why a woman may terminate her pregnancy.

In India, the right to choose does not flow from the constitution, but from an act of Parliament.[4] The Bombay High Court rejected the view that the prohibition of sex determination tests violates personal liberty or any other constitutional right.[5] However, the restrictions in the PCPNDT do deny women information about their body. This denial of information effectively prohibits sex-selective abortions. If the law is appropriately enforced, then to the extent a woman wants to have a boy child, she may need to have many children to ultimately give birth to a boy child.[6]

In addition, new data suggests that the ban on sex selection is chilling access to nonselective abortions. Some medical professionals have refused to provide second-trimester abortions altogether for fear that the patient may be intentionally aborting a female fetus.[7] Other evidence suggests that access to medication to induce abortion is more difficult to obtain as sex ratios continue to become more male-skewed in India. Some government and nongovernment programs implementing the ban are also coercive—they monitor and follow pregnant women in certain villages. In sum, both the prohibition on the information about the future sex of a fetus and the ban's implementation burden individual women's reproductive rights. Next I evaluate the impact of the practice of sex selection on women and girls in society.

How Does the Practice of Sex Selection in India Impact Women and Girls in Society?

In this section, I ascertain how sex selection as practiced impacts or harms women and girls in society. There are two parts to this inquiry. Under the feminist approach I proposed in Chapter 2, we first determine if sex selection is widespread in the jurisdiction. The next step is to evaluate the actual impact or harm to women and girls in society using empirical and context-specific information.

1. *Is the practice of sex selection widespread?*

The at-birth sex ratio is an indicator of the level of sex selection in any society. This ratio is the number of girls to boys born during any given time period in the society. However, a significant portion of births in India are not registered and as a result the at-birth sex ratio is not accurate. The "child sex ratio" is more reliable; it measures the ratio of girls to boys who are six years of age and younger. The Indian government generates this data when it undertakes a census.

The child sex ratios are calculated as the number of females for every 1000 males. Under the Indian convention, if there were no parental intervention, normal child sex ratios would be anywhere between 930 and 970 women to 1000 men. However, the actual child sex ratio in India is highly skewed in favor of boys. The child sex ratio in the 2011 census was 914, which dropped from 927 in the 2001 Census. This suggests that sex selection became more widespread since the period measured by the 2001 Census to the period measured by the 2011 Census. There is great regional variation in child sex ratios among the Indian states and territories. According to the 2011 Census, 10 states or territories had child sex ratios at or above 950 and 19 states had sex ratios above 930. Estimates of the annual number of "missing women" in India from 2000 to 2011 vary significantly from anywhere between 300,000 to 700,000.[8] Thus, the child sex ratio in India suggests that sex selection does occur widely in India.

2. *What is the consequence of sex selection (focusing on women and girls)?*

The choice made by hundreds of thousands of Indian women each year to abort female fetuses because they do not want to have a daughter has a number of societal consequences. A host of studies undertaken in multiple countries today have attempted to measure the consequences of sex selection. These studies generally examine how the surplus of men impacts the following groups: (1) men, (2) women, (3) girls that are born, and (4) society in general. In this section, I discuss all these findings, but focus my inquiry on the impact to women and girls.

Ineligible Bachelors

A significant number of men will never have female marriage partners in India as a result of sex selection. Christophe Guilmoto, a preeminent demographer, identified a phenomenon known as the "marriage squeeze."[9] Some believe that even if India's sex ratio returned to normal, by 2050 the country would still have 30% more single men hoping to marry than single women.[10] In some parts of India, a name has been coined for the plethora of aging single men. In the state of Haryana, they are called *malang*, and in the state of Punjab they are called *chhara*.[11] The marriage squeeze also impacts women. If the prevailing practice of women "marrying up" is followed, it is predicted that women at the highest rung (the highly educated) will not be able to find marriage partners.[12]

Girls Who Are Born Do Well

Another set of emerging studies examine how sex selection affects girls. These studies hypothesize that sex-selective abortions of female fetuses benefit girls that are born. These authors assume that this is because there are fewer unwanted girls as a result of sex selection. In places where there is greater sex selection against females, these authors predict that girls that are born are wanted and therefore will be treated better. One study found that an increase in the practice of sex selection in favor of boys is associated with the reduction in the incidence of malnutrition among girls.[13] On the other hand, a study by Arindam Nandi found that decreased sex selection did not increase infant mortality.[14] In other words, a more balanced sex ratio is not associated with a lower infant mortality rate. One study suggests that the practice of sex selection in India benefits the nutritional outcomes of girls and another suggests that the prohibition of sex selection does not harm the girls that are born (even if they were not wanted). Consequently, there are no clear results one way or another.

Crime in Society Increases

The other major category of studies has examined the impact of sex selection on crime in society. Hudson and Den Boer, international relations scholars, rang the alarm bell over a decade ago about the potential adverse impact of a surplus of unmarried men in Asia.[15] They argued that young men who lack stable bonds commit the most violent crimes. Another study showed how male-skewed sex ratios, particularly for those 18 to 25 years old, increased the rate of violent and property crimes in China.[16] The authors noticed that unskilled young men were increasingly resorting to crime to boost their incomes in order to fare better in the more competitive market for potential brides.[17]

Emerging studies about India have confirmed that a surplus of men is associated with more violent crime. In an article published in 2000, economists Jean Dreze and Reetika Khera, using 1991 Indian Census data, found a strong relationship between male-skewed sex ratios and murder.[18] Shareen Joshi recently updated their study using the 2001 Indian Census and also found a strong association between male-skewed sex ratios and murder, arson, robbery, and riots.[19] When she conducted a regression analysis to control for variables such as rural versus urban, percentage of people of scheduled castes in the region, and income, she found that while male-skewed sex ratios were not strongly associated with robberies, the association with murder remained strong.[20]

Authors have offered several strands of explanations for why a surplus of unmarried men leads to more crime. First, some argue that the biology of unmarried men—they have higher testosterone levels than married men—makes them more prone to commit crimes than married men.[21] But at least one other study did not find an association between testosterone levels and the commission of violent sexual crimes (including rape).[22] Second, others argue that when women are sparse, men compete for resources with each other to become more eligible. For example, crimes such as robbery might increase as men compete for limited resources to attract women.[23] A third explanation is known as the "supply of offenders," which suggests that when there are more men in society, the number of people who commit crimes will also increase given the fact that in most societies it is men who disproportionately commit crimes.[24] Whatever the most accurate explanation is, studies in parts of India have found a correlation between the rate of crime and male-skewed sex ratios in India.

Impact on Women

A host of studies examine the impact of sex selection on men, girls, and society in general, but fewer studies have focused exclusively on the impact on women. The view that sexual violence is on the rise in India has gained currency since the international media reported the December 16, 2012 rape and murder of Jyoti Singh. Some blame this rape on culture, but empirical studies are beginning to correlate violence against women with a male surplus. South and his colleagues' study of household surveys on victimization in India found that a surplus of men is associated with increased violence against women. They used household surveys instead of the number of reported crimes in assessing the rate of violence because the rate of reporting itself might be a function of a male-dominated society. In more male-dominated societies, women are less likely to report crimes.

By examining household survey results, the authors found that the "numerical abundance of males in the local area modestly but significantly increases the likelihood that members of Indian households are victimized by theft, breaking and entering, and assault, and also increases the probability that young women in the community are perceived to be harassed."[25] Some posit that sexual violence increases because of the unmet sexual gratification of unmarried men.[26]

In another study, Sunita Bose and her coauthors found a correlation between domestic violence and a shortage of women. Using survey data from the National Family and Health Survey, the authors found that a low community sex ratio is associated with a higher likelihood of wives being punched by their husbands.[27] Furthermore, wives in communities with a sex ratio imbalance in favor of men are more likely to be slapped, pushed, or shaken.[28] On the other hand, they found that other forms of domestic violence were not associated with community sex ratio changes. The authors conclude that "in a patriarchal society such as India a relative shortage of women will encourage men to resort to violence and control in order to constrain women's interactions with other nonrelated men and to confine women to traditional roles as wives and mothers."[29] Incidentally, quantitative empirical studies outside of India also suggest that a surplus of men leads to more violence toward women.[30]

Another consequence of sex selection in favor of boys in India is that dowry amounts have decreased and positive attitudes toward women's property rights have increased. A study by Larsen and Kaur surveyed 651 women, 1450 children, and 83 bachelors from 18 villages in three northern Indian states (Punjab, Haryana, and Himachal Pradesh). The authors found that there was a lowered demand for dowry, or no dowry was paid at all, because of a bride shortage.[31]

The authors also found a change in attitude toward women's inheritance rights. Where sex-selective practices favor boys, daughters are more willing to ask for their share, but they will receive it only if they have no brothers.[32] Relatedly, women are increasingly more likely to take on the responsibility of taking care of the parents, which in turn may indicate a weakening in "son necessity."[33] Overall, the authors conclude that the cumulative effects of these findings may result in an improved sex ratio and greater gender equality in the future.[34]

Yet another consequence of sex selection is that people are more willing to marry outside of their castes. Mishra studied 47 brides who were brought from different regions ("cross-region") to five villages in Haryana.[35] Mishra found that in less than ten years the number of cross-region brides increased.[36] Mishra attributes the increase in number to the effect of the sex ratio imbalance. People value marrying someone from the same cultural background as them because (among other things) they might believe that the same cultural values would be passed to the next generation.[37] However, Mishra found that people have been more willing to overlook the cross-region brides' lack of local cultural knowledge.[38]

In sum, on the whole, the findings of empirical studies lend support to the position that a male-skewed sex ratio in India negatively affects women and girls living in society. Harassment of women and domestic violence is correlated with regions in India where the sex ratios are more male-skewed. While in regions with male-skewed sex ratios, dowry amounts have decreased. This is a benefit to the parents of the daughters. An increase in intercaste marriage is a positive move toward a more equal society in India, but does not impact women directly in the way that violence does. The most positive impact on women is that parents are more likely to give women in male-surplus regions greater inheritance rights.

Writing decades ago, a number of scholars predicted the consequences of male-skewed sex ratios. I evaluated these theories in Chapter 2. Today there is data to test those theories. After decades of sex selection in favor of boys in India, most of the empirical studies published to date are not consistent with the theory that women, on the whole, will be better off if there is a shortage of them, because both public and private violence is likely to increase for many women.

Guttentag and Secord predicted that a male surplus decreases female literacy and lowers the age of marriage for women. According to UNICEF, India is the country with the sixth highest rate of child marriage in the world.[39] So while it is possible that Guttentag and Secord's predictions apply to India, more work needs to be done to confirm this. Empirical scholars should also study the impact of sex selection on trafficking and bride importation.[40]

Mary Warren's theory appears to be most consistent with what is happening in India. She predicted that a male surplus will negatively impact women in societies that are more male-dominated. While it is very difficult to measure whether societies are male-dominated, one way to do it is by referring to the United Nations gender inequality index, which measures women's reproductive health, political participation, workplace participation, and other relevant factors in countries around the world.[41] According to that global index, India ranks 130 out of 155 countries in terms of equality for women.[42] This suggests that India is a highly male-dominated society with high levels of gender inequality. Of course, the levels of inequality vary by class and other factors. Warren would predict that in such a country, sex selection in favor of men will actually harm women. The empirical studies discussed here, on the whole, are consistent with this prediction about India.

Balancing Burdens on Reproductive Rights and Harm to Women and Girls

The denial of information about the future sex of the fetus itself burdens women's reproductive rights in India. In addition, this ban has had a chilling impact on other reproductive care. Women who are not seeking to terminate their pregnancy due to the future sex of the fetus are finding it more difficult to obtain legal abortions. Even though the ban impinges on reproductive rights, the Indian government may still be justified in limiting such information if the practice by some women is harming women as a group in society.

Sex selection has been practiced by enough families in India that there are far fewer women than men in many regions. Emerging empirical studies suggest that the consequences of a male-skewed ratio in India are negative. There is more harassment in public spaces and an increase in some forms of domestic violence. The studies are far from complete on the topic—but if Warren's theory on sex ratios is correct, women and girls in society will continue to fare badly in Indian society.

In evaluating the ban in India, it is important to consider its effectiveness in actually curbing sex selection. The Indian Parliament first banned sex determination tests in 1994, the Indian Supreme Court ordered the law's full enforcement in 2002, and Parliament amended the law to strengthen it in 2003. However, according to the national census, the child sex ratio has become more male-skewed since the enactment of the ban. In 1991, the national child sex ratio was 945, in 2001 it was 927, and in 2011 it became 918. Even though the child sex ratio has become more male-skewed over time, this does not mean that the ban has been completely ineffective. Indeed, the ratios could have been worse were it not for the ban.

Arindam Nandi and Anil Deolalikar's empirical study of sex ratios in Maharashtra suggests that bans have at least some impact. The state of Maharashtra enacted a law banning sex detection tests six years before the central government. As a result, for a period of six years, Maharashtra was the only state in India to ban sex detection. The authors found that the sex ratio in Maharashtra, although worse after the ban's adoption as further discussed in Chapter 5, was better than the sex ratios in neighboring states.[43]

There are unintended consequences of the ban (chilling other reproductive care), and it has failed to achieve the intended impact (curb or significantly stop sex selection). These are also considerations that Indian advocates, policymakers, and scholars must look at in evaluating the ban. The transnational legal feminist perspective gives these stakeholders a new lens with which to understand the restriction and reassess whether or not it is appropriate. Advocates who support bans can use this framework to justify their goals in feminist terms rather than using anti-abortion rhetoric. Others can use this framework to call for repealing the ban. With this feminist framework, I propose to change the parameters of the debate among the relevant actors in India.

Beyond the factors articulated is the legal framework I propose, there are other reasons advocates may want a ban. A ban conveys a strong message that the society and government oppose the practice. Indeed, even at the time they were pushing for it, activists knew that the ban might not work to stop sex selection, but by criminalizing it, they thought that the government would send a strong message against the practice. The existence of a prohibition on sex selection also encourages organizations and government entities to work on changing the underlying structural inequalities that contribute to parents' desire to have at least one son.[44] Interviews with parents in rural parts of North India with the lowest child sex ratio even decades after the ban was adopted revealed that some parents refused to practice sex selection and proudly pointed to their daughters.[45] I do not definitively conclude whether or not a ban on sex selection in India is consistent with the framework I articulate. That determination should be made by stakeholders in India. I next turn to evaluating sex-selective abortion statutes in the United States and conclude that they are not justified under the legal framework I propose.

Evaluating Bans on Sex Selection in the United States

Nine states in the United States have adopted laws that prohibit medical professionals from terminating pregnancies when they suspect that a woman is seeking it due to the sex of the fetus. In this section, I evaluate the bans adopted in the United States from the transnational feminist legal perspective. The bans prohibit a woman from exercising her right to choose regardless of whether she is doing it for purposes of creating gender variety in her family or because of a preference for a certain gender. As I said before, I do not think any woman should terminate her pregnancy due to sex preference and not many women in the United States probably do so. Yet, these statutes burden reproductive rights in other ways. The at-birth sex ratio in the United States is close to the natural range, which suggests that sex selection does not occur widely. Consequently, the practice has no negative impact on women or girls in U.S. society as it does in India. Thus, the negative consequences or costs of these laws do not outweigh the benefits, of which there are few, if any. Thus, the bans do not promote women's equality.

Do the Anti–Sex-Selective Statutes Burden Women's Reproductive Rights?

Anti–sex-selective abortion statutes in the United States are "reason-based" restrictions on a woman's right to choose during the pre-viability and post-viability period. Unlike in India, where women strongly desire to have at least one son, most Americans do not feel strongly about the gender composition of their children.[46] A ban's intended impact will be minimal even if it could be enforced. It is, however, the other consequences of these bans that create obstacles to reproductive liberties. First, medical professionals may begin to profile Asian American women and restrict access to their reproductive rights even when they are not seeking sex-selective abortions. Second, the bans are meant to (and do) create barriers between all women and access to abortion services.

Profiling of Asian American Women

The legislative debates over the sex-selective abortion bans in the United States that have been proposed since 2009 point to the global problem of "missing women."[47] Two countries are singled out in the discourse—China and India. For example, the U.S. congressional bills introduced in 2015 and 2016 state that the "[c]ountries with long-standing experience with sex-selection abortion [are] the Republic of India . . . and the People's Republic of China."[48] Indeed, legislators use the perceived behavior of Asian Americans and what is understood about Indian culture to justify the need for the bans.[49]

There are references to India and China not just in the discussions on the federal legislation, but also in state legislative hearings. The bill proposed in Colorado contains virtually the same language as the preamble of PRENDA.[50] In Arizona, Sydney Hay, testified before the state's Committee on Health and Human Services, referred to an article in the *Economist* when she explained that:

> [W]hether overtly killed, aborted, or abandoned to die, well over 100 million girls [have] disappeared from the world, and many experts now believe sex selection abortion is the primary cause. And this is not just a hidden catastrophe in countries like India and China, where son preference, stemming from one-child policies and other cultural factors, has had a devastating impact on their societies.[51]

While it is true that sex ratios are heavily male-skewed in India and China, the legislative testimony, legislative hearings, and comments of legislators and advocates who support sex-selective abortion bans do not mention the male-skewed ratios that are emerging in countries like Armenia and Liechtenstein.

Indeed, the sex ratios in those countries show a stronger male skew than India and China's sex ratio. According to the U.S. Central Intelligence Agency's "World Factbook," Liechtenstein has the highest male-biased sex ratio at birth in the world, at 1.27.[52] It is believed that, absent manipulation, the standard range for male to female sex ratios at birth is approximately 1.03 to 1.07 males for every female, with an average of 1.05.

No one has provided an adequate explanation for why the at-birth sex ratio in Liechtenstein is so male-skewed.[53] The male-skewed sex ratio in the small European country is even more surprising given that abortion is banned there altogether.[54] This means that either sex selection is being achieved through means other than abortion or residents are crossing borders to neighboring countries to obtain abortions. Alternatively, the data may be flawed; countries self-report the data to the CIA World Factbook.

Leaving aside Liechtenstein, there are also several countries in the Caucasus region that have recently experienced increases in at-birth sex ratios. For example, the sex ratio at birth in Armenia is 1.14, higher than both India and China.[55] In Azerbaijan, the sex ratio is 1.12, well outside the standard range.[56] As shown in Table 5, at-birth sex ratios are skewed in favor of males in eleven countries. Six of these countries are in Europe. Of the remaining countries, four are in Asia, two are in the Caucasus region, and one is in the Caribbean. It is interesting to note that eleven countries—almost all of which are in Africa and the Caribbean—have sex ratios at birth below 1.03, indicating more girls than boys are born there, in comparison to the standard range. Table 6 lists the eleven countries and their sex rates at birth.

Sex-selective abortion ban proponents likely focus on Asians because it fits predominant stereotypes of Asian cultures as misogynist and because

Table 5. Countries with Sex Ratios at Birth Above the Standard Range

Country	*Sex Ratio at Birth*
Liechtenstein	1.26
Armenia	1.14
Hong Kong	1.13
Azerbaijan	1.12
India	1.12
Vietnam	1.12
Albania	1.11
China	1.11
San Marino	1.10
Grenada	1.10
Georgia	1.08
Kosovo	1.08
Macedonia	1.08

Source: CIA, Field Listing: Sex Ratio, The World FactBook, https://www.cia.gov/library/publications/resources/the-world-factbook/fields/2018.html.

Table 6. Countries with Sex Ratios at Birth Below the Standard Range

Country[1]	*Sex Ratio at Birth*
Kazakhstan	0.94
Barbados	1.01
Haiti	1.01
Cayman Islands	1.02
Kenya	1.02
Malawi	1.02
Mozambique	1.02
Puerto Rico	1.02
Qatar	1.02
Saint Kitts and Nevis	1.02
South Africa	1.02

Source: CIA, Field Listing: Sex Ratio, The World FactBook, https://www.cia.gov/library/publications/resources/the-world-factbook/fields/2018.html.

[1] The Republic of Nauru has a sex ratio at birth of 0.84 but is not included in the table because it has a population of less than 10,000 people. See Nauru, in THE WORLD FACTBOOK, CIA, https://www.cia.gov/library/publications/the-world-factbook/geos/nr.html.

these stereotypes do not hold for people who live in Europe and in the Balkan countries. The popular American media similarly focuses mainly on Asian countries and not on the sex ratio disparities in other countries.

The discourse on sex-selective abortion and the text of the bills are aimed at the behavior of Asian American women. Medical professionals might profile women of Asian descent by inaccurately assuming that these patients are seeking an abortion for sex-selective purposes when they are not. The statutes penalize medical professionals (not the patient). Consequently, medical professionals are incentivized to deny abortion access to Asian American women even if they have no cause to suspect that the women are seeking it for purposes prohibited by the statutes.

Access Barriers for All Women

Not only could sex-selective abortion bans lead to the profiling of Asian American women, but they also place access barriers on all women seeking an abortion. The bans place enforcement in the hands of medical professionals. Medical professionals are prohibited from performing an abortion on someone they know is seeking it for prohibited purposes. By making the medical professional fear for her own liability on the basis of the intent of the patient, these laws create a wedge in the relationship between the patient and the medical professional. Laws that interfere with this relationship jeopardize the quality of health care services.

Some states explicitly require medical professionals to inquire about the reasons a woman is seeking an abortion. South Dakota's law banning sex-selective abortion amended their abortion laws to require medical professionals to "[i]nquire into whether the pregnant mother knows the sex of her unborn child and if so, whether the mother is seeking an abortion due to the sex of the unborn child."[57] Oklahoma requires medical professionals to complete a form for each abortion, which includes a section on the reasons a woman obtained the abortion.[58]

For each abortion performed in Arizona, the medical professional must sign an affidavit certifying that the medical professional "is not aborting the child because of the child's sex or race and has no knowledge that the child to be aborted is being aborted because of the child's sex or race."[59] Arizona also requires health care professionals to report "known violations . . . to appropriate law enforcement authorities."[60]

These laws strain the relationship between the patient and doctor by making the woman cautious about what she discloses to her provider and by making the provider feel concerned that he or she could be subject to criminal sanctions based on the intent of the patient. While these intrusions may seem minor, they are barriers for a woman who has made the difficult decision to terminate her pregnancy. Thus, the anti–sex-selective statutes burden a woman's reproductive rights. Next I examine whether these prohibitions benefit women and girls in society.

What Is the Impact of Sex Selection on Women and Girls in the United States?

When reproductive technology enabling sex selection first emerged, there was a wellspring of feminist writing predicting a doomsday where people selected against girls.[61] A sociologist professor at Columbia predicted that there would be a 9.5% surplus of males in the United States if sex-selection technology became widely available.[62]

Jodi Danis predicted that the resulting male surplus would force women into traditional gender roles. She thought women would be valued only for their reproduction, violence against women would increase, and women would be increasingly underrepresented in positions of power.[63] Roberta Steinbacher pointed to public opinion polls in the 1970s that showed a preference for male firstborn children to argue that even if there were no male surplus, families would preselect for boys as firstborn children and girls as second-born children. [64] This, she asserted, would have negative consequences for girls because second-born children are more likely to have low self-esteem and be less intelligent.[65]

Even today Americans are more likely to desire to have a male child than a female child if they could only have one child, according to both the Gallup poll[66] and a poll conducted by the Cornell Social Science Research Institute.[67] Yet Americans do not appear to act on these preferences by sex-selecting for boys. Indeed, the at-birth sex ratio of the American population is not imbalanced. The ratio is in the natural range: 1.05.

The balanced sex ratio suggests that either sex selection is not practiced by a large number of people or, to the extent people are sex-selecting, about the same number of people are selecting for boys as they are for girls. Some studies have found that the few Americans who do use reproductive technology to sex-select are more likely to select for females.[68] Another study found that parents with two boys are more likely to use these reproductive technologies to select for a girl than families with two girls.[69] Sex selection, whether through pre-implantation or post-implantation methods, probably rarely occurs. Even if it does occur widely, it has not resulted in a male surplus or imbalanced sex ratios. Unlike in India, the practice of sex selection by some women does not negatively impact women's safety or cause women other actual harms.

In Chapter 4, I used data to demonstrate that sex selection among Asian Americans is limited and to the extent it occurs, a fair interpretation of the data suggests that those Asian Americans who sex-select do so to achieve gender balance within their families—families that have a girl select for a boy and families that have a boy select for a girl. Some feminists oppose all sex selection because those who engage in sex selection reject the notion that genders are fluid and not always tied to sex.

Other people who object to the practice altogether when it solely targets girls may be concerned that the empirical analysis of the recent U.S. census data I presented in Chapter 4 indicates that a few Asian Americans sex-select in favor of boys. Additionally, the data also suggests that more women who have two girl children will intervene to have a boy child than women who have two boy children will intervene to have a girl child. They may assume that the behavior of parents who sex-select when they have two girl children is inherently sexist. Drawing assumptions about their understanding of the horrors of the practice in India, they further misunderstand the practice in the United States.

Part of the reason feminists in India object to sex selection against girls is because they believe it occurs as a result of unequal societal institutions and that it also perpetuates those institutions. It may be true that the practice is discriminatory against women and girls in India, but that doesn't necessarily mean it is discriminatory in the United States. A practice gains meaning as discriminatory in the context in which it occurs. When traveling with my family members from New York City to upstate New York we would sometimes stop in fast-food restaurants along the way. We were often the only nonwhite people. On more than one occasion, I would hear someone say "dot-head" to us. Referring to the *bindis* Hindu women wear on their head, this is a derogatory term for Hindus. While this name-calling does not necessarily meet the legal definition of discrimination, because we were the only nonwhite people in the restaurant and part of a minority group in the United

States, I considered it to be discriminatory. The label separated me and my family from other Americans and made light of our cultural traits. This incident both reflects and reinforces racial inequality in the United States.

However, if that same person from upstate New York went to a restaurant in a small town in India and started to call people "dot-head," most people would probably look at him in puzzlement, but would not feel discriminated against. This is because the context is different. People at that restaurant in India are probably not familiar with what the term means and the fact that it is meant to be derogatory. Moreover, given that Hindus are the majority religion in India, they may be less likely to take offense at such a phrase even if they know its meaning and intent.

Similarly, many of the factors that define sex selection as discriminatory in India do not exist in the United States. The practice of sex selection reflects and further perpetuates gender inequalities in India. First, some argue that the practice of dowry causes people to prefer sons, but this practice is not common in the United States even among immigrants. Families in the United States often share the costs of marriage. Second, others argue that in India parents want to have at least one son because parents in India rely on their sons for support in old age given the lack of a national health care system. In the United States, although it is not necessarily adequate, the government does provide health care and other retirement benefits. Third, another argument advanced to explain "son preference" sex selection in India is the patrilocal system, where the daughter physically leaves her parents' family and joins her husband's family after marriage. In 2010, in the United States, 87% of households were comprised of the householder, his or her spouse, and his or her sons and daughters. Only 0.7% of households included a parent-in-law, son-in-law, or daughter-in-law.[70] Finally, in India, although property laws allow for inheritance by daughters, in practice that does not occur.[71] Daughters are often pressured by their fathers, mothers, and brothers to relinquish any claims to their share of paternal wealth. In the United States, daughters are not generally disinherited just because they are female. Thus, the societal motivations for sex selection and the institutions that shape our understanding of the practice as discriminatory in India are generally not present in the United States.

Comparing the practice of sex selection in India to the practice of sex selection in the United States is almost like comparing apples to oranges. In Chapter 4, I used empirical data to demonstrate that the scope of the practice in the United States is a tiny fraction of what it is in India. The data on sex ratios also shows that a few families who have boy children intervene to have girl children. I also relied on a poll of Asian Americans asking them about their preferences for the sex of their children. In this section, I have presented a comparative analysis of the Indian and American contexts. From this comparative study, I argue that many of the structural factors that contribute to sex selection are not present in the United States. I have also pointed out that a practice gains meaning as being discriminatory from the context and institutions in the country. Just because something is discriminatory in one country does not necessarily mean it will be discriminatory in another country. This comparative analysis, taken together with the empirical data in sex ratios and the poll results in Asian American preferences, suggests that the practice of sex selection in the United States is sharply distinct from the practice in India.

I am not suggesting that it is appropriate to sex select, but simply distinguishing how we should understand the practice in the two different countries. This sharper analysis assists people who are pro-choice and concerned about women's equality to better evaluate the bans. One might argue that even if no one sex-selects in the United States because of a hatred of girls, it may be still appropriate to ban it for symbolic reasons. Banning it sends a message that the practice is wrong. Similarly, we may oppose caste discrimination (which occurs in parts of India) and, notwithstanding the waste of legislative resources, some may support adopting bans that specifically address caste discrimination in the United States. But those bans do not restrict or burden other rights. On the other hand, bans on sex-selective abortion do burden the reproductive rights of all women without any consequent benefit for women's equality rights. Thus, adopting bans because of the symbolic harm from sex selection is problematic because there would be minimal benefit for doing so, and great harm.

Balancing Burdens on Reproductive Rights and Harm to Women and Girls

Sex-selective abortion statutes burden the legal right to choose. They will potentially limit abortion access to all women, even those seeking nonselective abortions—particularly Asian American women. Unlike in India, sex selection in America is not widely practiced. Moreover, to the extent people sex-select, the consequences of the practice do not harm women and girls in society.

In addition, commentators have correctly pointed out that it will be difficult to enforce prohibitions on sex-selective abortion because a woman who is seeking an abortion for sex-selective purposes may not disclose her true motives (especially if she is aware that a medical professional must refuse to provide the abortion if she desires to abort the fetus because of its future sex).[72] Indeed, in a paper I coauthored, we found that sex-selective abortion bans in adopted in Illinois in 1984 and in Pennsylvania in 1989 were not associated with reductions in male-biased sex ratios.[73]

Our study used annual birth data from the National Center for Health Statistics. Using the variation in the timing of each ban as a natural experiment, Nandi compared the pre-ban and post-ban sex ratios of certain Asian American newborn children in those states over 12-year periods. He then compared these ratios with the sex ratios of Asian American newborn children in neighboring states during the same period. He found that the bans in Illinois and Pennsylvania were not associated with any changes in sex ratios at birth among Asian Americans. In Illinois and its neighboring states, the sex ratio at birth of Asian children was not male-biased during the study period. On the other hand, the sex ratio at birth among Asian Americans in Pennsylvania and its neighboring states was skewed slightly in favor of boys, but the enactment of the ban did not normalize the sex ratio. Thus, sex-selective abortion bans in the United States have not achieved their intended result.

In balancing the burdens placed by sex-selective abortion bans on women's reproductive rights against the actual harm to women and girls, it is clear that the benefits of the bans do not outweigh their costs. They do no more than impinge on women's rights. Next, I consider whether or not prohibitions on sex-selective abortion in the United States are constitutional.

Are Sex-Selective Abortion Statutes in the United States Constitutional?

The transnational framework I proposed places women's rights at the center of evaluating whether or not a country should ban sex-selective abortions. The prescriptions of this approach may coincide with a constitutional analysis, but it is not designed to track the constitutional test. In the United States, the Supreme Court found that the right to choose is a constitutional right. The U.S. Supreme court will invalidate laws it deems to be contrary to constitutional rights. Pro-choice advocates have not challenged sex-selective abortion bans, and so the U.S. Supreme Court has yet to rule on their constitutionality. In this section, I evaluate whether or not the U.S. Supreme Court will uphold the sex-selective abortion statutes passed by nine state legislatures.

Pro-choice organizations have been reluctant to argue that bans on sex-selective abortions violate a woman's right to choose to terminate her pre-viability pregnancy. Planned Parenthood declined the opportunity to challenge sex-selective abortion bans adopted in 1989 by Pennsylvania in the seminal case *Planned Parenthood v. Casey*. Planned Parenthood challenged a host of restrictions Pennsylvania had adopted but did not challenge the sex-selective abortion ban.[74] Even in the recent suit brought by the ACLU against the sex-selective and race-selective bans adopted by Arizona, they do not argue that the bans contravene a woman's right to choose. In the American judicial system, typically if a litigant does not raise a specific argument, a court will not consider it. However, an Indiana Federal District Court judge who granted a preliminary injunction against sex-selective abortion bans (as well as race-selective and disability-selective bans) on the basis that they contravene *Roe v. Wade*, appeared to have done so *sua sponte*.[75] The plaintiffs in that suit, including Planned Parenthood, did not specifically challenge the constitutionality of the bans in their complaint.[76]

Lawyers representing pro-choice organizations are aware that the U.S. Supreme Court's ruling on sex-selective abortion statutes will depend primarily on the composition of the court at the time it hears the case. They are also right to be worried that the women's equality rhetoric surrounding the bans might appeal to the "swing votes" on the court—justices who have upheld some abortion restrictions and struck down others. Well before the question ever reaches the U.S. Supreme Court, though, lower courts, like the one in Indiana, may address the bans. Those who do will apply the court's existing jurisprudence in evaluating them. The existing jurisprudence strongly suggests that the bans are unconstitutional. Yet, a judge who opposes abortion rights or who is convinced by the decontextualized women's equality justifications for the bans will have no trouble finding them constitutional.

The main test that is now used by the U.S. Supreme Court in evaluating the constitutionality of abortion-restricting legislation is the "undue burden" test. In *Planned Parenthood v. Casey*, the court held that states' attempts to regulate abortion cannot create an "undue burden" on a woman's exercise of her right to an abortion. The court noted that "[a]n undue burden exists . . . if [a statute's] purpose or effect is to place substantial obstacles in the path of a woman seeking an abortion before the fetus attains viability."[77] Sex-selective abortion bans, like disability-selective and race-selective abortion bans, are complete prohibitions on abortion (even pre-viability abortions) for the reasons specified in the statutes. In the three major cases applying the "undue burden" test, none of the regulations in question were bans on abortion that take effect starting from conception.

In *Casey*, the court found that it was constitutional for Pennsylvania (1) to require parental consent for minors seeking an abortion, (2) to require providers to give a patient information about the procedure and require a short waiting period, and (3) to impose recordkeeping and reporting requirements.[78] They found the spousal notification requirement to be unconstitutional.[79] In the next major abortion case at the court, *Gonzales v. Carhart*,[80] the court was asked to determine whether a federal ban on a specific type of abortion procedure created an "undue burden" on the right to choose. The court held that a ban on that procedure did not create an "undue burden" on abortion access.[81]

Similarly, in the most recent landmark case, *Whole Woman's Health*,[82] the court evaluated two Texas regulations. The first regulation requires medical professionals who perform abortions to meet admitting requirements. The other regulation requires abortion clinics to satisfy the state requirements imposed on surgical centers. The majority of the court gave teeth to the "undue burden" test by framing it as a cost/benefit analysis. Supporters of the legislation argued that the strict health regulations were needed to protect the health of abortion-seekers. However, the court found that the Texas restrictions have no benefits since abortions are already fairly safe procedures in Texas.[83] On the other hand, they impose significant costs on women's access to abortion given that scores of clinics had already closed in Texas a result of the statute.[84]

There are several possible approaches the U.S. Supreme Court could take to sex-selective abortion statutes. First, they could apply the "undue burden" test to find that the bans are unconstitutional since those laws do more than create "obstacles" to abortion access, they completely prohibit the procedure. Under one version of the "undue burden" test, the court will have to conduct no further analysis to strike down the laws. Second, the court could use the most recent articulation of the "undue burden" test found in *Whole Woman's Health* to find that the costs of the bans are greater than the benefits. It is obvious that how they rule on the costs/benefits depends on how they define them. In an earlier section, I have argued that the costs of the bans are that they will lead to racial profiling and will burden the rights of women who desire to obtain nonselective abortions. The benefits will be to attempt to address the behavior of perhaps a few hundred people a year who are trying to gender balance their families.

If they agree with my analysis, they will likely find the anti–sex-selective laws unconstitutional. But they may instead agree with the framing that has gained currency in mainstream America about the benefits of the bans. The popular perception is that the bans prohibit Asian Americans from discriminating against their fetuses, a practice that is widespread in the United States and that they brought with them from their countries of origin. If the justices on the U.S. Supreme Court agree with this view, they will likely find the sex-selective abortion bans constitutional.

Third, the court could simply dismiss the "undue burden" test as inapplicable in evaluating the constitutionality of the bans. The costs and benefits that the court evaluated in *Whole Woman's Health* pertained to the same actor—the abortion-seeker. Texas justified the regulations on clinics and providers as needed to benefit the health of the patient, and the costs were to virtually eliminate abortion access. But for sex-selective bans, an evaluation of the costs and benefits involves different actors. The costs are imposed on the abortion-seeker, but the benefits would flow to the fetus—the fetus would be protected from sex discrimination.

Instead of the "undue burden" test, the lens through which courts could view these statutes is the balancing test articulated in *Roe v. Wade*,[85] the decision that legalized abortion access in the United States. In creating a right to abortion, the court balanced a woman's interests in privacy against the state's interest in protecting the life of the fetus. Indeed, the first lower court decision in the United States to directly address the constitutionality of sex-selective abortion bans relies largely on the *Roe* framework rather than using the "undue burden" standard. Judge Pratt of the United States Federal Court for the Southern District of Indiana granted a preliminary injunction that blocked an Indiana anti-abortion statute from becoming effective.[86] She prohibited Indiana from enforcing its bans on disability-selective, sex-selective, and race-selective abortions. Citing *Roe v. Wade* and *Casey*, she held that "the woman's right to choose to have an abortion pre-viability is categorical; a state cannot prohibit any woman from making the ultimate decision to terminate her pregnancy before viability."[87] The final decision in the case is still pending.

This holding is consistent with what happened to the sex-selective abortion statute in Indiana's neighboring state, Illinois. In 1984, Illinois adopted a ban on sex-selective abortion, but the state eventually agreed to limit the statute only to abortions post-viability after the U.S. Supreme Court's decision in *Casey* in 1993.[88] The American Academy of Medical Ethics objected to this settlement. In rejecting this objection, the United States Federal Court for the Northern District of Illinois stated that "[t]he *Casey* court made it clear that any pre-viability regulation which imposes a palpable restriction on a women's right to elect abortion would be prohibited."[89]

The Federal Court of Appeals for the Ninth Circuit has also interpreted *Casey* to mean that all pre-viability bans on abortion are unconstitutional.[90] Specifically, the Court notes:

> [A] woman has a constitutional right to choose to terminate her pregnancy before the fetus is viable. A prohibition on the exercise of that right is *per se* unconstitutional. While the state may *regulate* the mode and manner of abortion prior to fetal viability, it may not *proscribe* a woman from electing abortion, nor may it impose an undue burden on her choice through regulation.[91]

Thus, there is a strong basis for the court to find that all reason-based bans are unconstitutional because they are full bans even on pre-viability abortions. Notwithstanding these interpretations of *Casey*, there is language in that same decision that could be used to declare sex-selective bans constitutional. The *Casey* court also stated, "[T]he State has legitimate interests from the outset of the pregnancy in protecting the health of the woman and the life of the fetus that may become a child."[92] The focus then of a court's analysis would be to determine what legitimate state interest is being served by sex-selective abortion bans.

Anti-abortion advocates argue that the bans protect the fetus from sex discrimination. In evaluating these arguments, a court will consider whether the practice of gender-biased sex selection is widespread and the consequences of the bans. Again, I hope to change the popular perception in the United States. The practice is not widespread among Asian Americans in favor of either girls or boys according to an empirical study of recent census data. Data from a poll suggests that Asian Americans have no more of a preference for sons than Caucasian Americans. Through a comparative analysis of the practice in India, I have also argued that whether or not the practice is discriminatory should be considered in the context in which it occurs.

Another issue that a court will have to consider is whether a fetus should have a legal right to be free from discrimination. No American court has found that a state has an interest in protecting a fetus from discrimination. If a court were to extend this protection to a fetus, it would mean granting the fetus full personhood. To consider it discrimination when a mother terminates her pregnancy because she does not want to raise a boy or a child with severe disabilities will also extend discrimination law farther than it currently stands.

Bans on sex-selective abortion seem harmless. After all, most people do not approve of the practice. Very few women want to have an abortion for that purpose. But the right to choose could hinge on how the U.S. Supreme Court rules on sex-selective abortion bans if the issue ever reaches it. If the U.S. Supreme Court rules that sex-selective abortion bans are constitutional, then this will invite more states to adopt a host of other reason-based pre-viability prohibitions. On the other hand, if the U.S. Supreme Court does not accept decontextualized arguments about the practice and instead relies on evidence-based research about sex-selective abortions in the United States, then they are more likely to find them unconstitutional. The U.S. Supreme Court recognized that the justification for the Texas statute in *Whole Woman's Health* was nothing more than a fig leaf to restrict women's access to abortion. They should view sex-selective abortion bans the same way.

Conclusion

By examining the United States context using the transnational legal feminist approach, I have demonstrated that sex-selective bans do not address any harms to women caused by sex selection and instead only burden reproductive rights. The bans do not promote women's equality; rather, they infringe on women's rights. United States courts that have discussed sex-selective abortion bans have found them unconstitutional, but the U.S. Supreme Court has yet to rule on the issue.

In India, sex-selective abortions are more widespread. As a result of the magnitude of these abortions, there is a surplus of men in India. Emerging empirical studies from India have demonstrated that a male surplus is associated with violence against women. Preventing violence against living women and girls is a legitimate reason to prevent the practice. However, the ban in India appears to be having the unintended consequence of restricting non-selective abortions. While I think my feminist framework will assist Indian advocates and policymakers, I do not draw any conclusions about whether or not they should repeal the ban. This is a policy decision that should be made by local actors. The framework I propose is useful because it changes the terms of the conversation so that women's rights are on both sides of the equation.

CHAPTER 7

Transnational Legal Feminist Approach to the French Veil Ban

In this chapter, I examine the French ban on full-face veils from the perspective of the transnational feminist approach. I have argued in this book that commentators in migrant-receiving countries often lose sight of the importance of context in understanding, evaluating, and formulating appropriate policy responses to what they perceive to be harmful practices of some immigrants. Without much reflection, policymakers, scholars, media, and advocates often assume that "culture" motivates and defines the behavior of minority groups. In these formulations, culture is homogenous and fixed in time and space. People living in India are thought to share the same culture as people who live in the United States but whose parents trace their roots to India. I called this phenomenon "decontextualization." Certainly culture is relevant. But it is often overemphasized and used as a way to stereotype people's behavior.

The perspective I have developed in this work is also applicable to the discourse on other regulations in other migrant-receiving countries. Although some supporters of the full-face veil ban may have been motivated by anti-Muslim sentiment generally, many people who supported it claimed to do so on the grounds that the veil is oppressive to women. In the section "Decontextualization in the Full-Face Veil Ban Discourse in France," I examine how the discussions around France's adoption of a law that prohibits Muslim women from wearing the full-face veil used decontextualized arguments. In addition, in "Decontextualization and the European Court of Human Rights' Decision on France's Full-Face Veil Ban," I show how the European Court of Human Rights' decision on France's veil ban referred to veil bans in other countries in justifying its decision. Finally, I make preliminary observations about how a transnational feminist approach would evaluate bans on veiling. This chapter demonstrates that the transnational feminist perspective is useful in evaluating cross-border practices beyond sex selection in the United States.

Decontextualization in the Full-Face Veil Ban Discourse in France

In this section, I describe how behavior, motives, and harms were decontextualized in the debates around the banning of the full-face veil in France. In 2004, France prohibited girls from wearing headscarves in schools.[1] Six years later, in 2010, France banned women from covering their full faces in public spaces. The text of the law did not specifically target Muslims, but it was clear from discussions about the law that it was meant to address veils worn by Muslim women. The law applies only to full-face coverings and states that "[n]o one may, in public places, wear clothing designed to conceal the face."[2] These bans on full-face veils are largely justified in terms of women's equality.

During the discussions about the veil ban, the perception of the extent of the practice was greater than the reality. One of the justifications offered by policymakers for the ban was public safety.[3] In addition, the French government argued that someone could commit identity fraud by covering her face.[4] France could only have been concerned about public safety if policymakers thought that people were veiling in great numbers. But the reality is that very few women wore the full-face veil in France.

Indeed, a study cited by the European Court of Human Rights found that only 1900 women in France wore the full-face covering.[5] It seems that people who pushed for the law assumed that since the majority of women in some Muslim countries wear the veil, all or most Muslim women living in France must also veil.

Eva Brems points out that women who wore the veil were rarely consulted about their reasons for veiling. When the Parliamentary Commission of Inquiry in France evaluated the ban, they heard about 200 witnesses and experts. They sent out questionnaires to several French embassies. But the commission failed to seek a single woman who actually wore a face veil. The lone exception was a woman who appeared before them at her own request.[6]

Instead of conducting empirical research, many simply made assumptions about why women veiled based on stereotypes about why women in foreign countries wear veils. They perceive women in foreign countries as forced or coerced to wear them. Many scholars have argued that this perception is incorrect. Saba Mahmood, for example, has pointed out that wearing the veil is empowering to women even in countries where it is common practice.[7] Leila Ahmed's work about the resurgence of the veil also notes that for many women it is voluntary.[8]

The narrative that Muslim women are coerced into wearing a veil in Islamic countries is then projected onto Muslim women living in France. According to Joan Scott's work, *The Politics of the Veil*, two investigative bodies were appointed to look at the issue of headscarves in schools prior to the adoption the 2005 ban. They found that wearing headscarves was "either as a denial of freedom or a loss of reason."[9] Scott notes that in the French debate, the veil has never been seen as "reasonable choice."[10] While the investigative bodies admitted that "a few (*certains*) girls considered the veil a means of emancipation, the National Assembly study group insisted that many more (*beaucoup*) felt it oppressive."[11] According to psychoanalyst Elisabeth Roudinesco, the veil was thought to be a "curtain" that shrouds young girls in silence.[12] Of course, as Scott points out, there was no actual data to support the claim.[13] Yet the 2010 law itself contains a provision sanctioning people who force a woman to conceal her face.[14] There may be women who wear the face veil due to overt or implicit coercion, but those situations are overstated in the debates.

The coercion narrative prevailed in France despite the fact that many Muslim women argued that they wore the veil because of individual choice and not community pressure. Women who wore the veil in France also pointed out that they wore it for different reasons than women in Muslim-majority countries. In interviews, girls said they wore veils as an expression of self-identity in a country where they are a minority.[15] Some women wore it precisely because it was used to discriminate against Muslims in France.[16] By embracing a symbol that was used to discriminate against them, they lessened the power of its oppression. Yet, not all Muslim women oppose the ban. Some French Muslim women's rights activists agree that the veil is "a tool of oppression, alienation, discrimination, and an instrument of men's power over women."[17]

Unlike countries where the veil is required by law or by social pressure, women in France are exposed to the view that the veil is contrary to gender equality. While in some countries there may be societal pressure to veil, in France the mainstream societal pressure is the opposite. The only pressure to veil (if at all) in France would be from family, relatives, and other friends with the same beliefs. Although this pressure can be significant, it is not the same as the pressure to conform to norms that pervade the entire society.

Moreover, in many other countries, such as Iran, women are required to wear some form of veil by law.[18] By comparing the French situation to those countries, we are not able to clearly understand the reasons women in France veil. It is fair to say that a law that makes the veil mandatory is coercive. But it is problematic to assume that it is coercive in France just because of the context of other countries.

Many argued that women who claimed to veil voluntarily were under a "false consciousness" or duped by their own religion. The Belgian constitutional court's decision in upholding the veil ban in Belgium exemplifies this position:

> Even where the wearing of the full-face veil is the result of a *deliberate choice on the part of the woman*, the principle of gender equality, which the legislature has rightly regarded as a fundamental value of democratic society, justifies the opposition by the State, in the public sphere, to the manifestation of a religious conviction by conduct that cannot be reconciled with this principle of gender equality. . . . [T]he wearing of a full-face veil deprives women—to whom this requirement is solely applicable—of a fundamental element of their individuality which is indispensable for living in society and for the establishment of social contacts.[19]

The Belgian court argued that even if women chose to veil themselves, they are denying themselves gender equality. The court essentially imposed its version of gender equality on all women and refused to allow women to make their own decisions about the competing priorities (right to religion, right to identity, gender equality, etc.) that are at stake in the decision to wear the veil.

The idea that Muslim women who veil themselves have no agency was recently articulated by Laurence Rossignol, the French minister for Families, Children, and Women's Rights, in a controversy around women's fashion. Objecting to designer labels that have begun to create modest dress for women, including fashion styles that cover a woman's hair, Ms. Rossignol argued that "[w]hen brands invest in this Islamic garment market, they are shirking their responsibilities and are promoting women's bodies being locked up." She then compared Muslim women to "consenting slaves," but later recanted that part of her statement.[20] After the brutal massacre by a terrorist in Nice, France, by a terrorist, many French cities have begun to ban modest swimwear that Muslim women wear, known as the "burkini." [21]

In addition to ascribing motives based on their understanding of a practice in foreign countries, some people in France also assumed that the consequences of allowing women to veil in France would be similar to those in foreign countries. Caroline Fourest, a leading supporter of the headscarf ban in schools, insists that "Islamists were engaged in a political conspiracy, the aim of which was the oppression of women and the elimination of secularism—in short, the experience of Iran was about to be imported into France."[22] The claim, therefore, was that the veil was part of the oppression of women in Iran and that oppression would be replicated in France. In this section, I have demonstrated how perceptions about why women veil in other countries (perceptions themselves that were sometimes inaccurate) were used to further bans on veiling in France. With the emphasis on how the veil may be used as a tool of oppression by some governments, the voices of women in France who claim the veil as an expression of religion and identity were sidelined.

Decontextualization and the European Court of Human Rights' Decision on France's Full-Face Veil Ban

International courts and bodies adjudicate and evaluate practices that emerge in many different contexts. The European Court of Human Rights (ECHR) reviews petitions brought by individuals against countries that are signatories to the Convention for the Protection of Human Rights and Fundamental Freedoms (Convention) alleging violations under the Convention.[23]

In 2014, a French woman brought a petition to the ECHR arguing that France's veil ban violates a number of provisions of the Convention. The main claim addressed by the ECHR was whether the French veil ban violates a woman's right to express her religious views. I explain below how the court referred to a case from another context (Turkey) in justifying its decision to uphold the French veil ban, and I explore the problems that flow from doing so.

Article 9 of the Convention states that everyone has "[f]reedom to manifest one's religion or beliefs."[24] The ECHR agreed that the petitioner was indeed exercising her religion when she chose to wear the veil (which she noted she did only occasionally). But this right is not without limit in the Convention. The exercise of one's religion can be limited by the state if "necessary in a democratic society in the interests of . . . public safety . . . for the prevention of disorder or crime, for the protection of health or morals, or for the protection of the rights and freedoms of others."[25] France offered a number of reasons for the limitation, including a public safety rationale that allowing the covering of the face increases the risk of identity fraud. The court rejected the public safety rationale, finding that France could simply instead require women to remove their coverings when needed and that there was no general public safety threat being caused by women wearing veils.[26]

The court also rejected gender equality as an appropriate reason to limit exercise of religious liberty because the petitioner who was asking for the right to veil was a woman.[27] The court noted that "[France] cannot invoke gender equality in order to ban a practice that is defended by women—such as the applicant."[28] In rejecting gender equality as a rationale, the court avoided the objectionable presumption that women who veil do so because they are duped or have a "false consciousness."

But the court did find one justification offered by France to be persuasive. It found that wearing the veil contravenes the notion of "living together," stating:

> The Court takes into account the respondent State's point that the face plays an important role in social interaction. It can understand the view that individuals who are present in places open to all may not wish to see practices or attitudes developing there which would fundamentally call into question the possibility of open interpersonal relationships, which, by virtue of an established consensus, forms an indispensable element of community life within the society in question. The Court is therefore able to accept that the barrier raised against others by a veil concealing the face is perceived by the respondent State as breaching the right of others to live in a space of socialisation which makes living together easier.[29]

The court further pointed out that "[f]rom that perspective, the respondent State is seeking to protect a principle of interaction between individuals, which in its view is essential for the expression not only of pluralism, but also of tolerance and broadmindedness without which there is no democratic society."[30]

The court reasoned that although wearing the face veil was a valid exercise of the freedom of religion guaranteed under the Convention, the veil prevented people in France from living together. It further found that "living together" was an element of the "protection of the rights and freedom of others," which is a valid reason under the Convention for a state to limit a person's exercise of religion.[31] The court allowed for restrictions on religious freedom if, in exercising his or her religious freedom, a person infringes upon others' rights by creating barriers to interactions between people.

The dissent was quick to point out that "the very general concept of living together does not fall directly under any of the rights and freedoms guaranteed within the Convention."[32] Eva Brems, a human rights professor at Ghent University, is even more pointed—she correctly argues that there is no legal right to "see the face of others in a public space."[33] She further points out that in her empirical study she found that veil-wearers reported to have significant public exchanges and connections. She reports that many women she interviewed expressed a self-image that included them as open or sociable persons. The women felt communication was possible even when wearing a full-face veil.[34] The idea of equating social exchange with "face-to-face" interactions is a Western cultural notion.[35]

The court essentially found that a concept ("living together") that does not even rise to the level of a right trumps another person's fundamental right to religious expression. Upon finding that limiting the religious exercise of face veil wearers was permissible under the Convention, the court then gave wide latitude and deference to France's interpretation by using a doctrine called the "margin of appreciation." This doctrine gives countries great discretion in adopting laws in "grey areas" where there is not a clear contravention of the Convention.[36]

However, in this balancing of rights, it does not seem appropriate to me to deny someone her right to religion (which is an established fundamental and human right in most jurisdictions) in favor of others who feel they are not able to "live together" if another person covers her face. I think the court accepted a weak justification for the law. It may have done so because it agrees that full-face veil bans promote women's equality. However, it did not want to explicitly articulate that position, because it would require the court to hold that the woman who was challenging the veil ban was under a "false consciousness" or duped by her religion.

In holding in favor of France, the court refused to follow other commentators that had found that the veil ban contravened the Convention. For example, it rejected the Viewpoint of the Commissioner for Human Rights of the Council of Europe that "[p]rohibition of the burqa and the niqab will not liberate oppressed women, but might instead lead to their further exclusion and alienation in European societies."[37] They also refused to follow the Supreme Court of Spain, which found a veil ban unconstitutional because of the voluntary nature of the full-face veil.[38] In that case, the Spanish court found that it was not possible to restrict a constitutional freedom based on the mere supposition that the women who wore it did so under duress.[39] The Spanish court concluded that the limitations in question could not be regarded as necessary in a democratic society.[40] Lastly, the European court paid no heed to academic legal writings that cautioned that a ban on the wearing of the full-face veil would result in isolating the same women it was meant to protect and it would thus be incompatible with the objective of ensuring the social integration of groups of immigrant origin.[41]

In justifying its decision, the court cited *Sahin v. Turkey*, in which the ECHR found that Turkey's law banning headscarves in universities did not violate the Convention. Unlike most domestic courts, the ECHR is not bound by its prior decisions (i.e., they have no precedential value). However, in an empirical study of ECHR decisions, Yonatan Lupu and Erik Voeten argue that the court uses prior decisions much in the same way as U.S. courts and other common law courts do.[42] Moreover, even though the ECHR cites prior decisions, the court does so without consideration of the country context.[43]

The court cited *Sahin* 17 times in its decision on the French veil ban. Each time the court referred to *Sahin* it was to propositions that ultimately supported its legal conclusion in favor of France. For example, in citing *Sahin* as well as other cases, the court notes that "[i]n democratic societies, in which several religions coexist within one and the same population, it may be necessary to place limitations on freedom to manifest one's religion or beliefs in order to reconcile the interests of the various groups and ensure that everyone's beliefs are respected."[44] In addition, the court cites *Sahin* and a number of other cases to show that restrictions on religious garb do not violate Article 9 of the Convention.[45]

Moreover, even though the court extensively referred to *Sahin* in its opinion in which it found the French veil ban did not violate the Convention, it did not once distinguish the political and social context of Turkey from France. This is not because the court did not recognize the importance of social and political context. Indeed, it explicitly cited *Sahin* for the proposition that context matters in adjudicating bans on behavior in the name of women's rights.[46]

In *Sahin*, the ECHR found that Turkey's ban of headscarves only in universities was necessary to protect the "rights and freedoms of others" and to maintain "public order." The court agreed that "[i]mposing limitations on freedom in this sphere may, therefore, be regarded as meeting a pressing social need by seeking to achieve those two legitimate aims, especially since, as the Turkish courts stated . . . , this religious symbol has taken on political significance in Turkey in recent years."[47]

Karima Bennoune's reading of *Sahin*, on the other hand, stresses the gender equality logic. She believes that the Turkish ban was appropriate because "[e]ven to the extent that for some women, the choice to wear a headscarf is their own, and is for them an expression of religious belief, this limitation on that choice is necessary in context to protect the rights of others."[48] In particular, she notes that "[n]on-wearers of such garb risk becoming outsiders, seen as not fully or equally Muslim."[49] She goes on to say that bans are appropriate in public educational institutions since those institutions "shape the identities of future generations and forge the public consensus about gender roles and equality."[50]

Holding that a ban on a certain form of Muslim women's dress is appropriate in Turkey as well as in France suggests that the ECHR accepts a universal notion of women's rights. The court supports the view that veils (in any form and any place) are contrary to women's equality. Although the ECHR failed to mention it, the circumstances in the *Sahin* case are clearly distinguishable from those in the *S.A.S.* case. The court in *Sahin* justified its holding on the ground that there was evidence that the pressure to veil was in fact coming from a rising radical interpretation of Islam. Nevertheless, some commentators were skeptical of the *Sahin* Court's view that it was necessary to prohibit some girls and women from wearing headscarves to promote the rights and freedoms of others.[51] There is no such dominant political movement in France.

Moreover, where there is societal, political, or religious pressure to veil, it would seem appropriate for a government to desire to counter that pressure for the sake of promoting gender equality. On the other hand, because so few women in France wear the full-face veil or any veil, the dress of a certain group of women would not lead other women in French society to start veiling themselves. In France, as was the case in Turkey, there is no need to protect the nonveil wearers from the pressures that they would feel by seeing others veil themselves.

The ECHR, by relying on the *Sahin* decision in adjudicating a case arising in France, inaccurately tilted the equation toward upholding the ban. By relying on the rationale in *Sahin*, the court placed too little emphasis on other motives a woman may have to veil in a country where she is a member of a minority religion.

By making the comparison to Turkey, the court inadvertently suggested that the impact of a ban in Turkey would have the same benefits (e.g., promoting women's equality with men) as a ban in France. In addition, by its focus on the context in Turkey, the court also failed to give weight to the negative consequences the ban would have in France's specific political and social context (e.g., repressing minority immigrant women who wish to express their religion as distinct from the mainstream secular views).

It makes sense that the ECHR is not bound by its prior decisions. It adjudicates cases across many different countries and contexts. The court may come out one way in a case from one country and reach the opposite conclusion in a case from another with a similar set of facts depending on the larger social, historical, and economic context in those countries. Nevertheless, in its judicial opinions, the ECHR often refers to its prior cases. Indeed, the court supported and justified the legal conclusion it reached in the France veil ban case by referring to the Turkey veil ban case and its rationale. While upholding the headscarf ban in Turkey may have been perfectly appropriate to further gender equality, it should have no bearing on whether or not a full-face veil ban is permissible in France. But the ECHR's reliance on the decision about Turkey's law suggests that it failed to give due weight to the French context in determining whether or not the veil ban in France contravenes gender equality or women's rights.

Toward a Transnational Feminist Approach to Bans on Wearing Veils

What I have referred to as the "veil" takes many forms. It can involve wearing a loose headscarf, a cloth that covers all the hair, or a full-face covering, and it may also include a loose black covering over the entire body.[52] The veil also has many meanings. In one country, it may be a tool of political and gender repression; in another country, it may be an assertion of the religious identity of a minority. In this section, I make preliminary observations about how a transnational feminist perspective would evaluate veil bans.

The transnational feminist perspective helps evaluate bans on "cross-border practices" to determine if such bans promote women's rights or contravene them. A cross-border practice, as I defined it in Chapter 1, is a practice that is brought from one country to another by immigrants. Women who veil in one country migrate to another country and continue to veil. In some cases, women born in migrant-receiving countries also desire to wear a veil.

A transnational feminist approach to veil bans suggests that courts, policymakers, and feminists should be open to the possibility that a veil ban promotes equality in some contexts and not in others. Karima Bennoune's view, like mine, also recognized that veil bans should be evaluated within the context in which they emerge.[53] This defies the dominant paradigm that rights are universal. Many feminists and human rights advocates feel that veiling is oppressive no matter where the practice emerges. Others believe that bans violate women's rights no matter what country adopts them. For example, Amnesty International objected to the European Court of Human Rights' failure to find that France's full-face ban violated the European Convention of Human Rights and also objected when that same court failed to hold that Turkey's ban on headscarves in universities violated the Convention.[54]

However, consider the most extreme case where a country requires women to wear some form of veil by law and the practice has historically been used as tool of oppression. If that country passed a law prohibiting women from wearing any veil, few would decry the new law as a contravention of women's equality. Some women in that country might argue that the new ban violates their religious rights, but the government would have a strong argument that its veil ban is part of a larger strategy to combat structural inequality in society.

On the other hand, in a country where few women wear a veil, it is less plausible that a ban could be appropriate to promote women's rights. A migrant-receiving country might argue that its ban promotes the rights of women who would otherwise wear a veil, but that argument ignores those same women's rights to assert their religious identity. Assuming there is no larger structural problem that the migrant-receiving country is seeking to remedy with its ban, there is little to be gained from a ban in that country.

A transnational feminist approach would caution against making assumptions about why women veil in France based on the reasons for veiling in other countries. Instead, a transnational feminist methodology suggests that policymakers intensely focus on the context in which the bans arise. In "Decontextualization in the Full-Face Veil Ban Discourse in France," I pointed out the ways in which the discussions about the veil ban in France were decontextualized. This inappropriately tilted the balancing of rights in favor of prohibiting women from veiling in France.

During the public discussions about the full-face veil ban, proponents of the ban repeatedly argued that the veil was oppressive to women and the practice must be banned to promote women's equality. For example, in a resolution, the National Assembly in France stated that it "[c]onsiders that radical practices undermining dignity and equality between men and women, one of which is the wearing of the full veil, are incompatible with the values of the Republic."[55]

Legislatures, unlike courts, do not articulate the competing rights that may be at stake in adopting policies, nor do they explain how they have reconciled those competing rights. It may be that policymakers feel that the benefit of the ban was that it advanced women's equality by prohibiting a practice that is rooted in and causes gender oppression. That benefits then outweighed the cost of the ban. The cost of the veil ban is that it prevents some women from exercising their religious beliefs.

Policymakers and voters, however, have overvalued the benefits of the ban in France. In countries that require the veil by law—and even in countries that do not require it by law, but still punish uncovered women (e.g., there have been reports of Taliban members using sticks to beat parts of women's bodies that are exposed)—wearing the veil impinges on women's equality rights because women have no choice not to wear it.[56] Even in countries that have no mandatory veiling laws, women may feel intense pressure to veil if veiling is the generally accepted societal norm for women. Thus, in countries where women are required to veil in public or where societal norms dictate veiling, banning it may enhance gender equality in those countries. But this does not mean that it is harmful when women wear the veil in countries where it is not required to be worn by law or is not the prevalent practice. Thus, it is problematic to assume that a veil ban in France would have the same benefits as a veil ban in another country.

Relatedly, the costs associated with adopting the ban in France are undervalued. In part, by referring to the practice in other countries, supporters of the ban thought that all women who wore the veil were coerced to do so. By failing to consider the possibility that women who veil in France have different motives than women in certain Middle Eastern countries, supporters of the ban refused to accept Muslim women's claims that the veil was an expression of their religious identity. Thus, religious freedom and other motives for veiling in France were undervalued. By contextualizing practices, migrant-receiving countries and courts would make policy decisions that better promote women's equality and rights. While decontextualization should be resisted, this does not mean that it is not important to seek to gain accurate information about the significance of the practice in the contexts where it is widespread. Researchers could study one or more countries where veiling initially emerged to understand whether (and why) it is considered discriminatory or oppressive to women in that country. What is its scope? What are the relevant social and political institutions that give meaning to it as discriminatory? Once the practice is understood in these multiple contexts (i.e., migrant-sending countries and migrant-receiving countries), a comparative approach would help focus on factors that explain why a practice may be discriminatory or problematic in one context but not in another. This process would assist in formulating policies that further women's equality in migrant-receiving countries.

Conclusion

Veils are being debated in migrant-receiving countries around the world. Canada, for example, recently banned the full-face veil in citizenship ceremonies.[57] People who justified the veil ban made virtually the same arguments that were made in favor of bans in France. In evaluating bans on cross-border practices, I argue that stakeholders in migrant-receiving countries are informed by how the practice emerges in other countries. Because wearing the veil is considered to be historically repressive in Islamic societies, the practice may be assumed to carry that same meaning in migrant-receiving countries.

Part of the reason this decontextualization occurs is precisely because of the paradigm of universality that prevails in human rights scholarship and practice. Even feminists and human rights advocates make or accept or perpetuate decontextualized arguments about the harms of a cross-border practice since they accept the view that if a practice contravenes women's rights in a foreign country, it will also impinge on women's rights in their own country. On the other hand, the transnational feminist methodology presumes that practices that are oppressive in one context are not necessarily oppressive when they are undertaken by migrants in another country context. Using the methodology will not necessarily lead one to conclude that the human rights impact of the practice in question changes across contexts. But the methodology is still relevant and should be used because it grounds whatever conclusion is reached in solid, thorough analysis rather than assumptions and stereotypes.

Conclusion

Some of the most divisive issues about global women's rights today relate to bans on cross-border practices. Cross-border practices are practices of some migrants in migrant-receiving countries that are also undertaken by people who live in the country of origin of those immigrants. Many people in France and other migrant-receiving countries contend that practices such as the veil worn by first- and second- generation immigrants and some converts to Islam are oppressive to those women. Similarly, in the United States anti-abortion groups are calling for and succeeding in passing bans on sex-selective abortion because they believe that it manifests sexism and that many Asian American women are coerced to abort female fetuses. Others argue that prohibitions on sex selection and veiling are contrary to women's rights.

It is natural to look to feminist legal theory and international human rights law to help resolve these questions. American feminist legal theory developed in one country context and so it is natural that those theories did not take into account situations where practices emerge in such differing contexts. Under those theories, if a practice is viewed as harmful to women in one country context, it will likely also be harmful to women in another country context. Under international human rights doctrine, there are generally two ways human rights are framed: as universal or as culturally relative. The principle of universality—that everyone has the same basic human rights everywhere—has won the day among modern human rights organizations, institutions, and in scholarship. Any deviation from universality is thought to be an argument in favor of cultural relativism.

Under the extreme version of cultural relativism, human rights are subject to religious and cultural values in any given society. For example, if the prevailing religion dictates that women should not drive, then an extreme cultural relativist would say that to deny women (not men) the right to get a driver's license does not violate women's equality rights. Something is considered a human right in any given society only if it is consistent with its cultural values. The universalist paradigm in international human rights law and thinking is clearly important and necessary to counteract arguments that use cultural relativism to shield practices that are obviously oppressive to women.

There is a space, however, worth exploring between these polar opposites. Legal approaches that emerge in this space between universalism and cultural relativism would be open to the possibility that a practice that contravenes women's equality in one social and country context may not have the same impact in another. This approach would focus on multiple country contexts in determining how to craft regulation in one domestic context. American feminist legal theory examined only the context where a law was enacted or proposed to be enacted. International human rights law and practice, on the other hand, focuses on the context where a practice first emerges and is identified as oppressive to women.

Cross-border practices implicate concerns that cannot be solved just by international law or by domestic law developed in isolation from the transnational practice. The growing field of transnational law fills the gap between a purely international legal approach and a domestic approach to lawmaking. Transnational law lies at the interaction and overlap of domestic law and international laws. Peer Zumbansen, an important scholar of transnational law, recently described transnational law more as a methodology than a substantive legal field like contract law or property law.[1] It is a way to approach problems like cross-border practices that are carried from one country to another by immigrants, but often evolve and modify in the new environment.

I build on the insights about transnational law as a methodological approach to develop a framework to evaluate one specific issue—cross-border practices. Bans on practices such as veiling and sex-selective abortion are often justified to promote the rights of the women who engage in those practices. I propose a feminist framework to evaluate and assess those arguments and resolve the competing rights at stake for women's equality when jurisdictions adopt bans on sex-selective abortion and veiling. Regulations on cross-border practice should be enacted only after considering and comparing the context from where the practice originally emerges and the context where the regulation is being considered.

This methodology can be used in evaluating other cross-border practices beyond sex selection and veiling. I am not suggesting that all cross-border practices should be permitted. Nor am I arguing that all cross-border practices are morally acceptable. I am simply ascertaining whether banning them does more harm to women's rights than permitting them. The principles articulated here present a new lens to evaluate whether or not a cross-border practice is discriminatory or oppressive to women.

I use sex-selective abortion bans in the United States to elucidate and develop a transnational legal feminist methodology. First, I suggest that it is important for policymakers to understand the actual scope and magnitude of the practice and the motives of those who engage in it. Instead of doing this, people in migrant-receiving countries may instead decontextualize. By this I mean that people assume that immigrants undertake any given practice at the same magnitude and with the same motives as those who live in the immigrant's country of origin. I have shown how proponents of sex-selective abortion bans are quick to point to the scope and reasons for sex-selective abortions in India and China in explaining immigrant behavior in the United States. I also demonstrate that this occurs in France in the veil ban debates.

People in migrant-receiving countries also sometimes erroneously assume that a practice undertaken by people in a foreign country will have the same negative consequences when it is undertaken in their own country. Supporters of sex-selective abortion bans argue that sex selection among the Asian American community will lead to a significant number of "missing women" and that this behavior is harmful because it manifests discrimination against girls in the same way as it does in parts of Asia where it occurs. This overestimates the magnitude of sex selection in the United States and fails to appreciate that a practice is considered discriminatory only by reference to the social and historical context of a society.

This decontextualization sometimes occurs because of a static view of culture—the "culture" of people who live in Asia is thought to be the same as the "culture" of people who live in the United States but who trace their origin to Asia. Culture is also overemphasized in explaining the motives or reasons for the behavior of immigrants and context is underemphasized. The current empirical data on sex ratios of Asian Americans as well as the survey of their attitudes challenges this view. At best the data shows that a small number of Asian Americans sex-select in favor of both boys and girls. Those handful of people who intervene desire to balance their families—some sex-select for a boy when they have two prior girls and some sex-select for a girl when they have two prior boys. They are not acting out of misogynist hatred for girls. This demonstrates that behaviors and practices and the reasons for those practices change when people are exposed to a new social context.

Second, a transnational legal feminist approach calls for critically examining the context of the country of origin of the immigrant whose behavior is subject to regulation. The in-depth study of India presented here demonstrates the complex societal and historical factors that led to the high rates of sex-selective abortion in some parts of India. From the in-depth study of India, it is also clear that the knowledge that prevails in the United States about the practice in India is itself often distorted. It is channeled through the sound bites of the media and stereotypes about foreign people. This knowledge should be interrogated and questioned through an in-depth examination of the context of the country of origin of the migrant.

Third, I propose a comparative examination of the societal context, individual motives, and other factors that contribute to the occurrence of the cross-border practice in both contexts. Part of the reason sex selection in favor of a boy (whether it occurs through pre-implantation or post-implantation means) is sexist in India is because it is a reflection of unequal social institutions such as dowry, the custom of patrilocal residence, and the fewer economic opportunities for women. But these social institutions (even in immigrant communities) by and large do not exist in the United States. By a comparative study of India, I demonstrate that the historic, economic, and social reasons that some people in India sex-select are very different from those in the United States.

By focusing on the multiple contexts in which sex-selective abortion emerges, I have developed a specific feminist framework to evaluate bans on sex-selective abortion that emerge across multiple country contexts. I argue that the reproductive rights of women should only be burdened if it can be proven that the way in which sex selection is being practiced by large numbers of women in any particular country negatively impacts women and girls in that country. From this perspective, it seems appropriate to ban sex determination in India because sex selection in favor of boys is associated with increasing violence against living women. Though I leave it to Indian policymakers to make conclusions about their law, the transnational legal feminist framework to sex-selective abortion bans reorients the dialogue.

When examining the U.S. context from the transitional feminist perspective, it is clear that sex-selective abortion bans do nothing to promote women's equality and only impact it negatively. The bans burden women's reproductive rights without any consequent benefit to other women. I do not support sex selection and few women want the right to sex-select. But the reason to oppose bans is that they will lead to the profiling of Asian American women, hinder access to abortion for all women, and potentially erode even pre-viability rights to abortion, particularly if the U.S. Supreme Court finds them to be constitutional.

Notwithstanding this, bans on sex-selective abortion are spreading like wildfire in the United States today. Nearly half of the state legislatures in the United States have considered legislation banning sex-selective abortion, and nine states have adopted the ban. Although it is hard to imagine an issue on which pro-choice and pro-life people will agree, a ban on sex-selective abortion appears to be one. Some pro-choice state legislative representatives have voted for the bans. Some people who are otherwise pro-choice also support the bans. Although pro-choice organizations oppose the bans, it is not a priority issue for them and they are reluctant to argue in court that the bans violate a woman's right to choose.

People who are pro-choice are typically concerned about women's equality. Indeed, many believe that the right to abortion access is a key to ensuring women's equality. On the other hand, although they appeal to a liberal notion of women's equality rights, pro-life advocates' primary objective in pushing for anti–sex-selective laws is to forge a path toward a total prohibition on legal abortion rights. There appears to be a Rawlsian "overlapping consensus" on sex-selective abortion bans in the United States where groups with opposing conceptions of justice support the same policy.

But this consensus is based on a number of false premises. The national discourse on sex-selective abortion (largely framed by the anti-abortion movement) stereotypes the behavior of Asian Americans. Moreover, the release of an empirical study on sex ratios of Asian Americans in 2008 propelled the legislative campaign to enact bans across the country. This study demonstrated that when some groups of Asian Americans have one or two girl children, the next child they have is more likely to be a boy as compared to the next child born to similarly situated Caucasian American parents. The empirical findings of the study were widely exaggerated by anti-abortion advocates and the national media. The behavior of a small group of Asian Americans was seen as proof that "son preference" existed in the entire community.

A team of economists I collaborated with made a surprising discovery by analyzing more recent U.S. Census data—we found that some Asian Americans who had two boy children were more likely to have a girl child than similarly situated Caucasian Americans. A survey of the views of Asian Americans suggests that, for some, it is important to have gender-balanced families. To that extent, a few families sex-select and do so, by and large, because they want their third child to be of a different sex than their first two. Those practicing sex selection could be using a variety of methods in addition to abortion, including pre-implantation methods such as sperm sorting together with artificial insemination and PGD together with IVF. To repeat, I am not suggesting that I endorse any form of sex selection; I am simply pointing out that the motives for sex selection should inform whether or not we view it as a discriminatory practice.

Both pro-choice and pro-life advocates use the language of discrimination when talking about sex selection. Pro-life advocates claim that the object of discrimination in sex-selective abortion is the fetus. They believe that if an Asian American aborts a fetus because its future sex is female, then that is sex discrimination against the fetus. On the other hand, pro-choice advocates make two variations of the discrimination argument. Some pro-choice advocates sometimes go so far as to say that parents who undertake sex selection discriminate. But a person can discriminate against something only if that something (in this case the fetus) has the right to be free from discrimination. In a sense, then, this pro-choice view accepts the pro-life framing and is the opposite side of the same coin as the pro-life argument. The more popular sentiment among pro-choice scholars and advocates is the proposition that the practice of "son-preference" sex selection reflects sex discrimination in society.

Pro-choice advocates are usually careful not to explicitly endorse the view that the fetus has a right to be free from discrimination. Accepting this view (which no court has yet accepted in the United States or elsewhere) essentially grants a fetus the human rights protections of a person. It will also open the door to a host of other pre-viability reason-based restrictions such as on disability-selective abortion. Two states in the United States have already banned a woman from terminating her pregnancy if she is doing it because the fetus has genetic or other disabilities. My proposal rejects the discrimination approach and instead calls for a focus on the consequences of sex selection. When many people practice sex selection in favor of one sex, this can lead to severe sex ratio imbalances in that society and create social instability.

Certainly sex selection can reflect discriminatory social institutions and structures. In India, the causes of sex selection include dowry, significantly fewer economic opportunities for women than in the United States, lack of property ownership, and other social institutions. Many of these social norms do not exist in the United States. Thus, those who do practice sex selection are not doing it in response to the same problematic social norms found in some communities in India.

While the practice of selective abortion of female fetuses not only reflects but also furthers women's oppression in India, it does not have that impact in the United States. Empirical evidence suggests that only a small number of people engage in it and that they do so to obtain boys and girls. The practice has not led to sex ratio imbalances. It does not reflect structural discrimination in society nor will it perpetuate it. Thus, it does not serve to oppress women as it may do in other countries.

The decontextualized narrative that is used to push for sex-selective abortion bans in the United States forecloses important meaningful conversations about sex selection. Should parents have the liberty to preselect the sex of their children using sperm sorting and IVF? Is sex selection a gateway to selection for other traits? Is sex selection sexist? Instead, the only conversation that is happening in the United States is based on false assumptions. I welcome a broader conversation about the morality and ethics of sex selection in the legislative debates about the bans.

As immigration continues unabated, more practices will test the limits of universality and require a focus beyond the domestic and the international. Although beyond the scope of this work, the approach and methodology outlined here could be used to examine other cross-border practices such as female genital cutting (FGC). It occurs both in parts of Africa as well as among immigrants in other countries. As I did with sex-selective abortion, the occurrence, magnitude, and motives of FGC need to be examined both in how it is practiced in the United States and in other countries. In evaluating the practice, it is important to resist making assumptions about how the practice is undertaken in the United States on the basis of information available to us about the practice in African countries. In line with this view, some advocates in the United States argue that the procedure should not be banned altogether.[2]

It may very well be that after closer examination, it is determined that FGC is harmful to women both in the United States and outside of it. Any practice like FGC that involves removing parts of genitalia or making other physical changes to a person's body should not be performed on anyone under the age of 18. Even those over 18 should be informed of the consequences and have a real opportunity to refuse it.

I explained how the debates around the veil ban in France and the European Court of Human Rights opinion upholding the ban decontextualize. Using the features of a transnational feminist legal approach, I encourage others to construct a legal framework to evaluate bans in migrant-receiving countries as well as migrant-sending countries. In undertaking this task, it is important to generate empirical evidence about the practice in the migrant-receiving country, compare it to the practice in the migrant-sending country, and evaluate the competing rights in question with a focus on the impact on women as a group. I have employed this methodology in this book to examine sex selection among Asian Americans in the United States.

Many countries around the world are considering bans on sex-selective abortion and veiling to address the practices (or perceived practices) of immigrants.[3] The European Court of Human Rights will soon consider bans on sex-selective abortion.[4] I hope that the lens for understanding cross-border practices and the methodology for evaluating bans on such practices suggested in this book will be relevant for scholars, policymakers, international organizations, and judges who are concerned about women's equality. By failing to examine and compare the multiple contexts where the practice subject to proposed regulation emerges, many immigrant-receiving countries are adopting prohibitions that undermine women's rights.

NOTES

Preface

1. *See* Makau W. Mutua, *Savages, Victims, and Saviors: The Metaphor of Human Rights*, 42 Harv. Int'l. L.J. 201, 201 (2001).

2. Sital Kalantry, *It's a Trick: Pro-Choice Group Love This Movie. Its Director Worked for a Pro-Life Ministry. How Did That Happen?*, Slate (May 6, 2013), http://www.slate.com/articles/double_x/doublex/2013/05/it_s_a_girl_a_pro_life_movie_embraced_by_pro_choice_groups.html [hereinafter Kalantry, *It's a Trick*].

3. Kalantry, *It's a Trick*, *supra* note 2.

4. Prenatal Nondiscrimination Act of 2012 (PRENDA), H.R. 3541, 112th Cong. (2012). Each year since then PRENDA has been reintroduced in Congress.

5. *India's Missing Girls, Hearing Before Subcomm. on Afr., Global Health, Global Human Rights, and Int'l Org. of the H. Comm. on Foreign Affairs*, 113th Sess. 1 (2013), http://foreignaffairs.house.gov/hearing/subcommittee-hearing-indias-missing-girls.

6. Prenatal Nondiscrimination Act of 2013, H.R. 447, 113th Cong. § 2(a)(1)(J) (2013).

7. Sital Kalantry & Miriam Yeung, U. Chi. L. Sch. Int'l Hum. Rts. Clinic, Nat'l Asian Pac. Women's F. & Advancing New Standards for Reprod. Just., Replacing Myths with Facts: Sex Selective Abortion Laws in the United States 23 (2014), https://ihrclinic.uchicago.edu/page/replacing-myths-facts-sex-selective-abortion-laws-united-states.

8. Planned Parenthood of Ind. & Ky. v. Comm'r, No. 1:16-cv-00763-TWP-DML, 2016 U.S. Dist. LEXIS 84917 (S.D. Ind. June 30, 2016).

9. Sital Kalantry, *Sex Selection in the United States and India: A Contextualized Feminist Approach*, 18 UCLA J. Int'l L. & Foreign Aff. 61 (2013); Sital Kalantry, *Sex-Selective Abortion Bans: Anti-Immigration or Anti-Abortion?*, 16 Geo. J. Int'l Aff. 140 (2015).

Introduction

1. Noah Berlatsky, *Neither Pro-Life Nor Pro-Choice Can Solve the Selective Abortion Crisis*, Atlantic (Mar. 6, 2013), http://www.theatlantic.com/sexes/archive/2013/03/neither-pro-life-nor-pro-choice-can-solve-the-selective-abortion-crisis/273704/.

2. Mary Ann Warren, Gendercide: The Implications of Sex Selection 104 (1985).

3. Prenatal Nondiscrimination Act of 2015, S. 48, 114th Cong. § 2(a)(13) (2015).

4. "[T]he magnitude of the deviations we find for second and third children [of Chinese, Indian, and Korean Americans] is comparable to that documented for India, China and South Korea." Douglas Almond & Lena Edlund, *Son-Biased Sex Ratios in the 2000 United States Census*, 105 Proc. Nat'l Acad. Sci. 5681, 5681 (2008), http://www.pnas.org/content/105/15/5681.full.pdf.

5. Randolph E. Schmid, *Some Asian Couples in U.S. Opt for Sons; If Daughters Born First, Sex Selection More Common*, Hous. Chron., Apr. 5, 2008, at A8 ("We should emphasize that our paper does not imply that sex selection is practiced by all or even most Asian-Americans.").

6. While the discourse in the United States on sex-selective abortion legislation consistently makes reference to both China and India, I focus only on India given my professional and personal expertise.

7. *The Marriage Squeeze in India and China: Bare Branches, Redundant Males,* Economist (Apr. 18, 2015), http://www.economist.com/news/asia/21648715-distorted-sex-ratios-birth-generation-ago-are-changing-marriage-and-damaging-societies-asias.

8. *See, e.g.*, Wency Leung, *Some Couples in Canada Practising Prenatal Sex Selection in Favour of Male Fetuses, Studies Suggest*, Globe & Mail (Apr. 11, 2016, 12:00 PM), http://www.theglobeandmail.com/life/health-and-fitness/health/some-couples-in-canada-practising-prenatal-sex-selection-in-favour-of-male-fetuses-studies-show/article29583670/.

9. *See, e.g.*, Pallavi Jain, *Could Gender-Selective Abortions Be Happening in Australia?*, SBS (Aug. 28, 2015, 9:58 AM), http://www.sbs.com.au/news/article/2015/08/17/could-gender-selective-abortions-be-happening-australia.

10. *See, e.g.*, Rowena Mason, *The Abortion of Unwanted Girls Taking Place in the UK*, Telegraph (Jan. 10, 2013 10:00 PM), http://www.telegraph.co.uk/news/uknews/crime/9794577/The-abortion-of-unwanted-girls-taking-place-in-the-UK.html.

Chapter 1

1. *The Prenatal Nondiscrimination Act (PRENDA) of 2016: Hearing of the H. Judiciary Comm., Subcomm. on Constitution and Civil Justice*, 114th Cong. 1 (2016).

2. Whole Women's Health v. Hellerstedt, 136 S. Ct. 2292 (2016).

3. *Whole Woman's Health*, 136 S. Ct. at 2300.

4. *Whole Women's Health*, 136 S. Ct. at 2300.

5. *See* F.J. Beernink et al., *Sex Preselection through Albumin Separation of Sperm*, 59 Fertility & Sterility 382, 382 (1993) (stating that the Ericsson Method of sperm sorting uses the difference in swimming speed between the X and Y chromosome-bearing sperm to separate the two groups, resulting in a 71% accuracy rate for the desired sex).

6. M. Ruth Nentwig, *Technical Aspects of Sex Preselection*, in The Custom-Made Child? Women-Centered Perspectives 183 (Humana Press Inc. 1981) (*citing* Gordon, M.J., *The Control of Sex*, 236 Sci. Am. 87 (1977)).

7. *Purity and Results*, MICROSORT, http://www.microsort.com/?page_id=453 (last visited May 30, 2015); *see also* Al Kalfoglou et al., *Ethical Arguments for and Against Sperm Sorting for Non-Medical Sex Selection: A Review*, 26 REPROD. BIOMED. ONLINE 231, 232 (2013).

8. *Purity and Results*, *supra* note 7.

9. *See* Marcy Darnovsky, *FDA Questions Sex Selection for "Family Balancing,"* BIO-POL. TIMES (Apr. 11, 2011), http://www.biopoliticaltimes.org/article.php?id=5668.

10. *Requirements and Recommendations*, MICROSORT, http://www.microsort.com/?page_id=281 (last visited May 29, 2015).

11. *Pricing for Gender Selection Sperm Sorting in Our Office*, GENDER SELECT, http://chooseagender.com/Pricing.aspx (last visited May 29, 2015).

12. *Intrauterine Insemination (IUI) Fact Sheet*, AM. SOC'Y REPOD. MED., https://www.asrm.org/FACTSHEET_Intrauterine_Insemination_IUI/ (last visited Aug. 13, 2016).

13. *See, e.g.*, *In Vitro Fertilization (IVF)*, MEDLINE PLUS, http://www.nlm.nih.gov/medlineplus/ency/article/007279.htm (last visited May 29, 2015).

14. *See* Susannah Baruch et al., *Genetic Testing of Embryos: Practices and Perspectives of U.S. IVF Clinics*, 89 FERTILITY & STERILITY 1053 (2006).

15. *See, e.g.*, *Pre-implantation Genetic Diagnosis (Embryo Screening)*, PENN FERTILITY CARE, http://www.pennmedicine.org/fertility/patient/clinical-services/pgd-pre-implantation-genetic-diagnosis/ (last visited May 29, 2015).

16. *See, e.g.*, *In Vitro Fertilization (IVF)*, MEDLINE PLUS, http://www.nlm.nih.gov/medlineplus/ency/article/007279.htm (last visited May 29, 2015).

17. *See* Baruch et al., *supra* note 14, at 1053.

18. Deborah Netburn, *In IVF, Frozen Embryos May Lead to More Live Births Than Fresh Embryos*, LA TIMES: SCI. NOW (Aug. 10, 2016), http://www.latimes.com/science/sciencenow/la-sci-sn-ivf-frozen-embryos-20160809-snap-story.html.

19. *See, e.g.*, *Gender Selection*, SAN DIEGO FERTILITY CTR., http://www.sdfertility.com/gender_selection.htm (last visited May 29, 2015); *see also Selecting the Sex of Your Baby*, FERTILITY AUTH., https://www.fertilityauthority.com/fertility-treatment/gender-selection-options/selecting-sex-your-baby (last visited May 29, 2015); Katie Moisse, *Fertility Clinic Offers Gender Selection, Draws Women from Abroad*, ABCNEWS (Sept. 24, 2012), http://abcnews.go.com/Health/Wellness/fertility-clinic-offers-gender-selection-draws-women-abroad/story?id=17219176.

20. *See Ultrasound: Sonogram*, AM. PREGNANCY ASSOC., http://americanpregnancy.org/prenatal-testing/ultrasound/ (last visited May 29, 2015).

21. *See Induced Abortion in the United States*, GUTTMACHER INSTITUTE, www.guttmacher.org/fact=sheet/induced-abortion-united-states (last visited Jan. 17, 2017).

22. Ceara O'Brien, *Social Implications of Non-Invasive Blood Tests to Determine the Sex of Fetuses*, THE EMBRYO PROJECT ENCYCLOPEDIA (Mar. 23, 2014), http://embryo.asu.edu/handle/10776/7648.

23. O'Brien, *supra* note 22.

24. *See Chorionic Villus Sampling*, Mayo Clinic, http://www.mayoclinic.org/tests-procedures/chorionic-villus-sampling/basics/definition/prc-20013566 (last updated Oct. 17, 2015).

25. O'Brien, *supra* note 22.

26. Stephanie A. Devaney et al., *Noninvasive Fetal Sex Determination Using Cell-Free Fetal DNA*, 306 JAMA 627, 636 (2011); *see* O'Brien, *supra* note 22.

27. I use the term "Asian American" to refer to people who live in the United States but either migrated from parts of Asia or trace their ancestry to people who migrated from Asia.

28. Prenatal Nondiscrimination Act of 2016, H.R. 4924, 114th Cong. § 2(a)(1)(F) (2016) (emphasis added).

29. H.R. Rep. No. 112-496, at 2 (2012).

30. H.R. Rep. No. 112-496, at 2 (2012).

31. Prenatal Nondiscrimination Act of 2015, S. 48, 114th Cong. § 2(a)(12)–(13) (2015).

32. James F.X. Egan et al., *Distortions of Sex Ratios at Birth in the United States: Evidence for Prenatal Gender Selection*, 31 Prenatal Diagnosis 560, 565 (2011).

33. Melissa Stillman et al., Guttmacher Inst., Abortion in India: A Literature Review 18 (2014), https://www.guttmacher.org/pubs/Abortion-India-Lit-Review.pdf.

34. Prenatal Nondiscrimination Act of 2015, S. 48, 114th Cong. § 2(a)(12) (2015).

35. I discuss the importance of this documentary to the genesis of this project in this book's "Introduction."

36. It's a Girl (Shadowline Films 2012), http://www.itsagirlmovie.com/ (last visited Aug. 13, 2016). See the Preface for a further discussion of this film.

37. Sunita Puri et al., *There Is Such a Thing as Too Many Daughters, but Not Too Many Sons: A Qualitative Study of Son Preference and Fetal Sex Selection Among Indian Immigrants in the United States*, 72 Soc. Sci. & Med. 1169, 1170 (2011). Some of the women they interviewed were suggested by other women in the study (snowball sample).

38. Puri et al., *supra* note 37, at 1173.

39. Prenatal Nondiscrimination Act of 2012 (PRENDA), H.R. 3541, 112th Cong. § 2(a)(1)(L)(iii) (2012).

40. *See* Ariz. Rev. Stat. § 13-3603.02 (A)(2) (2013); Okla. Stat. tit. 63, § 1-740.2A (B) (2013); N.D. Cent. Code § 14-02.1-03 (3) (2013); S.D. Codified Laws § 34-23A-56 (4)(a) (2014).

41. H.R. Rep. No. 112-496, at 15 (2012) (submission of Rep. Lamar Smith, Chairman, H. Comm. On Science, Space, & Technology).

42. *See, e.g.*, Prenatal Nondiscrimination Act of 2013, H.R. 447, 113th Cong. (2013) ("To prohibit discrimination against the unborn on the basis of sex or race, and for other purposes").

43. *See, e.g.*, National Asian Pacific Women's Forum, http://napawf.org/ (last visited Aug. 12, 2016).

44. *See, e.g.*, Nat'l Ass'n Asian Am. Professionals, http://www.naaap.org/ (last visited Aug. 12, 2016).

45. *E.g.*, UCLA Dep't Asian Am. Stud., http://www.asianam.ucla.edu (last visited Aug. 12, 2016); Cornell U. Asian Am. Stud. Program, http://www.asianamerican studies.cornell.edu (last visited Aug. 12, 2016).

46. Pei-Te Lien, Making of Asian America: Through Political Participation 2–3 (2001).

47. George Gao, *The Challenges of Polling Asian Americans*, Pew Res. Ctr. (May 11, 2016), http://www.pewresearch.org/fact-tank/2016/05/11/the-challenges-of-polling-asian-americans/.

48. Kishwer Vikaas, *ABCD: Who Are You Calling Confused?*, Asian Am. Writers' Workshop (July 24, 2014), http://aaww.org/abcd-a-short-history/.

49. In her study of Italian immigrants, Caroline Ware finds that the new generation is more likely to reject patriarchal family structures than older generations of Italians. Caroline F. Ware, Greenwich Village, 1920–1930, at 196 (1932) ("Masculine authority continued to be accepted by a larger proportion than held to the ideal of a large family, but it was challenged by two thirds of the younger and a third of the older groups").

50. Donald B. Kraybill et al., The Amish, 251–53, 269 (2013) ("Minister Joseph Stoll echoed Amish anxiety about the threat of cultural assimilation: 'How can we parents expect our children to grow up untainted by the world if we voluntarily send them into a worldly environment, where they associate with worldly companions, and are taught by men and women not of our faith six hours a day, five days a week, for the greater part of the year.' ").

51. Kraybill et al., *supra* note 50, at 269.

52. Clifford Geertz, The Interpretation of Culture 44 (1973).

53. Karen Knop et al., *From Multiculturalism to Technique: Feminism, Culture and Conflict of Laws Style*, 64 Stan. L. Rev. 589, 602 (2012).

54. Uma Narayan, Dislocating Cultures: Identities, Traditions and Third World Feminism 81–117 (1997)

55. Leti Volpp, *Blaming Culture for Bad Behavior*, 12 Yale J.L. & Human. 89, 94–95 (2000) (footnote omitted).

56. Volpp, *supra* note 55, at 94–95.

57. Volpp, *supra* note 55, at 108–09 (footnotes omitted).

58. Volpp, *supra* note 55, at 115.

59. Anna C. Korteweg, *"Honour Killing" in the Immigration Context: Multiculturalism and the Racialization of Violence Against Women*, *in* Gender and Multiculturalism: North-South Perspectives 228 (Amanda Gouws & Daiva Stasiulis eds. 2014).

60. Korteweg, *supra* note 59, at 229.

61. Korteweg, *supra* note 59, at 230–31.

62. Korteweg, *supra* note 59, at 231.

63. Korteweg, *supra* note 59, at 237.

64. Doriane Lambelet Coleman, *Individualizing Justice Through Multiculturalism: The Liberal's Dilemma*, 96 Colum. L. Rev. 1093 (1996).

65. Leti Volpp, *(Mis)identifying Culture: Asian Women and the "Cultural Defense,"* 17 Harv. Women's L.J. 57 (1994).

66. Holly Maguigan also proposed a middle-ground solution to allow cultural evidence for purposes of evaluating *mens rea*. Holly Maguigan, *Cultural Evidence and Male Violence: Are Feminist and Multiculturalist Reformers on a Collision Course in Criminal Courts?*, 70 N.Y.U. L. Rev. 36, 87 (1995) ("The starting point for achieving a balanced approach is the courts' application of existing precedents for the admissibility of cultural evidence, not to support a separate defense, but as part of a challenge to the sufficiency of the prosecution's proof of mens rea.").

67. Knop et al., *supra* note 53, at 591.

68. Knop et al., *supra* note 53, at 610–32.

69. Knop et al., *supra* note 53, at 636.

70. *E.g.*, Ala. Code §§ 30-2-51 to -53 (1975), *invalidated by* Orr v. Orr, 440 U.S. 268 (1979).

71. Reed v. Reed, 404 U.S. 71 (1971).

72. Katharine T. Bartlett & Carol B. Stack, *Joint Custody, Feminism, and the Dependency Dilemma*, *in* Joint Custody & Shared Parenting 63, 63–87 (Jay Folberg ed., 2d ed. 1991).

73. *See, e.g.*, Robin West, *Jurisprudence and Gender*, 55 U. Chi. L. Rev. 1 (1988).

74. Verta Taylor & Leila J. Rupp, *Women's Culture and Lesbian Feminist Activism: A Reconsideration of Cultural Feminism*, 19 U. Chi. L. Rev. 32, 42 (1993).

75. It should be noted that context (though not geographic context) was very important to feminist legal methods. In describing the various feminist legal methods, Professor Bartlett discusses context in the following ways: the context of multiple identities, the social context, the factual context of a case, context of community norms, and the historical context. Katharine T. Bartlett, *Feminist Legal Methods*, 103 Harv. L. Rev. 848, 851, 854 (1990).

76. Katharine T. Bartlett et al., Gender and Law: Theory, Doctrine & Commentary 1193–95 (3d ed. 2002).

77. Angela Harris, *Race and Essentialism in Feminist Legal Theory*, 42 Stan. L. Rev. 581 (1990).

78. Harris, *supra* note 77, at 598.

79. Patricia Cain, *Feminist Jurisprudence: Grounding the Theories*, 4 Berkeley Women's L.J. 191 (1989–90).

80. Halley et al., *From the International to the Local in Feminist Legal Responses to Rape, Prostitution/Sex Work, and Sex Trafficking: Four Studies in Contemporary Governance Feminism*, 29 Harv. J.L. & Gender 335, 380 (2006).

81. Halley et al., *supra* note 80, at 394.

82. Halley et al., *supra* note 80, at 346.

83. Halley et al., *supra* note 80, at 347–68.

84. Halley et al., *supra* note 80, at 349 (*citing* Catharine A. MacKinnon, *Prostitution and Civil Rights*, 1 MICH. J. GENDER & L. 13–14 (1993)).

85. Halley et al., *supra* note 80, at 350.

86. Halley et al., *supra* note 80, at 350.

87. Halley et al., *supra* note 80, at 356.

88. Halley et al., *supra* note 80, at 356.

89. Halley et al., *supra* note 80, at 358.

90. Francis G. Snyder, *The Failure of "Law and Development,"* 1982 WIS. L. REV. 373, 373 (1982) (reviewing JAMES A. GARDNER, LEGAL IMPERIALISM: AMERICAN LAWYERS AND FOREIGN AID IN LATIN AMERICA (1980)).

91. Snyder, *supra* note 90, at 392.

92. Karima Bennoune, *Secularism and Human Rights: A Contextual Analysis of Headscarves, Religious Expression, and Women's Equality Under International Law*, 45 COLUM. J. TRANSNAT'L L. 367, 367 (2007).

93. Bennoune, *supra* note 92, at 369.

94. Sahin v. Turk., App. No. 44774/98 (Eur. Ct. H.R. Fourth Section June 29, 2004), http://minorityrights.org/wp-content/uploads/old-site-downloads/download-386-Leyla-Sahin-v.-Turkey.pdf [hereinafter Sahin, Fourth Section]. The judgment was affirmed by the Grand Chamber in Sahin v. Turk., App. No. 44774/98 (Eur. Ct. H.R. Nov. 10, 2005), http://hudoc.echr.coe.int/eng?i=001-70956.

95. Bennoune, *supra* note 92, at 410.

96. Bennoune, *supra* note 92, at 414.

97. European Convention on Human Rights, Nov. 4, 1950, 213 U.N.T.S. 221.

98. Sahin, Fourth Section, *supra* note 94, at ¶¶ 108–14.

99. Bennoune, *supra* note 92, at 386.

100. Bennoune, *supra* note 92, at 413.

101. Bennoune, *supra* note 92, at 386.

102. Bennoune, *supra* note 92, at 389–90.

103. Bennoune, *supra* note 92, at 416.

104. *See, e.g.*, Jack Donnelly, *Cultural Relativism and Universal Human Rights*, 6 HUM. RTS. Q. 400 (1984); Christopher C. Joyner & John C. Dettling, *Bridging the Cultural Chasm: Cultural Relativism and the Future of International Law*, 20 CAL. W. INT'L L.J. 275 (1990); John Kleinig, *Cultural Relativism and Human Rights*, *in* TEACHING HUMAN RIGHTS 111 (Alice Erh-Soon Tay ed. 1981); Fernando R. Tesón, *International Human Rights and Cultural Relativism*, 25 VA. J. INT'L L. 869 (1985).

105. Nancy Kim, *Toward a Feminist Theory of Human Rights: Straddling the Fence between Western Imperialism and Uncritical Absolutism*, 25 COLUM. HUM. RTS. L. REV. 49, 56 (1993).

106. Kim, *supra* note 105, at 63–64.

107. Kim, *supra* note 105, at 61.

108. Kim, *supra* note 105, at 61.

109. Tracy E. Higgins, *Anti-Essentialism, Relativism, and Human Rights*, 19 Harv. Women's L.J. 89 (1996).

110. Higgins, *supra* note 109, at 102–03 (footnotes omitted).

111. Higgins, *supra* note 109, at 125–26 (footnotes omitted).

112. Cynthia Grant Bowman & Elizabeth M. Schneider, *Feminist Legal Theory, Feminist Lawmaking, and the Legal Profession*, 67 Fordham L. Rev. 249 (1998).

113. Bowman and Schneider, *supra* note 112, at 253.

114. Bowman and Schneider, *supra* note 112, at 251.

115. *Modern Immigration Wave Brings 59 Million to U.S., Driving Population Growth and Change Through 2065*, Pew Res. Ctr. (Sept. 28, 2015), http://www.pewhispanic.org/2015/09/28/chapter-5-u-s-foreign-born-population-trends/.

116. Michael Dimock, *Global Migration's Rapid Rise*, Trust Mag. (July 5, 2016), http://magazine.pewtrusts.org/en/archive/trend-summer-2016/global-migrations-rapid-rise.

117. *See, e.g.*, Sheryl J. Grana et al., The Social Context of Law (Prentice Hall, 2d ed. 2002).

118. Bringing Human Rights Home: A History of Human Rights in the United States (Cynthia Soohoo, Catherine Albisa & Martha F. Davis eds., University of Pennsylvania Press 2009).

119. See generally Chapter 2.

120. In feminist studies literature, some scholars use the term "transnational feminism" as a way to de-emphasize the importance of the "nation-state." To some, the nation-state is viewed as an outdated or regressive political formation. Leela Fernandes, Transnational Feminism in the United States: Knowledge, Ethics, Power 6 (2013). In my approach, the nation-state plays a primary role. The nation-state is the source of regulations on the behavior of people living within its borders. Under the label of transnational feminism, some feminist authors also critique global movements of capital and goods or object to the neoliberal economic framing to the exclusion of other economic models such as socialism. Maylei Blackwell et al., *Transnational Feminisms Roundtable*, 36 Frontiers 1 (2015). I do not take a normative view on this phenomenon, but take it as a given.

121. *See generally* Peer Zumbansen, *Transnational Law* in Encyclopedia Comp. L. 738–54 (Jan Smits ed., Edward Elgar Publishing 2006).

122. Harold Hongju Koh, *Transnational Legal Process*, 75 Neb. L. Rev., 181 (1996).

123. Carrie Menkel-Meadow, *Why and How to Study "Transnational" Law*, 1 U.C. Irvine L. Rev. 97, 104 (2011).

124. Peer Zumbansen, *Defining the Space of Transnational Law: Legal Theory, Global Governance, and Legal Pluralism*, 21 Transnat'l L. & Contemp. Probs. 305, 307 (2012) (footnotes omitted).

125. Knop et al., *supra* note 53, at 595.

126. Ann Oakley, Gender, *Methodology and People's Ways of Knowing: Some Problems with Feminism and the Paradigm Debate in Social Science*, 32 Soc. 707, 708-09 (1998).

Chapter 2

1. In this section, I refine the framework I developed in the following article: Sital Kalantry, *Sex Selection in the United States and India: A Contextualized Feminist Approach,* 18 UCLA J. INT'L L. & FOREIGN AFF. 61 (2013).

2. April L. Cherry, *A Feminist Understanding of Sex-Selective Abortion: Solely a Matter of Choice?*, 10 WISC. WOMEN'S L.J. 161, 166 (1995).

3. Cherry, *supra* note 2, at 222–23.

4. Farhat Moazam, *Feminist Discourse on Sex Screening and Selective Abortion of Female Foetuses*, 18 BIOETHICS 205 (2004).

5. Some parents might refuse to vaccinate their children for religious reasons as well.

6. See also Thaddeus Mason Pope, *Balancing Public Health Against Individual Liberty: The Ethics of Smoking Regulations,* 61 U. PITT. L. REV. 419 (2000) (arguing that the individual autonomy rights of smokers can be limited from a public health perspective).

7. RUTH MACKLIN, AGAINST RELATIVISM: CULTURAL DIVERSITY AND THE SEARCH FOR ETHICAL UNIVERSALS IN MEDICINE 158 (Oxford Univ. Press 1999).

8. Whole Woman's Health v. Hellerstedt, 136 S. Ct. 2292 (2016).

9. Nivedita Menon, *Abortion As a Feminist Issue: Who Decides, and What?*, OUTLOOK INDIA (May 12, 2012), http://www.outlookindia.com/article/abortion-as-a-feminist-issue/280902 [hereinafter Menon, *Abortion As a Feminist Issue*].

10. Menon, *Abortion As a Feminist Issue, supra* note 9. ("I believe feminists must defend women's access to legal and safe abortions whenever they decide to have them—whatever the reason for their decision.") In an earlier piece in 1993, Nivedita Menon appears to have been more ambivalent about whether or not bans on the practice were appropriate. Nivedita Menon, *Abortion and the Law: Questions for Feminism,* 6 CAN. J. WOMEN & L. 103, 117 (1993).

11. Mallika Kaur Sarkaria, Comment, *Lessons from Punjab's "Missing Girls": Toward a Global Feminist Perspective on "Choice" in Abortion*, 97 CALIF. L. REV. 905, 910-11 (2009).

12. M. Ruth Nentwig, *Technical Aspects of Sex Preselection,* in THE CUSTOM-MADE CHILD? WOMEN-CENTERED PERSPECTIVES 181 (Humana Press Inc. 1981) (citing Gordon, M.J., *The Control of Sex*, 236 SCIENT. AMER. 87 (1977)).

13. Nentwig, *supra* note 12, at 181.

14. Nentwig, *supra* note 12, at 181.

15. Nentwig, *supra* note 12, at 181.

16. Tabitha M. Powledge, *Unnatural Selection: On Choosing Children's Sex, in* THE CUSTOM-MADE CHILD?: WOMEN-CENTERED PERSPECTIVES 193, 196–97 (Helen B. Holmes et al. eds., 1981).

17. ROSALIND P. PETCHESKY, ABORTION AND WOMEN'S CHOICE: THE STATE, SEXUALITY AND REPRODUCTIVE FREEDOM 7 (1984).

18. MARY ANNE WARREN, GENDERCIDE: THE IMPLICATIONS OF SEX SELECTION 104 (1985).

19. Generations Ahead, *Sex Selection Can Lead to Gender Discrimination, reprinted in* Should Parents be Allowed to Choose the Sex of Their Children? 28, 29 (Tamara Thompson ed., 2012).

20. *See generally* Judith Butler, Gender Trouble: Feminism and the Subversion of Identity (2006).

21. Jonathan M. Berkowitz & Jack W. Snyder, *Racism and Sexism in Medically Assisted Conception*, 12 Bioethics 25 (1998). Others have argued that the concept of family balancing creates this idea that an appropriate family has at least one boy and one girl, Soren Holm, *Like a Frog in Boiling Water: The Public, the HFEA, and Sex Selection*, 12 Health Care Analysis, 27 (2004); but why would those who balance their family have more gender expectations than those who don't?

22. Jasmeet Sidhu, *How to Buy a Daughter: Choosing the Sex of Your Baby Has Become a Multimillion-Dollar Industry*, Slate (Sept. 14, 2012, 3:30 AM), http://www.slate.com/articles/health_and_science/medical_examiner/2012/09/sex_selection_in_babies_through_pgd_americans_are_paying_to_have_daughters_rather_than_sons_.html (Megan Simpson changed her name to protect her identity in this article.).

23. Michael Bayles, Reproductive Ethics 35 (1984).

24. ACOG Committee Opinion No. 360: Sex Selection, Am. Congress Obstetricians & Gynecologists (ACOG) 3 (Feb. 2007) (reaffirmed 2014), http://www.nzord.org.nz/__data/assets/pdf_file/0018/4239/co360.pdf.

25. Powledge, *supra* note 16, at 196–97.

26. Powledge, *supra* note 16, at 197.

27. Bernard Dickens et al., *Sex Selection: Treating Different Cases Differently*, 90 Int'l J. Gynecology & Obstetrics 171, 171 (2005).

28. Dickens et al., *supra* note 27, at 176.

29. Dickens et al., *supra* note 27, at 176.

30. Johanna Westeson, Regional Director for Europe, Center for Reproductive Rights, *Rights-based Approach to Sex Selection* (Jan. 23, 201), http://www.reproductiverights.org/press-room/intlawgrrls-rights-based-approach-to-sex-selection.

31. *See, e.g., Statement of Policies and Principles on Discrimination Against Women and Sex-Selective Abortion Bans,* Ctr. Reprod. Rts. (Sept. 29, 2009), http://reproductiverights.org/sites/crr.civicactions.net/files/documents/Statement%20on%C20Sex%C20Selective%C20Abortion%C20Bans%FIN_1.pdf.

32. Rachel Rebouché, *Testing Sex*, 49 U. Rich. L. Rev. 519, 553 (2015).

33. 410 U.S. 113 (1973).

34. *See, e.g.*, Reva B. Siegel, *Abortion as Sex Equality Right: Its Basis in Feminist Theory, in* Mothers in Law, Feminist Theory and the Legal Regulation of Motherhood 43 (Martha A. Fineman et al. eds., 1995).

35. Ruth Bader Ginsburg, *Some Thoughts on Autonomy and Equality in Relation to* Roe v. Wade, 63 N.C. L. Rev. 375, 383 (1985).

36. Sylvia A. Law, *Rethinking Sex and the Constitution*, 132 U. Pa. L. Rev. 955, 962–63 (1984).

37. Planned Parenthood v. Casey, 505 U.S. 833, 856 (1992).

38. *See generally* Jaime S. King, *Not This Child: Constitutional Questions in Regulating Non-Invasive Prenatal Genetic Diagnosis and Selective Abortion*, 60 UCLA L. Rev. 2 (2012).

39. Catharine A. MacKinnon, *Reflections on Sex Equality Under Law*, 100 Yale L.J. 1281, 1317 n.157 (1991). *See also* Catharine A. MacKinnon, Toward a Feminist Theory of the State 115–16 (1989).

40. Mary John, U.N. Population Fund (UNFPA), Sex Ratios and Gender Biased Sex Selection: History, Debates and Future Directions 24–25 (2014), http://asiapacific.unfpa.org/webdav/site/asiapacific/shared/Publications/2014/Sex-Ratios-and-Gender-Biased-Sex-Selection.pdf.

41. Bijayalaxmi Nanda, *Campaign Against Female Foeticide: Perspectives, Strategies and Experiences*, *in* Sex-Selective Abortion in India: Gender, Society and New Reproductive Technologies 361 (Tulsi Patel ed., 2007).

42. *See generally* John A. Robertson, Children of Choice: Freedom and the New Reproductive Technologies (1994); Tom L. Beauchamp & James F. Childress, Principles of Biomedical Ethics (4th ed. 1994); David McCarthy, *Why Sex Selection Should Be Legal*, 27 J. Med. Ethics 302, 306 (2001).

43. Robertson, Children of Choice, *supra* note 42, at 4.

44. Robertson, Children of Choice, *supra* note 42, at 156.

45. John A. Robertson, *Ethics and the Future of Preimplantation Genetic Diagnosis*, 10 Reprod. Biomed. Online 97, 100 (2005), http://www.utexas.edu/law/faculty/jrobertson/RB1626Robertson.pdf.

46. Guido Pennings, *Ethics of Sex Selection for Family Balancing*, 11 Hum. Reprod. 2339, 2342 (1996).

47. Pennings, *supra* note 46, at 2342.

48. Al Kalfoglou et al., *Ethical Arguments for and Against Sperm Sorting for Non-Medical Sex Selection*, 26 Reprod. BioMed. Online 231, 233 (2013) (citing Jenny Dai, *Preconception Sex Selection: The Perspective of a Person of the Undesired Gender*, 1 Am. J. Bioethics 37, 37–38 (2001)).

49. *See generally* Amel Alghrani & John Harris, *Reproductive Liberty: Should the Foundation of Families Be Regulated*, 18 Child & Fam. L. Q. 175, 191 (2006).

50. Alghrani & Harris, *supra* note 51, at 192.

51. Michelle L. McGown & Richard R. Sharp, *Justice in the Context of Family Balancing*, 38 Sci., Tech. & Hum. Values 271, 286 (2012).

52. Elisabeth Boetzkes, *Symbolic Harm and Reproductive Practices*, 3 L. & Med. 327, 337–40 (2000).

53. Maura A. Ryan, *The Argument for Unlimited Procreative Liberty: A Feminist Critique*, Hastings Ctr. Rep., July–Aug. 1990, at 8.

54. Immaculada de Melo-Martin, *Sex Selection and Procreative Liberty Framework*, 23 Kennedy Inst. Ethics J. 1, 13 (2013).

55. Christine Hicks, *Women Should Have the Right to Choose the Sex of Their Children*, *in* Should Parents be Allowed to Choose the Sex of Their Children? 48,

51 (Tamara Thompson ed., 2012). *See also* Rosamond Rhodes, *Acceptable Sex Selection*, 1 AM. J. BIOETHICS. 31, 31 (2001).

56. Arindam Nandi, *The Unintended Effects of a Ban on Sex-Selective Abortion on Infant Mortality: Evidence from India*, OXFORD DEV. STUD. 10, 11 (2013), http://www.tandfonline.com/doi/full/10.1080/13600818.2014.973390.

57. Lynne Marie Kohm, *Sex Selection Abortion and the Boomerang Effect of a Woman's Right to Choose: A Paradox of the Skeptics*, 4 WM. & MARY J. WOMEN & L. 91, 109 (1997) ("Those who oppose abortion believe abortion terminates life, not that it prevents life from beginning at all. In other words, procreation has already occurred.").

58. THE VATICAN, CATECHISM OF THE CATHOLIC CHURCH, ¶ 2377 (English ed., Libreria Editrice Vaticana 1993), http://www.vatican.va/archive/ccc_css/archive/catechism/p3s2c2a6.htm (footnotes omitted).

59. Edgar Dahl, *Sex Selection Will Not Lead to Gender Discrimination*, *in* SHOULD PARENTS BE ALLOWED TO CHOOSE THE SEX OF THEIR CHILDREN? 40, 43 (Tamara Thompson ed., 2012) (arguing that the argument that sex selection should be prohibited because it is unnatural is simply a gut reaction and not a principled argument).

60. One commentator argues that sex selection "involves a failure to accept the child-to-be as a gift. For, seen as a gift—a gift from God—the child will be unconditionally welcomed and accepted as a member of the human family, possessing the same inherent dignity as the rest of us." Agneta M. Sutton, *Sex Selection via "Sperm-Sorting": A Morally Acceptable Option?*, CTR. BIOETHICS & HUM. DIGNITY (Nov. 3, 2002), https://cbhd.org/content/sex-selection-sperm-sorting-morally-acceptable-option.

61. *See* H.R. Rep. No. 112-496, at 15 (2012) (submission of Rep. Lamar Smith, Chairman, H. Comm. on Science, Space, & Technology).

62. American Convention on Human Rights, *opened for signature* Nov. 22, 1969, art. 4, 9 I.L.M. 101 (1970).

63. See CTR. REPROD. RTS., WHOSE RIGHT TO LIFE?: WOMEN'S RIGHTS AND PRENATAL PROTECTIONS UNDER HUMAN RIGHTS AND COMPARATIVE LAW 7 n.18 (2012), http://www.reproductiverights.org/sites/crr.civicactions.net/files/documents/RTL_3%2014%2012.pdf, for a citation to the Baby Boy case.

64. LYNN M. PALTROW, ACLU, CRIMINAL PROSECUTIONS AGAINST PREGNANT WOMEN: NATIONAL UPDATE AND OVERVIEW (1992), http://advocatesforpregnantwomen.org/file/1992%20State-by-State%20Case%20Summary.pdf.

65. *See, e.g.*, Thornburgh v. American College of Obstetricians & Gynecologists, 476 U.S. 747, 779 n.8 (1986).

66. Guatam Naik, *Sex Selection Can Lead to Trait-Based Eugenics*, in SHOULD PARENTS BE ALLOWED TO CHOOSE THE SEX OF THEIR CHILDREN? 54, 56 (Tamara Thompson ed., 2012).

67. Naik, *supra* note 66, at 55.

68. Naik, *supra* note 66, at 55.

69. *See* Convention for the Protection of Human Rights and Dignity of the Human Being With Regard to the Application of Biology and Medicine art. 14, Apr. 4, 1997,

E.T.S. No. 164, http://conventions.coe.int/Treaty/en/Treaties/Html/164.htm [hereinafter Oviedo Convention].

70. Roberto Andorno, *The Oviedo Convention: A European Legal Framework at the Intersection of Human Rights and Health Law*, 2 J. Int'l Biotech. L. 133, 141 (2005).

71. Kelly M. Plummer, *Ending Parents' Unlimited Power to Choose: Legislation is Necessary to Prohibit Parents' Selection of Their Children's Sex and Characteristics*, 47 St. Louis U. L.J. 517, 553–54 (2003).

72. *See* Ed O'Keefe, *Bill Banning "Sex-Selection Abortions" Fails in the House*, Wash. Post (May 31, 2012), http://www.washingtonpost.com/politics/bill-banning-sex-selection-abortions-fails-in-the-house/2012/05/31/gJQAaWFd5U_story.html. *See also* John Parkinson, *House Rejects Ban on Sex-Selection Abortions*, ABC News (May 31, 2012), http://abcnews.go.com/blogs/politics/2012/05/house-rejects-ban-on-sex-selection-abortions/ ("Canada, the United Kingdom, France, Germany, Switzerland, Sweden, Norway, Finland and the Netherlands all have laws banning sex-selection abortions.").

73. The U.K. government interprets its existing laws to prohibit abortion for solely sex selection purposes. *MPs Reject Backbench Bid to Amend Abortion Laws*, BBC News (Feb. 24, 2015), http://www.bbc.com/news/uk-politics-31596968.

74. *Susan B. Anthony and Frederick Douglass Prenatal Nondiscrimination Act of 2011: Hearing before the S. Comm. on the Constitution of the Comm. on the Judiciary*, 112th Cong. 1 (2011) (statement of Steven W. Mosher, President, Population Research Institute), http://judiciary.house.gov/_files/hearings/pdf/Mosher12062011.pdf.

75. *See* Prenatal Nondiscrimination Act of 2016 (PRENDA), H.R. 4924, 114th Cong. § 2(a)(1)(J) (2016).

76. World Health Org., Preventing Gender-Biased Sex Selection: An Interagency Statement OHCHR, UNFPA, UNICEF, UN Women and WHO 1, 3 (2011), http://whqlibdoc.who.int/publications/2011/9789241501460_eng.pdf [hereinafter Interagency Statement].

77. Status of *Convention on the Elimination of All Forms of Discrimination Against Women*, United Nations Treaty Collections, https://treaties.un.org/doc/Publication/MTDSG/Volume%20I/Chapter%20IV/IV-8.en.pdf (last visited July 6, 2016).

78. Convention on the Elimination of All Forms of Discrimination Against Women, art. 5(a), G.A. Res. 34/180, U.N. GAOR, 34th Sess., Supp. No. 46, at 193, U.N. Doc. A/34/46 (1979) [hereinafter CEDAW].

79. Sherry Colb & Michael Dorf, Beating Hearts: Abortion and Animal Rights 89–90 (2016).

80. Harold Hongju Koh, *Why America Should Ratify the Women's Rights Treaty (CEDAW)*, 34 Case W. Res. J. Int'l L. 263, 272 (2002).

81. *See* CEDAW, *supra* note 78, at art. 12(1) ("States Parties shall take all appropriate measures to eliminate discrimination against women in the field of health care in order to ensure, on a basis of equality of men and women, access to health care services,

including those related to family planning."); *see also* CEDAW, *supra* note 78, at art. 16(1)(e) (stating that women must have the "rights to decide freely and responsibly on the number and spacing of their children and to have access to the information, education and means to enable them to exercise these rights").

82. Interagency Statement, *supra* note 76, at 12.

83. Human Rights Committee, General Comment 28, Equality of Rights between Men and Women (art. 3), U.N. HRC, 68th Sess., U.N. Doc. CCPR/C/21/Rev.1/Add.10 (2000), at ¶ 5.

84. Interagency Statement, *supra* note 76, at 4 (emphasis added).

85. *See* U.N. Comm. on Econ., Soc. & Cultural Rights, *Concluding Observations on the Combined Second and Third Periodic Reports of Armenia*, ¶ 22, U.N. Doc. CESCR/C.12/ARM/CO/2-3 (July, 16, 2014). *See also* Report of the Special Rapporteur on Violence Against Women, Its Causes and Consequences, Rashida Manjoo, *Addendum: Mission to Azerbaijan*, ¶¶ 19–20 U.N. Doc. A/HRC/26/38/Add.3 (June 18, 2014); U.N. Human Rights Council, Report of the Working Group on the Issue of Discrimination Against Women in Law and in Practice, ¶¶ 73–74, U.N. Doc. A/HRC/26/39 (Apr. 1, 2014); CEDAW, *Concluding Observations on the Combined Fourth and Fifth Periodic Reports of Georgia*, ¶¶ 30–31, U.N. Doc. CEDAW/C/GEO/CO/4-5 (July 2014); CEDAW, *Concluding Observations on the Combined Seventh and Eighth Periodic Reports of China*, ¶¶ 24–25, U.N. Doc. CEDAW/C/CHN/CO/7-8 (Nov. 7, 2014); Human Rights Committee, *Concluding Observations on the Fourth Periodic Report of Georgia*, ¶¶ 7–8, U.N. Doc. CCPR/C/GEO/CO/4 (July 23, 2014); U.N. Comm. on Econ., Soc. & Cultural Rights, *Concluding Observations on the Initial Report of Montenegro*, ¶ 24, U.N. Doc. E/C.12/MNE/CO/1 (Dec. 15, 2014).

86. U.N. Comm. on the Rights of the Child, *Concluding Observations on the Combined Third and Fourth Periodic Reports of India*, ¶¶ 33–34, U.N. Doc. CRC/C/IND/CO/3-4 (July 7, 2014).

87. Each of the four current conservative justices of the U.S. Supreme Court has expressed strong opposition to citing foreign law in U.S. constitutional cases. Zachary D. Kaufman, *From the Aztecs to the Kalahari Bushmen: Conservative Justices' Citation of Foreign Sources: Consistency, Inconsistency, or Evolution*, 41 Yale J. Int'l L. Online 1, 2, https://campuspress.yale.edu/yjil/files/2012/09/kaufman-macro-proof-07-31-15-1ca947b.pdf.

88. Prenatal Nondiscrimination Act of 2016 (PRENDA), H.R. 4924, 114th Cong. § 2(a)(1)(H) (2016).

89. *The World's Abortions Laws 2015*, Ctr. for Reprod. Rts., http://worldabortionlaws.com/map (last visited May 31, 2015).

90. See Chapter 5 for a discussion of India's law; *see also* Population and Family Planning Law of the People's Republic of China (promulgated by the Standing Comm. Nat'l People's Cong., Dec. 29, 2001, effective Sept. 1, 2002), at art. 35, *translated in* http://www.hsph.harvard.edu/population/policies/china.pop.pdf; Country Code (Eleventh Amendment) and Women's Right, No Abortion on the Basis of Sex Identification,

http://nepal.ohchr.org/en/resources/Documents/English/other/2009/March%2009/1.Country%20Code%20amendment.pdf (last visited May 29, 2015).

91. Population and Family Planning Law of the People's Republic of China, *supra* note 90, at art. 35 ("Use of ultrasonography or other technologies to identify fetal gender for non-medical purposes is strictly prohibited").

92. Law No. 03/L-110 on the Termination of Pregnancy (promulgated by the Government of Kosovo, Jan. 22, 2009, effective Feb. 4, 2009), at art. 14, *translated in* http://www.hsph.harvard.edu/population/abortion/KOSOVO.abo.htm. ("Termination of pregnancy by the motive of selecting the gender of the embryo is prohibited.").

93. *See* Prabhat Lamichhane et al., *Sex-Selective Abortion in Nepal: A Qualitative Study of Health Workers' Perspectives*, 21 Women's Health Issues S37, S38 (2011), http://www.whijournal.com/article/S1049-3867(11)00013-2/pdf ("The 2002 law that legalized abortion in Nepal expressly prohibits sex determination and sex-selective abortion."); Ctr. for Research on Env't Health & Population Activities, Sex Selection: Pervasiveness and Preparedness in Nepal 9 (2007), http://www.unfpa.org/sites/default/files/resource-pdf/nepal.pdf ("Conducting (or facilitating) sex-determination tests alone is punishable with imprisonment of 3–6 months" and doing the same for sex-selective abortion is punishable with imprisonment of one year.). For an excerpt of Nepal's abortion laws, see *The World's Abortion Laws 2015*, *supra* note 89.

94. Decree No. 104/2003/Nd-Cp Detailing and Guiding the Implementation of a Number of Articles of the Population Ordinance (promulgated by the Government of Vietnam, Sept. 16, 2003), at art. 10, *translated in* www.hsph.harvard.edu/population/policies/vietnam2.03.doc ("To strictly prohibit acts of selecting fetus gender, including: . . . Getting rid of fetuses for reason of gender selection by methods of abortion, supply and use of assorted chemicals, drugs and other measures."). In 2008, an amendment was made to the 2003 Population Ordinance followed by a new decree guiding its implementation.

95. *MPs Reject Backbench Bid to Amend Abortion Laws*, BBC News (Feb. 24, 2015), http://www.bbc.com/news/uk-politics-31596968.

96. *See, e.g.*, Albania, Law on Reproductive Health (2002), No. 8876, at art. 37; Canada, Assisted Human Reproduction Act (S.C. 2004, c. 2), at art. 5(e); Germany, Act for Protection of Embryos (The Embryo Protection Act) (1990), at § 3; Great Britain, Human Fertilisation and Embryology Act (1990) (as amended), at Interpretation of Mandatory Requirements 10D; Netherlands, Embryos Act; New Zealand, Human Assisted Reproductive Technology Act (2004), 2004 N.Z. Stat. No. 92, at § 11; Oman, Code of Practice for Assisted Conception Unit (2002) of Muscat Hospital; Saudi Arabia, Regulation of IVF Units, Embryos, and Infertility Management No. 2870/1/12; South Korea, Bioethics and Safety Act (Revised as of June 5, 2008), Act No. 9100, at art. 13; Spain, Law 14/2006 of 26 May on Assisted Human Reproduction Techniques, at ch. VIII, art. 26(c)(10); Switzerland, Federal Act on Medically Assisted Reproduction (Reproductive Medicine Act) (1998), at art. 5(2); Taiwan, Artificial Reproduction Act, (promulgated under Presidential Decree Hua-Tsong 1 Yi No.09600035251 on Mar. 21, 2007), at art. 16; Tunisia,

Tunisian National Committee on Medical Ethics Opinion No. 1 (Dec. 12, 1996) and Medically Assisted Procreation Decree No. 2003-1027 (Apr. 28, 2003).

97. Heather Strange & Cesagen, *Non-Medical Sex Selection: Ethical Issues*, 94 Brit. Med. Bull. 7, 8 (2010).

98. Strange & Cesagen, *supra* note 97, at 8.

99. Oviedo Convention, *supra* note 69.

100. *See Sweden Rules "Gender-Based" Abortion Legal,* Local (May 12, 2009), http://www.thelocal.se/20090512/19392.

101. Elisabeth Garber-Paul, *Gender-Based Abortions: A Slippery Slope*, RH Reality Check (May 14, 2009), http://rhrealitycheck.org/article/2009/05/14/genderbased-abortions-a-slippery-slope/.

102. Mark Levels et al., *A Review of Abortion Laws in Western-European Countries. A Cross-National Comparison of Legal Developments Between 1960 and 2010*, 118 Health Pol'y 97, 103 (2014). *See also* Emily Matchar, *In Liberal Europe, Abortion Laws Come With Their Own Restrictions*, Atlantic (Aug. 5, 2013), http://www.theatlantic.com/international/archive/2013/08/in-liberal-europe-abortion-laws-come-with-their-own-restrictions/278350/.

103. Jeremy Williams, *Sex-Selective Abortion: A Matter of Choice*, 31 L. & Phil. 125, 131 (2012).

104. Williams, *supra* note 103, at 132.

105. Williams, *supra* note 103, at 133.

106. Williams, *supra* note 103, at 146.

107. Williams, *supra* note 103, at 157.

108. It should be noted that social scientists can only tell if there is a correlation between the imbalanced sex ratio and any given consequence. For example, let's assume that we can determine that a society with a male surplus has a higher rate of violence against women than a society with a balanced ratio. Here we can only make a statement that the imbalance is correlated with increased violence—we cannot know with certainty that the imbalance causes the violence.

109. Gary Becker, *Is Sex Selection of Births Undesirable?*, Becker-Posner Blog (Feb. 12, 2007), http://www.becker-posner-blog.com/2007/02/is-sex-selection-of-births-undesirable-becker.html.

110. Hrishikesh D. Vinod, *Newborn Sex Selection and India's Overpopulation Problem*, 4 Mod. Econ. 102, 105 (2013).

111. *See generally* Marcia Guttentag & Paul F. Secord, Too Many Women? The Sex Ratio Question (1983).

112. Guttentag & Secord, *supra* note 111, at 182, 188.

113. Guttentag & Secord, *supra* note 111, at 185–186.

114. Scott J. South & Katherine Trent, *Sex Ratios and Women's Roles: A Cross-National Analysis*, 93 Am. J. Soc. 1096 (1988) [hereinafter *Sex Ratios and Women's Roles*].

115. *Sex Ratios and Women's Roles*, *supra* note 114, at 1102.

116. *Sex Ratios and Women's Roles*, *supra* note 114, at 1108.

117. *Sex Ratios and Women's Roles*, *supra* note 114, at 1108.

118. *Sex Ratios and Women's Roles*, *supra* note 114, at 1111–13.

119. Mary Ann Warren, Gendercide: The Implications of Sex Selection 134 (1985).

120. Some might argue that another problem with operationalizing the transnational feminist framework is that the category "women" is hard to define and is not fixed. Are transgender people like *Hijras* considered to be women? The fact that the line between genders is blurred, making it difficult to define precisely who fits within the category of "women," does not undermine the entire project.

121. King, *supra* note 38, at 48.

122. Whole Woman's Health v. Hellerstedt, 136 S. Ct. 2292 (2016).

123. Bendix Autolite Corp. v. Midwesco Enterprises, 486 U.S. 888, 896 (1988) (Scalia, J., concurring).

Chapter 3

1. Careen Oppenheim, *Kim Kardashian and Kanye West Only Had Male Embryos Implanted for a Son*, US Wkly. (June 24, 2015), http://www.usmagazine.com/celebrity-news/news/kim-kardashian-and-kanye-west-only-had-male-embryos-implanted-2015246.

2. Oppenheim, *supra* note 1.

3. *See* Ind. Code § 16-34-4-1 (2016), *enjoined from taking effect by* Planned Parenthood of Ind. & Ky v. Comm'r, No. 1:16-cv-00763-TWP-DML, 2016 U.S. Dist. LEXIS 84917 (S.D. Ind. June 30, 2016); Ariz. Rev. Stat. § 13-3603.02 (2013); 720 Ill. Comp. Stat. § 510/6-8 (2013); Kan. Stat. § 65-6726 (2013); N.C. Gen. Stat. § 90-21.121 (2013); N.D. Cent. Code § 14-02.1-04.1 (2013); Okla. Stat. tit. 63, § 1-731.2 (2013); 18 Pa. Cons. Stat. § 3204 (2013); H.B. 1162, 89th Leg., Reg. Sess. (S.D. 2014) (enacted).

4. *See, e.g.*, Prenatal Nondiscrimination Act of 2015, S. 48, 114th Cong. (2015); California, A.B. 2336, 2013–2104 Leg., Reg. Sess. (Cal. 2014); Colorado, *see, e.g.*, H.B. 1131 and S.B. 56, 70th Gen. Assemb., Reg. Sess. (Colo. 2013), H.B. 1162, 70th Gen. Assemb. 1st Reg. Sess (Colo. 2015); Florida, *see, e.g.*, H.B. 845 and S.B. 1072, 115th Leg., Reg. Sess. (Fla. 2013); Georgia, H.B. 1155 and S.B. 529, 2009 Leg., Reg. Sess. (Ga. 2010); Iowa, S.F. 13, 85th Gen. Assemb. (Iowa 2014), S.F. 44, 86th Gen. Assemb. Reg. Sess. (Iowa 2015); Idaho, H.B. 693, 60th Leg., Reg. Sess. (Idaho 2010); Indiana, H.B. 1430 and S.B. 183, 118th Gen. Assemb., Reg. Sess. (Ind. 2013), S.B. 334, 119th Gen. Assemb., Reg. Sess. (Ind. 2015); Louisiana, H.B. 701, 2015 Leg., Reg. Sess. (La. 2015); Massachusetts, H.B. 1567, 188th Leg., Reg. Sess. (Mass. 2014); Michigan, *see, e.g.*, H.B. 5731, 96th Leg., Reg. Sess. (Mich. 2012); Minnesota, *see e.g.*, H.F. 1196 and S.F. 1073, 86th Leg., Reg. Sess. (Minn. 2010); Missouri, *see, e.g.*, H.B. 1585, 97th Gen. Assemb., Reg. Sess. (Mo. 2014), H.B. 439, 98th Gen. Assemb., Reg. Sess. (Mo. 2015); Mississippi, *see, e.g.*, S.B. 2790, 129th Leg., Reg. Sess. (Miss. 2014), S.B. 2767, 2015 Leg., Reg. Sess. (Miss, 2015); New Jersey, *see, e.g.*, A.B. 2157, 215th Leg., Reg. Sess. (N.J. 2013); New York, *see, e.g.*, A.B. 2533 and S.B. 2286, 237th Leg., Reg. Sess. (N.Y. 2014), A.B.

6545, 238th Leg., Reg. Sess. (N.Y. 2015); Ohio, H.B. 570, 129th Gen. Assemb., Reg. Sess. (Ohio 2012); Oregon, *see, e.g.*, H.B. 4034, 78th Leg. Assemb., Reg. Sess. (Or. 2014), H.B. 3458, 78th Leg. Assemb., Reg. Sess. (Or. 2015); Rhode Island, *see, e.g.*, H.B. 7383 and S.B. 2376, 2014 Leg., Reg. Sess. (R.I. 2014); Texas, *see, e.g.*, H.B. 309, 83d Leg., Reg. Sess. (Tex. 2013), H.B. 113, 84th Leg., Reg. Sess. (Tex. 2015); Virginia, *see, e.g.*, H.B. 98, 2014 Leg., Reg. Sess. (Va. 2014); West Virginia, *see, e.g.*, H.B. 2371, 81st Leg., Reg. Sess. (W. Va. 2014), H.B. 2031, 82d Leg., Reg. Sess. (W. Va. 2015); Wisconsin, *see, e.g.*, A.B. 217 and S.B. 201, 101st Leg., Reg. Sess. (Wis. 2014). A Utah state senator initially proposed a sex-selective abortion ban but changed the proposed legislation to a bill to collect statistics on the reasons women report for seeking abortions. *See* S.B. 60, 60th Leg., Gen. Sess (Utah 2013).

5. 158 Cong. Rec. H3289 (daily ed. May 31, 2012) (recorded vote).

6. *See* Jennifer Steinhauer, *House Vote 299—Rejects Ban on Sex-Selective Abortions*, N.Y. Times (May 31, 2012), http://www.nytimes.com/2012/06/01/us/politics/house-rejects-bill-to-ban-sex-selective-abortions.html.

7. House Committee on the Judiciary Hearings, *H.R._ the Prenatal Nondiscrimination Act (PRENDA) of 2016*, YouTube (Apr. 14, 2016), https://www.youtube.com/watch?v=6AyJKNjW0Ec.

8. *See supra* note 3.

9. Phillip Lentz & Michael Lang, *Abortion Foes Push Bill Through House*, Chi. Trib., Apr. 27, 1984, at A1.

10. *Pennsylvania Abortion Limits Become Law*, N.Y. Times (Nov. 19, 1989), http://www.nytimes.com/1989/11/19/us/pennsylvania-abortion-limits-become-law.html.

11. *See* Tamar Lewin, *States Testing the Limits on Abortion*, N.Y. Times (Apr. 2, 1990), http://www.nytimes.com/1990/04/02/us/states-testing-the-limits-on-abortion.html; *see also* John F. Harris, *Abortion Curb Debated in Richmond*, Wash. Post (Feb. 7, 1990), http://www.washingtonpost.com/archive/local/1990/02/07/abortion-curb-debated-in-richmond/a0e1d52a-4a88-4c44-88ca-5d8256390fb7/; Lisa M. Fleischman, *"Good" vs. "Bad" Abortion: The Matter of Motives*, L.A. Times (May 20, 1990), http://articles.latimes.com/1990-05-20/opinion/op-41_1_abortion-debate.

12. Douglas Almond & Lena Edlund, *Son-biased Sex Ratios in the 2000 United States Census*, 105 Proc. Nat'l Acad. Sci. 5681, 5681 (2008), http://www.pnas.org/content/105/15/5681.full.pdf.

13. Representative Van Zant sponsored the Termination of Pregnancy Based on Sex or Race of Unborn Child Act, H.B. 845, 115th Leg., Reg. Sess. (Fla. 2013); the Susan B. Anthony and Frederick Douglass Prenatal Nondiscrimination and Equal Opportunity for Life Act, H.B. 1327, 114th Leg., Reg. Sess. (Fla. 2012); and the Florida for Life Act, H.B. 1151 114th Leg., Reg. Sess. (Fla. 2012) (banning all abortion unless it is to save the life of the mother). Representative Dennis Kruse sponsored S.B. 183, 118th Gen. Assemb., Reg. Sess. (Ind. 2013) (prohibiting sex- and genetic-selective abortions); S.B. 290, 117th Gen. Assemb., Reg. Sess. (Ind. 2011) (prohibiting abortion except to save a mother's life); and S.B. 116, 117th Gen. Assemb., Reg. Sess. (Ind. 2011) (prohibiting

qualified health plans under the federal health care reform law from providing coverage for abortion). Senator Chris McDaniel sponsored S.B. 2790, 2014 Leg., Reg. Sess. (Miss. 2014) (prohibiting abortion of a human being based upon a determination of the gender or race of the human being); S.B. 2297, 2008 Leg., Reg. Sess. (Miss. 2008) (prohibiting abortion of a human being based upon a determination of the gender or race of the human being); and S.B. 2692, 2012 Leg., Reg. Sess. (Miss. 2012) (prohibiting abortion of a fetus with a detectable heartbeat without informed written consent). Representative Bette Grande sponsored H.B. 1305, 63d Leg. Assemb., Reg. Sess. (N.D. 2013) (prohibiting sex- and genetic-selective abortions) and H.B. 1456, 63d Leg. Assemb., Reg. Sess. (N.D. 2013) (prohibiting abortions if fetal heartbeat is detected). Representative Allen Fletcher sponsored H.B. 17, H.B. 55 and H.B. 309, 83d Leg., Reg. Sess. (Tex. 2013) (prohibiting abortion based on the sex of the unborn child); H.B. 59, 83d Leg., Reg. Sess. (Tex. 2013) (prohibiting abortion after detection of a fetal heartbeat); and H.B. 2364, 83d Leg., Reg. Sess. (Tex. 2013) (prohibiting abortion of an unborn child at or after 20 weeks postfertilization).

14. *See* Prenatal Nondiscrimination Act of 2012, H.R. 3541, 112th Cong. (2011); Susan B. Anthony and Frederick Douglass Prenatal Nondiscrimination Act of 2009, H.R. 1822, 111th Cong. (2009).

15. *Right to Life*, U.S. Congressman Trent Franks, http://franks.house.gov/issues/life/right-life (last visited Jan. 26, 2017). Similarly, Representative John MacCaherty, the sponsor of a proposed sex-selective abortion ban in Missouri, has been quoted as saying: "We can't legally . . . stop [a woman] from aborting a child. But we can restrict what doctors do. . . . Obviously, I'm pro-life and my intent would be to limit the number of abortions happening." Sam Levin, *Abortion Ban Bill: John McCaherty Wants to Limit Sex Selection and Genetic Terminations*, Riverfront Times (Feb. 5, 2013), http://www.riverfronttimes.com/newsblog/2013/02/05/abortion-ban-bill-john-mccaherty-wants-to-limit-sex-selection-and-genetic-terminations.

16. *See Christopher Smith on Abortion*, On the Issues, http://www.ontheissues.org/NJ/Christopher_Smith_Abortion.htm (last visited May 31, 2015).

17. Jeff Sagnip, *Legacy of Abortion: 40 Years of Victims*, U.S. Congressman Chris Smith (Jan. 25, 2013), http://chrissmith.house.gov/news/documentsingle.aspx?DocumentID=317730.

18. Representative Bette Grande sponsored H.B. 1305, 63d Leg. Assemb., Reg. Sess. (N.D. 2013) (prohibiting sex- and genetic-selective abortions) and H.B. 1456, 63d Leg. Assemb., Reg. Sess. (N.D. 2013) (prohibiting abortions if fetal heartbeat is detected). Representative Allen Fletcher sponsored H.B. 17, H.B. 55, and H.B. 309, 83d Leg., Reg. Sess. (Tex. 2013) (prohibiting abortion based on the sex of the unborn child) and H.B. 59, 83d Leg., Reg. Sess. (Tex. 2013) (prohibiting abortion after detection of a fetal heartbeat).

19. H.R. Rep. No. 112-496, at 50 (2012) (quoting Steven W. Mosher, *A New Front in the Abortion Wars: PreNDA Seeks Race and Sex-Based Equality for the Unborn*, 18 PRI Rev. (Nov./Dec. 2008), http://www.pop.org/content/a-new-front-in-abortion-wars-prenda-seeks-1602.

20. Steven G. Calabrasi, *How to Reverse Government Imposition of Immorality: A Strategy for Eroding Roe v. Wade*, 31 Harv. J.L. & Pub. Pol'y 85, 89–90 (2008).

21. *See* Americans United for Life, Prenatal Nondiscrimination Act (Bans on Abortions for Sex Selection and Genetic Abnormalities): Model Legislation and Policy Guide Model for the 2014 Legislative Year (2014), http://www.aul.org/downloads/2014-Legislative-Guides/abortion/Prenatal_Nondiscrimination_Act_%28Sex_Selective_and_Genetic_Abnormality_Ban%29_-_2014_LG.pdf [hereinafter Americans United for Life].

22. *See* Americans United for Life, *supra* note 21, at 2 ("In 2011, author Mara Hvistendahl reported in her book, *Unnatural Selection*, that 163 million girls are missing in the world because of sex-selection abortions. . . . While the practice of sex-selection abortions is common in some Asian countries, such as China and India, it is also being practiced in the United States, often by people who trace their ancestry to countries that commonly practice sex-selection abortions.").

23. Jaime Staples King, *Not This Child: Constitutional Questions in Regulating Noninvasive Prenatal Genetic Diagnosis and Selective Abortion*, 60 UCLA L. Rev. 2, 29 (2012). The language used in laws banning sex-selective abortion also suggests that lawmakers are concerned primarily with restricting access to abortion generally. For instance, the language used in the bill pending in the U.S. Congress consistently refers to the "unborn child" and defines abortion sought based on the sex of the fetus as "the intentional killing of unborn females." Prenatal Nondiscrimination Act of 2013, H.R. 447, 113th Cong. § 2(a)(5) (2015).

24. Press Release, Ctr. for Reprod. Rts., Dangerous and Cynical Sex and Race-Selective Abortion Ban Continues to Move through House of Representatives (Feb. 16, 2012), http://www.reproductiverights.org/press-room/dangerous-and-cynical-sex-and-race-selective-abortion-ban-continues-to-move-through-house.

25. Generations Ahead, Nat'l Asian Pac. Am. Women's F. (NAPAWF) & Asian Communities for Reprod. Just. (ACRJ), Taking a Stand: Tools for Action on Sex Selection (2009), http://napawf.org/wp-content/uploads/2010/01/Toolkit-final.pdf [hereinafter Taking a Stand].

26. Taking a Stand, *supra* note 25.

27. Sital Kalantry & Miriam Yeung, U. Chi. L. Sch. Int'l Hum. Rts. Clinic, Nat'l Asian Pac. Women's F. & Advancing New Standards for Reprod. Just., Replacing Myths with Facts: Sex Selective Abortion Laws in the United States (2014), https://ihrclinic.uchicago.edu/page/replacing-myths-facts-sex-selective-abortion-laws-united-states [hereinafter Replacing Myths].

28. Tara Culp-Ressler, *6 Victories for Reproductive Freedom You May Not Realize Happened This Year*, ThinkProgress (Dec. 4, 2014), http://thinkprogress.org/health/2014/12/04/3598996/victories-reproductive-rights-2014/.

29. Anti-abortion groups have successfully launched a campaign at the state level where they have proposed numerous abortion restrictions. *See* Erik Eckholm, *Access to Abortion Falling as States Pass Restrictions*, N.Y. Times, (Jan. 3, 2014), http://www

.nytimes.com/2014/01/04/us/women-losing-access-to-abortion-as-opponents-gain-ground-in-state-legislatures.html.

30. See Chapter 2 for a detailed discussion on the ethics of sex selection.

31. Letter to the Editor, *Planned Parenthood Does Not Support Sex-Selection Abortion*, WASH. POST (June 4, 2012), http://www.washingtonpost.com/opinions/planned-parenthood-does-not-support-sex-selection-abortion/2012/06/04/gJQAKHTVEV_story.html.

32. Susan Sachs, *Clinics' Pitch to Indian Émigrés: It's a Boy*, N.Y. TIMES (Aug. 15, 2001), http://www.nytimes.com/2001/08/15/nyregion/clinics-pitch-to-indian-emigres-it-s-a-boy.html.

33. Sachs, *supra* note 32.

34. Sneha Barot, *A Problem-and-Solution Mismatch: Son Preference and Sex-Selective Abortion Bans*, 15 GUTTMACHER POL'Y REV. 18 (2012), https://www.guttmacher.org/pubs/gpr/15/2/gpr150218.html.

35. Chris Bodenner, *The Gendercide Crisis in Asia*, ATLANTIC (May 23, 2016, 12:25 PM), http://www.theatlantic.com/notes/2016/05/abortion/483866/.

36. I published an article in Slate connecting the filmmaker and its funding sources to an anti-abortion group. Since then, the links have been removed, but I have copies in my records.

37. Sital Kalantry, *It's a Trick: Pro-Choice Group Love This Movie. Its Director Works for a Pro-Life Ministry. How Did That Happen?*, SLATE (May 6, 2013), http://www.slate.com/articles/double_x/doublex/2013/05/it_s_a_girl_a_pro_life_movie_embraced_by_pro_choice_groups.html [hereinafter Kalantry, *It's a Trick*].

38. Kalantry, *It's a Trick*, *supra* note 37.

39. Kalantry, *It's a Trick*, *supra* note 37.

40. Susan Moller Okin, *Is Multiculturalism Bad for Women?*, *in* IS MULTICULTURALISM BAD FOR WOMEN? 7 (Princeton Univ. Press 1999).

41. Leti Volpp, *Blaming Culture for Bad Behavior*, 12 YALE J.L. & HUMAN. 89, 110 (2000) (quoting Okin, *supra* note 40, at 9).

42. Volpp, *supra* note 41, at 110 (footnotes omitted).

43. REPLACING MYTHS, *supra* note 27, at 23.

44. *See Oklahoma Political Information and Measures*, NARAL PRO-CHOICE AMERICA, http://www.prochoiceamerica.org/government-and-you/state-governments/state-profiles/oklahoma.html (last visited Jan. 26, 2017); *South Dakota Political Information and Measures*, NARAL PRO-CHOICE AMERICA, http://www.prochoiceamerica.org/government-and-you/state-governments/state-profiles/south-dakota.html (last visited Jan. 26, 2017).

45. For instance, in the same year that the Oklahoma state legislature passed its sex-selective abortion ban, it also passed—over an executive veto—a statute requiring women seeking an abortion to fill out an "Individual Abortion Form," and instituted a fine for failure to do so. *See* H.B. 3284, 52d Leg., 2d Sess. (Okla. 2010). The statute received the

support of 42% of Democrats in the Oklahoma Senate and 66% of Democrats in the Oklahoma House of Representatives. *See HB 3284—Requiring Women Seeking Abortions to Answer Questionnaire—Key Vote*, VoteSmart (Mar. 25, 2010), https://votesmart.org/bill/11419/30534/requiring-women-seeking-abortions-to-answer-questionnaire#.U1hp4fldUuc (last visited May 31, 2015). And in the South Dakota state legislature, 95.7% of the legislators who voted in favor of the sex-selective abortion ban also voted to pass H.B. 1180, 89th Leg., Reg. Sess. (S.D. 2014)—a bill providing that no organization that places children up for adoption or that performs abortions may be registered as a pregnancy help center. *See* NARAL Pro-Choice South Dakota, 2014 Legislative Recap (on file with author).

46. *State Facts About Abortion: Oklahoma*, Guttmacher Inst., https://www.guttmacher.org/pubs/sfaa/oklahoma.html (last visited May 31, 2015).

47. *State Facts About Abortion: South Dakota*, Guttmacher Inst., https://www.guttmacher.org/pubs/sfaa/south_dakota.html (last visited May 31, 2015).

48. *Elected Pro-Life Democrats*, Democrats for Life Am., https://web.archive.org/web/20150516222530/http://www.democratsforlife.org/index.php/elected-pro-life-dems/pro-life-democrats (last visited Jan. 26, 2017).

49. Mitch Smith, *Indiana Governor Signs Abortion Bill with Added Restrictions*, N.Y. Times (Mar. 24, 2016), http://www.nytimes.com/2016/03/25/us/indiana-governor-mike-pence-signs-abortion-bill.html.

50. *After Pence Signed HEA 1337, Women's Rights in Indiana Are Dead*, NUVO (Mar. 25, 2016), http://www.nuvo.net/indianapolis/after-pence-signed-hea-1337-womens-rights-in-indiana-are-dead/Content?oid=3880183.

51. Republicans may have become more educated as well. Representative Ed Clere, one of the few Republicans voting against the ban, had this to say: "The best way for us to reduce the number of abortions in Indiana is to empower girls and women. The best way to do that is through education and access to services and support, while also working long-term to empower and improve the status of girls and women in Indiana. That's where our policy focus should be." *Id.*

52. The study described in this section was original published in the Georgetown Journal of International Affairs. Sital Kalantry, *Sex-Selective Abortion Bans: Anti-Immigration or Anti-Abortion?*, 16 Geo. J. Int'l Aff. 140 (2015).

53. Molly Redden, *GOP Lawmaker: We Need to Ban Sex-Selective Abortions Because of Asian Immigrants*, Mother Jones (Feb. 25, 2014), http://www.motherjones.com/politics/2014/02/south-dakota-stace-nelson-ban-sex-based-abortions-because-asian-immigrants (last visited May 29, 2015).

54. Press Release, U.S. Census Bureau, Asians Fastest-Growing Race or Ethnic Group in 2012, Census Bureau Reports (June 13, 2013), http://www.census.gov/newsroom/press-releases/2013/cb13-112.html.

55. Press Release, U.S. Census Bureau, *supra* note 54.

56. Elizabeth M. Hoeffel et al., *The Asian Population: 2010*, in 2012 Census Briefs, U.S. Census Bureau 1, 14 (2012), http://www.census.gov/prod/cen2010/briefs/c2010br-11.pdf.

57. Hoeffel et al., *supra* note 56, at 7.

58. S.B. 6612, 64th Leg., Reg. Sess. (Wash. 2016).

59. The p-value is .337. The p-value was obtained using the Fisher's exact two-tailed test. In small data sets p-values that are below .1 are considered to be statistically significant. I would like to thank Marty Wells, Charles A. Alexander Professor of Statistical Sciences, Cornell University, for reviewing and giving me comments on this analysis.

60. *See* Igor Volsky, *Interactive Map: The Most Restrictive Abortion Measures in the States*, ThinkProgress (Mar. 7, 2012), http://thinkprogress.org/health/2012/03/07/439383/interactive-map-abortion/.

61. The p-value here was .089. The p-value was obtained using Fisher's exact two-tailed test. In exact small-sample tests it is typical to see p-values that are not below the standard .05 significance level; the marginal significance is considered sufficient evidence of an effect. *See* B. Burt Gerstman, Basic Biostatistics: Statistics for Public Health Practice (Jones & Bartlett 2008).

62. The p-value is .098. The p-value was obtained from exact two-sample proportion tests. *See* Alan Agresti, Categorical Data Analysis (2d ed. 2003). In exact small-sample tests it is typical to see p-values that are not below the standard .05 significance level; the marginal significance is considered sufficient evidence of an effect. *See* B. Burt Gerstman, Basic Biostatistics: Statistics for Public Health Practice (Jones & Bartlett 2008).

63. The p-value is .449. The p-value was obtained from exact two-sample proportion tests.

64. *See, e.g.*, Ariz. Rev. Stat. § 13-3603.02 (2013); Kan. Stat. § 65-6726 (2013).

65. *See, e.g.*, Ariz. Rev. Stat. § 13-3603.02 (2013); N.C. Gen. Stat. § 90-21.121 (2013).

66. *See, e.g.*, H.B. 1162, 89th Leg., Reg. Sess. (S.D. 2014) (enacted).

67. *See Mens Rea*, Cornell Legal Info. Inst., https://www.law.cornell.edu/wex/mens_rea (last visited May 30, 2015).

68. *See Actus Reus*, Cornell Legal Info. Inst., https://www.law.cornell.edu/wex/actus_reus (last visited May 30, 2015).

69. Sonu Bedi, *Why a Criminal Prohibition on Sex Selective Abortions Amounts to a Thought Crime*, 5 Crim. L. & Phil. 349 (2011).

70. Okla. Stat. tit. 63, § 1-731.2 (B)(4) (2013); 720 Ill. Comp. Stat. § 510/6(8) (2013).

71. *Sex-Linked Disorder*, Biology Online, http://www.biology-online.org/dictionary/Sex-linked_disorder (last visited May 29, 2015).

72. Prenatal Nondiscrimination Act (PRENDA) of 2016, H.R. 4924, 114th Cong. (2016).

73. Ind. Code § 16-34-4-1 (2016), *enjoined from taking effect by* Planned Parenthood of Ind. & Ky v. Comm'r, No. 1:16-cv-00763-TWP-DML, 2016 U.S. Dist. LEXIS 84917 (S.D. Ind. June 30, 2016); Ariz. Rev. Stat. Ann. § 13-3603.02 (2011)

74. Florida, *see, e.g.*, H.B. 845, 2013 Leg., Reg. Sess. (Fla. 2013); H.B. 1327, 2012 Leg., Reg. Sess. (Fla. 2012); Georgia, *see, e.g.*, S.B. 529, 150th Gen. Assemb., Reg. Sess.

(Ga. 2010); Idaho, *see, e.g.*, H.B. 693, 60th Leg., 2d Reg. Sess. (Idaho 2010); Michigan, *see, e.g.*, S.B. 799, 2009 Leg., Reg. Sess. (Mich. 2009); Minnesota, *see, e.g.*, S.B. 1073, 86th Leg., Reg. Sess. (Minn. 2009); Mississippi, *see, e.g.*, S.B. 2166, 2010 Leg., Reg. Sess. (Miss. 2010); New Jersey, *see, e.g.*, Gen. Assemb. 162, 214th Leg., Reg. Sess. (N.J. 2010); West Virginia, *see, e.g.*, S.B. 62, 77th Leg., Reg. Sess. (W. Va. 2010). The selective abortion bills in Florida, Georgia, Idaho, Mississippi, and New Jersey include race provisions.

75. Susan B. Anthony and Frederick Douglass Prenatal Nondiscrimination Act of 2009, H.R. 1822, 111th Cong. (2009).

76. Prenatal Nondiscrimination Act of 2013, H.R. 447, 113th Cong. § 2(a)(1)(D).

77. Complaint, Ex. B at 8, NAACP, et al. v. Tom Horne, et al., No. CV13-01079-PHX-DGC (D. Ariz. Oct. 3, 2013), *appeal docketed*, No. 13-17247 (9th Cir. Nov. 4, 2013), https://www.aclu.org/legal-document/naacp-et-al-v-tom-horne-et-al-exhibits-e [hereinafter Complaint]. It is interesting to note that the data supporting the claim that there is a disproportionate number of fetuses aborted of African American mothers compared to white mothers is more substantiated than the data on sex-selective abortion. This is because providers have to keep data about race of the woman seeking the abortion, but there is no requirement that data be kept on the sex of the fetus that is aborted. Jason Abrevaya, *Are There Missing Girls in the United States? Evidence from Birth Data*, 1 Am. Econ. J.: Applied Econ. 1, 7 (2009). Even if providers were required to document it, in most cases, the sex of the fetus may not be known when the abortion is obtained.

78. Complaint, *supra* note 77, Ex. B at 8.

79. Complaint, *supra* note 77, Ex. C at 63–64.

80. Prenatal Nondiscrimination Act (PRENDA) of 2016: Hearing on H.R. 4924 Before the Subcomm. on the Constitution and Civil Justice, 114th Cong. 62 (2016) (testimony of Catherine Davis, Founding Core Member, National Black Pro-Life Coalition).

81. Prenatal Nondiscrimination Act of 2016, H.R. 4924, 114th Cong. § 3(a) (2016). *See, e.g.*, Ariz. Rev. Stat. § 13-3603.02(A) (2013).

82. Caitlin Coakley Beckner, *House OKs Outlawing of Race- and Gender-selection Abortion*, Ariz. Capitol Times (Feb 21, 2011), http://azcapitoltimes.com/news/2011/02/21/bill-to-ban-selection-abortion-gets-initial-oks/#ixzz2KLO6v3Tl.

83. Complaint, *supra* note 77, at 13, ¶ 55.

84. *National Association for the Advancement of Colored People, Maricopa Country Branch, National Asian Pacific American Women's Forum vs. Tom Horne, et al.*, ACLU (March 12, 2014), https://www.aclu.org/cases/reproductive-freedom/national-association-advancement-colored-people-maricopa-county-branch.

85. NAACP v. Horne, 626 Fed. Appx. 200 (9th Cir. 2015).

86. Planned Parenthood of Ind. & Ky v. Comm'r, No. 1:16-cv-00763-TWP-DML, 2016 U.S. Dist. LEXIS 84917 (S.D. Ind. June 30, 2016).

87. Susan A. Cohen, *Abortion and Women of Color: The Bigger Picture*, 1, 11 Guttmacher Pol'y Rev. (2008), https://www.guttmacher.org/pubs/gpr/11/3/gpr110302.html.

88. Cohen, *supra* note 87, at 11.

Chapter 4

1. Unless I specify otherwise, I use the category of Asian Americans to include people who live in the United States but who migrated from Asia or whose ancestors migrated from Asia.

2. Tufuku Zuberi & Eduardo Bonilla-Silva, *Towards a Definition of White Logic and White Methods*, *in* WHITE LOGIC, WHITE METHODS: RACISM AND METHODOLOGY 3 (Tufuku Zuberi & Eduarado Bonilla-Silva eds., 2008).

3. Zuberi & Bonilla-Silva, *supra* note 2, at 17.

4. Zuberi & Bonilla-Silva, *supra* note 2, at 18.

5. Zuberi & Bonilla-Silva, *supra* note 2, at 6.

6. Zuberi & Bonilla-Silva, *supra* note 2, at 9.

7. Zuberi & Bonilla-Silva, *supra* note 2, at 7.

8. See Mario L. Barnes, *Empirical Methods and Critical Race Theory: A Discourse on Possibilities for a Hybrid Methodology*, 2016 WIS. L. REV. 443, for an excellent description of the emergence of this movement.

9. Barnes, *supra* note 8, at 447.

10. Barnes, *supra* note 8, at 451.

11. Barnes, *supra* note 8, at 451.

12. Douglas Almond & Lena Edlund, *Son-Biased Sex Ratios in the 2000 United States Census*, 105 PROC. NAT'L ACAD. SCI. 5681, 5681–82 (2008), http://www.pnas.org/content/105/15/5681.full.pdf.

13. Jason Abrevaya, *Are There Missing Girls in the United States? Evidence from Birth Data*, 1 AM. ECON. J.: APPLIED ECON. 1, 23 (2009).

14. Abrevaya, *supra* note 13, at 27.

15. James F.X. Egan et al., *Distortions of Sex Ratios at Birth in the United States: Evidence for Prenatal Gender Selection*, 31 PRENATAL DIAGNOSIS 560, 565 (2011).

16. Elizabeth M. Hoeffel et al., *The Asian Population: 2010*, in 2012 CENSUS BRIEFS, U.S. CENSUS BUREAU 1, 14 (2012), http://www.census.gov/prod/cen2010/briefs/c2010br-11.pdf.

17. Abrevaya, *supra* note 13, at 7.

18. Abrevaya, *supra* note 13, at 8.

19. Abrevaya, *supra* note 13, at 6.

20. *See supra* "New U.S. Data on Sex Selection among Asian Americans: Son Preference or Family Balancing?" on page 116.

21. Egan et al., *supra* note 15, at 565.

22. *See* Amadu Jacky Kaba, *Sex Ratio at Birth and Racial Differences: Why Do Black Women Give Birth to More Females Than Non-Black Women?*, 12 AFR. J. REPROD. HEALTH 139 (2008), http://works.bepress.com/cgi/viewcontent.cgi?article=1027&context=amadu_kaba.

23. Although Almond and Edlund's first footnote cites a paper that notes that sex ratios vary by race, Almond and Edlund do not specifically mention this fact in their

paper. They instead state that 1.05 is "the biological norm." Almond & Edlund, *supra* note 12, at 5681, 5682 n.1 (citing Anouch Chahnazarian, *Determinants of the Sex Ratio at Birth: Review of Recent Literature*, 35 SOC. BIOLOGY 214 (1988)).

24. Egan et al., *supra* note 15, at 564.

25. *Guidance Note on Prenatal Sex Selection*, UNITED NATIONS POPULATION FUND 1, 11 (2010), http://www.unfpa.org/webdav/site/global/shared/documents/publications/2010/guidenote_prenatal_sexselection.pdf.

26. Gretchen Livingston, *The Odds That You Will Give Birth to a Boy or Girl Depend on Where in the World You Live*, PEW RES. CTR. (Sept. 24, 2013), http://www.pewresearch.org/fact-tank/2013/09/24/the-odds-that-you-will-give-birth-to-a-boy-or-girl-depend-on-where-in-the-world-you-live; Natalie Wolchover, *Why Are More Boys Born Than Girls?*, LIVESCIENCE (Sept. 9, 2011), http://www.livescience.com/33491-male-female-sex-ratio.html.

27. Steven Hecht Orzack et al., *The Human Sex Ratio from Conception to Birth*, 112 PROC. NAT'L ACAD. SCI. E2102 (2015), http://www.pnas.org/content/112/16/E2102.full.

28. Almond & Edlund, *supra* note 12, at 5681.

29. Almond & Edlund, *supra* note 12, at 5681.

30. Almond & Edlund, *supra* note 12, at 5681.

31. Prabhat Jha et al., *Low Male-to-Female Sex Ratio of Children Born in India: National Survey of 1.1 Million Households*, 367 LANCET 211 (2006).

32. Almond & Edlund, *supra* note 12, at 5681.

33. Jae Woo Lim, *The Changing Trends in Live Birth Statistics in Korea, 1970 to 2010*, 54 KOREAN J. PEDIATRIC 429 (2011), http://www.ncbi.nlm.nih.gov/pmc/articles/PMC3254888/.

34. *See* Woojin Chung & Monica Das Gupta, *Why Is Son Preference Declining in South Korea? The Role of Development and Public Policy, and the Implications for China and India* (World Bank, Working Paper No. 4373, 2007), https://openknowledge.worldbank.org/bitstream/handle/10986/7367/wps4373.pdf?sequence=1.

35. Egan et al., *supra* note 15, at 563.

36. Egan et al., *supra* note 15, at 565.

37. Abrevaya, *supra* note 13, at 10 n.15.

38. Abrevaya, *supra* note 13, at 10 n.15.

39. MALCOLM NICOLSON & JOHN E.E. FLEMING, IMAGING AND IMAGINING THE FETUS: THE DEVELOPMENT of OBSTETRIC ULTRASOUND 7 (2013) ("By the late 1970s, the ultrasound scanner had become a medical white good, a standardized commodity in the mass marketplace.").

40. Abrevaya, *supra* note 13, at 16–17.

41. Abrevaya, *supra* note 13, at 18.

42. *Field Listing: Sex Ratio*, *in* THE WORLD FACTBOOK, CIA, https://www.cia.gov/library/publications/the-world-factbook/fields/2018.html (last visited May 31, 2015).

43. For example, the sex ratio in both Kenya and Malawi is 1.02. *Field Listing: Sex Ratio*, *supra* note 42.

44. Almond & Edlund, *supra* note 12, at 5681.

45. *Male Birth Rate Among Asian Americans Studied*, NPR (Apr. 1, 2008), http://www.npr.org/templates/story/story.php?storyId=89284549.

46. Sam Roberts, *U.S. Asians Show Bias for Boys; Census Data on Births Also Reflects Embrace of Sex Selection, Experts Say*, Int'l Herald Trib., June 16, 2009, at 2.

47. William Saletan, *Fetal Subtraction*, Slate (Apr. 3, 2008), http://www.slate.com/articles/health_and_science/human_nature/2008/04/fetal_subtraction.html.

48. *Asians Bring Preference for Sons to U.S.; Likelihood of Male Births Rises After Having Girls, Study Finds*, Record, Apr. 1, 2008, at A05; *Preference for Sons Revealed in Study*, Charleston Daily Mail, Apr. 1, 2008, at P3A; *Some Asian Couples in U.S. Opt for Sons*, Hous. Chron., Apr. 5, 2008, at 8.

49. *Race- and Sex-Selection Abortion Bans: A False Solution to the Real Problems of Racism and Sexism*, NARAL Pro-Choice America (Jan. 1, 2016), http://www.prochoiceamerica.org/media/fact-sheets/race-and-sex-selection-abortion.pdf.

50. Marcelo L. Urquia et al., *Sex Ratios at Birth After Induced Abortion*, 188 Can. Med. Assoc. J. E181 (2016), http://www.cmaj.ca/content/early/2016/04/12/cmaj.151074.short.

51. *Sex-Selective Abortion May Be Driving Boy Boom Among Indian-Born Moms in Canada: Study*, Nat'l Post (Apr. 11, 2016), http://news.nationalpost.com/news/canada/sex-selective-abortion-may-be-driving-boy-boom-among-indian-born-moms-in-canada-study.

52. *4,472 'Missing' Daughters*, Waterloo Reg'l Rec., Apr. 12, 2016, at A3.

53. H.R. Rep. No. 112-496, at 50 (2012) (quoting Steven W. Mosher, *A New Front in the Abortion Wars: PreNDA Seeks Race and Sex-Based Equality for the Unborn*, 18 Pri. Rev. (Nov./Dec. 2008), http://www.pop.org/content/a-new-front-in-abortion-wars-prenda-seeks-1602).

54. Anti-abortion groups began a concerted effort only in 2011 to pass state-level abortion restrictions. Frances Robles, *State Legislatures Put Up Flurry of Roadblocks to Abortion*, N.Y. Times (May 8, 2015), http://www.nytimes.com/2015/05/09/us/politics/state-legislatures-put-up-flurry-of-roadblocks-to-abortion.html ("The 37 new rules in 11 states are part of a strategy accelerated by abortion opponents in 2011, when provisions restricting abortion access began sweeping state legislatures").

55. *See supra* Table 3 in Chapter 3 (the numbers in the text include those state legislatures that considered the bills more than once).

56. Planned Parenthood of Ind. & Ky. v. Comm'r, No. 1:16-cv-00763-TWP-DML, 2016 U.S. Dist. LEXIS 84917 (S.D. Ind. June 30, 2016).

57. Florida, H.B. 845, 115th Leg., Reg. Sess. (Fla. 2013). *See also* Prenatal Nondiscrimination Act of 2013, H.R. 447, 113th Cong. § 2(a)(1)(F) (citing the Almond and Edlund study as showing an "obvious 'son preference' in the form of unnatural sex-ratio imbalances within certain segments of the United States population, primarily those segments tracing their ethnic or cultural origins to countries where sex-selection abortion is prevalent"); New Jersey, A.B. 2157(1)(f), 215th Leg., Reg. Sess. (N.J. 2013) ("[I]n a March

2008 report published in the Proceedings of the National Academy of Sciences, two economists from Columbia University examined the sex ratio of children born in the United States and found 'evidence of sex selection, most likely at the prenatal stage'").

58. Phillip Lentz & Michael Lang, *Abortion Foes Push Bill Through House*, Chi. Trib., Apr. 27, 1984, at A1.

59. *Pennsylvania Abortion Limits Become Law*, N.Y. Times (Nov. 19, 1989), http://www.nytimes.com/1989/11/19/us/pennsylvania-abortion-limits-become-law.html.

60. Lentz & Lang, *supra* note 58, at A1; H.R. 173-65, 1989 Sess., at 1743-44 (Pa. 1989), http://www.legis.state.pa.us/WU01/LI/HJ/1989/0/19891024.pdf. The abortion laws in Pennsylvania amended Pennsylvania's existing abortion laws in light of the Supreme Court's decision in Webster v. Reproductive Health Services, 492 U.S. 490 (1989).

61. State of Ill. Gen. Assemb., S. Transcripts Discussing H.B. 1399, 83d Gen. Assemb., at 36–38 (June 25, 1983); State of Ill. Gen. Assemb., S. Transcripts Discussing H.B. 1399, 83d Gen. Assemb., at 222–23 (June 29, 1983); State of Ill. Gen. Assemb., S. Transcripts Discussing H.B. 1399, 83d Gen. Assemb., at 17–33 (Apr. 30, 1984); State of Ill. Gen. Assemb., S. Transcripts Discussing H.B. 1399, 83d Gen. Assemb., at 142–51 (June 30, 1984); State of Ill. Gen. Assemb., H. Transcripts Discussing H.B. 1399, 83d Gen. Assemb., at 175–79 (May 27, 1983); State of Ill. Gen. Assemb., H. Transcripts Discussing H.B. 1399, 83d Gen. Assemb., at 81–86 (Apr. 26, 1984); State of Ill. Gen. Assemb., H. Transcripts Discussing H.B. 1399, 83d Gen. Assemb., at 50–64 (June 29, 1984).

62. H.R. 173-65, 1989 Sess., at 1743–44 (Pa. 1989), http://www.legis.state.pa.us/WU01/LI/HJ/1989/0/19891024.pdf (last visited June 7, 2015).

63. H.R. 173-65, at 1744.

64. *In Support of H.B. 1979: "1989 Abortion Control Act": Hearing on H.B. 1979 Before the H. Comm. on the Judiciary*, H.R. 173-65, 1989 Sess. 5 (Pa. 1989) (testimony of Pennsylvania Pro-Life Federation) [hereinafter *In Support of H.B. 1979 Hearing*].

65. *In Support of H.B. 1979 Hearing*, *supra* note 64, at 5.

66. H.R. 173-65, at 1749.

67. Nicholas D. Kristof, *The Chosen Sex—A Special Report; Chinese Turn to Ultrasound, Scorning Baby Girls for Boys*, N.Y. Times (July 21, 1993), http://www.nytimes.com/1993/07/21/us/chosen-sex-special-report-chinese-turn-ultrasound-scorning-baby-girls-for-boys.html.

68. Kristof, *supra* note 67.

69. *See* Tamar Lewin, *States Testing the Limits on Abortion*, N.Y. Times (Apr. 2, 1990), http://www.nytimes.com/1990/04/02/us/states-testing-the-limits-on-abortion.html (last visited July 30, 2015); John F. Harris, *Abortion Curb Debated in Richmond*, Wash. Post (Feb. 7, 1990), http://www.washingtonpost.com/archive/local/1990/02/07/abortion-curb-debated-in-richmond/a0e1d52a-4a88-4c44-88ca-5d8256390fb7/; Lisa M. Fleischman, *"Good" vs. "Bad" Abortions: The Matter of Motives*, L.A. Times (May 20, 1990), http://articles.latimes.com/1990-05-20/opinion/op-41_1_abortion-debate.

70. Egan et al., *supra* note 15, at 564.

71. *Testimony to the South Dakota House of Representatives*, 89th Leg., 19th Sess. (S.D. 2014) (statement of Spencer Cody, Vice President of South Dakota Right to Life), http://sdpb.sd.gov/SDPBPodcast/2014/hju19.mp3 (last visited Jan. 27, 2017) (emphasis added).

72. *Susan B. Anthony and Frederick Douglass Prenatal Nondiscrimination Act of 2011: Hearing before the S. Comm. on the Constitution of the Comm. on the Judiciary*, 112th Cong. 1, 1 (2011) (statement of Steven W. Mosher, President, Population Research Institute), http://judiciary.house.gov/_files/hearings/printers/112th/112-74_71599.pdf (last visited July 26, 2016).

73. Prenatal Nondiscrimination Act of 2013, H.R. 447, 113th Cong. § 2(a)(1)(L)(i), (iii) (2013).

74. Jonathan V. Last, *The War Against Girls: Since the Late 1970s, 163 Million Female Babies Have Been Aborted by Parents Seeking Sons*, Wall St. J., (June 24, 2011) submitted in the record of the *Susan B. Anthony and Frederick Douglass Prenatal Nondiscrimination Act of 2011: Hearing before the S. Comm. on the Constitution of the Comm. on the Judiciary*, 112th Cong. 1, 36 (2011) (statement of Rep. Trent Franks), http://judiciary.house.gov/_files/hearings/printers/112th/112-74_71599.pdf [hereinafter *PRENDA 2011 Hearing*].

75. See Chapter 1 for a detailed discussion of the methods for sex selection.

76. *See* F.J. Beernink et al., *Sex Preselection through Albumin Separation of Sperm*, 59 Fertility & Sterility 382 (1993) (stating that the Ericsson method of sperm sorting uses the difference in swimming speed between the X- and Y-chromosome–bearing sperm to separate the two groups, resulting in a 71% accuracy rate for the desired sex).

77. *In Vitro Fertilization (IVF)*, MedlinePlus, http://www.nlm.nih.gov/medlineplus/ency/article/007279.htm (last visited June 7, 2015).

78. *See* Susannah Baruch et al., *Genetic Testing of Embryos: Practices and Perspectives of U.S. IVF Clinics*, 89 Fertility & Sterility 1053 (2006), http://www.fertstert.org/article/S0015-0282(07)01216-2/fulltext.

79. *See, e.g.*, *Gender Selection*, San Diego Fertility Ctr., http://www.sdfertility.com/gender_selection.htm (last visited June 7, 2015); *see also Selecting the Sex of Your Baby*, Fertility Authority, https://www.fertilityauthority.com/fertility-treatment/gender-selection-options/selecting-sex-your-baby (last visited June 7, 2015); Katie Moisse, *Fertility Clinic Offers Gender Selection, Draws Women from Abroad*, ABCNews (Sept. 24, 2012), http://abcnews.go.com/Health/Wellness/fertility-clinic-offers-gender-selection-draws-women-abroad/story?id=17219176. For a fuller discussion of the methods of sex selection, see Chapter 1.

80. Hoeffel et al., *supra* note 16, at 7.

81. *Latest Data, 2013—Clinic Tables and Data Dictionary*, Ctrs. for Disease Control & Prevention, http://www.cdc.gov/art/reports/index.html (scroll down to Latest Data, 2013).

82. Susan Sachs, *Clinics' Pitch to Indian Émigrés: It's a Boy*, N.Y. Times (Aug. 15, 2001), http://www.nytimes.com/2001/08/15/nyregion/clinics-pitch-to-indian-emigres-it-s-a-boy.html.

83. Sachs, *supra* note 82.

84. Sital Kalantry & Miriam Yeung, U. Chi. L. Sch. Int'l Hum. Rts. Clinic, Nat'l Asian Pac. Women's F. & Advancing New Standards for Reprod. Just., Replacing Myths with Facts: Sex Selective Abortion Laws in the United States (2014), https://napawf.org/wp-content/uploads/2014/06/Replacing-Myths-with-Facts-final.pdf.

85. The full study is on file with the author and is also under review for publication at peer-reviewed demographic journals.

86. Although data on births in the United States is available from the National Center for Health Statistics (NCHS), we cannot use that data to analyze the sex of children at different birth parities of the same family, because that database does not provide information about the sexes of the prior births of the mother.

87. Almond & Edlund, *supra* note 12, at 5682.

88. Abrevaya, *supra* note 13, at 19; Egan et al., *supra* note 15, at 561.

89. Egan et al., *supra* note 15, at 564–65.

90. *See* Frank Newport, *Americans Prefer Boys to Girls, Just as They Did in 1941*, Gallup (June 23, 2011), http://www.gallup.com/poll/148187/americans-prefer-boys-girls-1941.aspx.

91. Newport, *supra* note 90.

92. Hoeffel et al., *supra* note 16, at 7.

Chapter 5

1. *See Amniocentesis*, Mayo Clinic, http://www.mayoclinic.org/tests-procedures/amniocentesis/basics/definition/prc-20014529 (last visited Aug. 6, 2016).

2. Mara Hvistendahl, Unnatural Selection 80 (2011).

3. Hrishikesh D. Vinod, *Newborn Sex Selection and India's Overpopulation Problem*, 4 Mod. Econ. 102, 103 (2013).

4. Vinod, *supra* note 3, at 103.

5. Hvistendahl, *supra* note 2, at 82–89.

6. The Lawyers Collective: Women's Rights Initiative, Pre-conception & Pre-natal Diagnostic Techniques Act: A Users Guide to the Law 1 (Indira Jaising ed., 2004) [hereinafter PCPNDT Act: A Users Guide].

7. Ceara O'Brien, *Social Implications of Non-Invasive Blood Tests to Determine the Sex of Fetuses*, Embryo Project Encyclopedia (Mar. 24, 2014), http://embryo.asu.edu/handle/10776/7648 (last visited Aug. 6, 2016).

8. Hvistendahl, *supra* note 2, at 49.

9. *See* Christophe Z. Guilmoto, Characteristics of Sex-Ratio Imbalance in India, and Future Scenarios 4–8 (2007), http://www.unfpa.org/gender/docs/studies/india.pdf.

10. William E. Hudson, Global Issues: Selections from CQ Researcher 286 (2012).

11. Amartya Sen, *More Than 100 Million Women Are Missing*, 37 N.Y. Rev. Books 61 (1990).

12. Amartya Sen, *Missing Women: Social Inequality Outweighs Women's Survival Advantage in Asia and North Africa*, 304 Brit. Med. J. 587, 587–88 (1992).

13. *See generally* Stephan Klasen & Claudia Wink, *"Missing Women": Revisiting the Debate*, 9 Feminist Econ. 263 (2003).

14. *See, e.g.*, Jason Abrevaya, *Are There Missing Girls in the United States? Evidence from Birth Data*, 1 Am. Econ. J.: Applied Econ. 1, 23 (2009).

15. Melissa Stillman et al., Guttmacher Inst., Abortion in India: A Literature Review 1, 18 (2014), https://www.guttmacher.org/pubs/Abortion-India-Lit-Review.pdf.

16. Stillman et al., *supra* note 15, at 18.

17. Stillman et al., *supra* note 15, at 18.

18. Monica Das Gupta & P.N. Mari Bhat, *Fertility Decline and Increased Manifestation of Sex Bias in India*, 51 Population Stud. 307, 307–09 (1997).

19. *See generally* Satish Balram Agnihotri, Sex Ratio Patterns in the Indian Population: A Fresh Exploration (2000).

20. Mary John, U.N. Population Fund (UNFPA), Sex Ratios and Gender Biased Sex Selection History, Debates and Future Directions 18 (2014), http://asiapacific.unfpa.org/webdav/site/asiapacific/shared/Publications/2014/Sex-Ratios-and-Gender-Biased-Sex-Selection.pdf.

21. Veena Talwar Oldenburg, Dowry Murder: The Imperial Origins of a Cultural Crime 41 (2002).

22. Oldenburg, *supra* note 21, at 37–38.

23. Hvistendahl, *supra* note 2, at 64.

24. Oldenburg, *supra* note 21, at 66–67.

25. Oldenburg, *supra* note 21, at 67–68.

26. L.S. Vishwanath, Female Infanticide and Social Structure: A Socio-Historical Study in Western and Northern India 6, 13 (2000).

27. Oldenburg, *supra* note 21, at 129–30.

28. Oldenburg, *supra* note 21, at 134.

29. Oldenburg, *supra* note 21, at 8.

30. Annie Cossins, Female Criminality: Infanticide, Moral Panics and the Female Body 78 (2015).

31. Hvistendahl, *supra* note 2, at 62.

32. Hvistendahl, *supra* note 2, at 62.

33. Hvistendahl, *supra* note 2, at 63.

34. Hvistendahl, *supra* note 2, at 63.

35. Hvistendahl, *supra* note 2, at 63.

36. Hvistendahl, *supra* note 2, at 65.

37. Pravin M. Visaria, The Sex Ratio of the Population of India, Census of India 1961, Volume 1, Monograph No. 10, at 65 (1968).

38. John, *supra* note 20, at 5.

39. Hvistendahl, *supra* note 2, at 71.

40. Geetanjali Misra et al., *Poor Reproductive Health and Environmental Degradation: Outcomes of Women's Low Status in India*, 6 Colo. J. Int'l Envtl. L. & Pol'y 273, 280 (1995).

41. India Code Crim. Proc. § 125 (1973).

42. Mallika Kaur Sarkaria, Comment, *Lessons from Punjab's "Missing Girls": Toward a Global Feminist Perspective on "Choice" in Abortion*, 97 Calif. L. Rev. 905, 910-11 (2009).

43. *See* Rita Patel, *The Practice of Sex Selective Abortion in India: May You Be the Mother of a Hundred Sons*, Ctr. Global Initiatives 1, 7 (1996).

44. *See, e.g.*, Ashok Sircar, *Emerging Voices: Ashok Sircar on Women's Right to Inherit Land in India*, Landesa (June 12, 2013), http://www.landesa.org/emerging-voices-ashok-sircar-womens-right-inherit-land-india-blog/.

45. Nitya Rao, UN Women, *Women's Access to Land: An Asian Perspective*, 12 tbl.1, U.N. Doc. EGM/RW/2011/EP.3 (Sept. 2011), http://www.un.org/womenwatch/daw/csw/csw56/egm/Rao-EP-3-EGM-RW-30Sep-2011.pdf.

46. Kirti Singh, U.N. Population Fund (UNFPA), Laws and Son-Preference in India: A Reality Check 51 (2013), http://www.unfpa.org/sites/default/files/jahia-news/documents/publications/2013/LawsandSonPreferenceinIndia.pdf.

47. *Satyamev Jayate: Female Foeticide, Daughters Are Precious* (television broadcast May 6, 2012), http://www.satyamevjayate.in/watch-the-episodes/female-foeticide/watch-full-episode-hindi.aspx.

48. Kumkum Sangari, *Settled Alibis and Emerging Contradictions: Sex Selection, Dowry and Domestic Violence*, 47 Econ. & Pol. Wkly. 39, 44 (2012).

49. John, *supra* note 20, at 35.

50. Mallika Kaur Sarkaria's study of Punjab describes the violence women face if they do not have sons. *See* Mallika Kaur Sarkaria, Comment, *Lessons from Punjab's "Missing Girls": Toward a Global Feminist Perspective on "Choice" in Abortion*, 97 Calif. L. Rev. 905, 910-11 (2009).

51. Christophe Z. Guilmoto, UNFPA Asia & Pac. Reg'l Off., Sex Imbalances at Birth: Current Trends, Consequences and Policy Implications 10 (2012), http://www.unfpa.org/publications/sex-imbalances-birth.

52. Carl Haub & James Gribble, Population Reference Bureau, Population Bulletin: The World at 7 Billion, at 9 (2011), http://www.prb.org/pdf11/world-at-7-billion.pdf.

53. John, *supra* note 20, at 42–43.

54. Ravinder Kaur, *Dispensable Daughters and Bachelor Sons: Sex Discrimination in North India*, 43 Econ. & Pol. Wkly. 109, 114 (2008.)

55. *See China Reforms: One-Child Policy to be Relaxed*, BBC (Nov. 15, 2013), http://www.bbc.com/news/world-asia-china-24957303.

56. Singh, *supra* note 46, at 80.

57. *Follow Himachal and Abolish Two Child Norm, Panchayat Minister Urges MP*, Infochange Population (June 27, 2005), http://infochangeindia.org/index.php

?option=com_content&view=article&id=4408:follow-himachal-and-abolish-two-child-norm-panchayat-minister-urges-mp&catid=198:news&Itemid=44.

58. Javed v. State of Haryana, A.I.R. 2003 S.C. 3057 (India).

59. *See* Mevlude Akbulut-Yuksel & Daniel Rosenblum, *The India Ultrasound Paradox*, IZA, Jan. 2012 at 1, http://ftp.iza.org/dp6273.pdf.

60. Mary E. John et al., *Dispensing with Daughters: Technology, Society, Economy in North India*, 44 Econ. & Pol. Wkly 18 (2009).

61. Navtej K. Purewal, Son Preference: Sex Selection, Gender and Culture in South Asia 14–16 (2010).

62. Gita Aravamudan, Disappearing Daughters: The Tragedy of Female Foeticide 27 (2007). *See also* Chander Suta Dogra, *Death Becomes Her*, Outlook India (Feb. 27, 2006), http://www.outlookindia.com/article/death-becomes-her/230331; Sunita Puri et al., *"There Is Such a Thing as Too Many Daughters, But Not Too Many Sons": A Qualitative Study of Son Preference and Fetal Sex Selection Among Indian Immigrants in the United States*, 72 Soc. Sci. & Med. 1169, 1174 (2011), http://www.nrlc.org/uploads/sexselectionabortion/TooManyDaughtersSunitaPuri.pdf.

63. Jaising et al., From the Abnormal to the Normal: Preventing Sex Selective Abortions Through the Law 108 (2007), http://www.lawyerscollective.org/publications/abnormal-normal-preventing-sex-selective-abortions-law.html.

64. Jaising et al., *supra* note 63, at 143, tbl.34.

65. Jaising et al., *supra* note 63, at 117.

66. Jaising et al., *supra note* 63, at 117–18.

67. Jaising et al., *supra note* 63, at 117.

68. John et al., *supra* note 60, at 17.

69. Prabhat Jha et al., *Low Male-to-Female Sex Ratio of Children Born in India: National Survey of 1.1 Million Households*, 367 Lancet 211, 214 (2006).

70. Jha et al., *supra* note 69, at 211–12.

71. Jha et al., *supra* note 69, at 211.

72. Tulsi Patel, *The Mindset Behind Eliminating the Female Foetus*, *in* Sex-Selective Abortion in India, Gender, Society and New Reproductive Technologies 135, 143 (Tulsi Patel ed., 2007).

73. *Missing Sisters*, Economist (Apr. 17, 2003), http://www.economist.com/node/1715401.

74. *Sex Ratio in India*, Census 2011, http://www.census2011.co.in/sexratio.php (last visited Oct. 4, 2013).

75. Vibhuti Patel, *Sex Tests Endanger Women's Rights*, Times India, Jan. 14, 1989, at 12.

76. John, *supra* note 20, at 8.

77. John, *supra* note 20, at 8.

78. Bijayalaxmi Nanda, *Campaign Against Female Foeticide: Perspectives, Strategies and Experiences*, *in* Sex-Selective Abortion in India: Gender, Society and New Reproductive Technologies 361 (Tulsi Patel ed., 2007).

79. Nanda, *supra* note 78, at 361.

80. India Const. art. 32.

81. Centre for Enquiry into Health and Allied Themes (CEHAT) v. Union of India, (2001) 3 S.C.R. 534 (India), *in* PCPNDT Act: A Users Guide, *supra* note 6, at 106–08.

82. CEHAT v. Union of India, (2001) 3 S.C.R. 534 (India), *in* PCPNDT Act: A Users Guide, *supra* note 6, at 106–08.

83. CEHAT v. Union of India, 2003 SOL Case No. 547 (2003), *in* PCPNDT Act: A Users Guide, *supra* note 6, at 109–16.

84. *See generally* KPMG & Federation of Indian Chambers of Commerce and Industry (FICCI), Medical Value Travel in India (2014), http://www.travelbizmonitor.com/images/kpmg_ficci_heal_sep_2014_271014.pdf.

85. CEHAT v. Union of India, 2003 SOL Case No. 547 (2003), *in* PCPNDT Act: A Users Guide, *supra* note 6, at 109–16.

86. The Pre-Natal Diagnostic Techniques (Regulation and Prevention of Misuse) Amendment Act, No. 14 of 2003, India Code (2003) [hereinafter 2003 PNDT Amendment Act].

87. 2003 PNDT Amendment Act, *supra* note 86.

88. ILO Reg'l Off. for Asia & Pac., Int'l Labour Org., Wages in Asia and the Pacific: Dynamic but Uneven Process 2 (2014), http://www.ilo.org/wcmsp5/groups/public/---asia/---ro-bangkok/---sro-bangkok/documents/publication/wcms_325219.pdf.

89. *IVF*, Global Dr. Options, http://www.globaldoctoroptions.com/ivf-cost/424 (last visited Aug. 15, 2016).

90. 2003 PNDT Amendment Act, *supra* note 86, at ch. VI (18).

91. 2003 PNDT Amendment Act, *supra* note 86, at ch. V (17).

92. 2003 PNDT Amendment Act, *supra* note 86, ch. II (3)(B).

93. 2003 PNDT Amendment Act, *supra* note 86, ch. VII (22).

94. 2003 PNDT Amendment Act, *supra* note 86, ch. VII (24).

95. Singh, *supra* note 46, at 58, 73 & n.94.

96. Medical Termination of Pregnancy (MTP) Act, No. 34 of 1971, India Code (1971).

97. PCPNDT Act: A Users Guide, *supra* note 6, at 62.

98. MTP Act, No. 34 of 1971, India Code (1971).

99. MTP Act, No. 34 of 1971, India Code (1971), § 3(2)(b)(i).

100. MTP Act, No. 34 of 1971, India Code (1971), § 3(2)(b)(ii), Explanation 1.

101. John, *supra* note 20, at 11–12.

102. Jaising et al., *supra* note 63, at 77–78.

103. Jaising et al., *supra* note 63, at 81.

104. Jaising et al., *supra* note 63, at 61–62.

105. PCPNDT Act: A Users Guide, *supra* note 6, at 1.

106. PCPNDT Act: A Users Guide, *supra* note 6, at 46–47.

107. D.Y. Chandrachud, *Foreword* to Shalini Phansalkar Joshi, Compilation and Analysis of Case-laws on Pre-conception and Pre-natal Diagnostics Techniques (Prohibition of Sex Selection) Act, 1994, at iv (2011) ("There are few convictions under the Act.").

108. Asian Ctr. for Hum. Rts., The State of Female Infanticide in Himachal Pradesh 10 (2016), http://www.stopfemaleinfanticide.org/files/HimachalPradesh.pdf (stating that there have been 206 convictions for violations of PCPNDT between the years 2009–2014).

109. Jaising et al., *supra* note 63, at 160.

110. Jaising et al., *supra* note 63, at 161.

111. John, *supra* note 20, at 12–13.

112. Swapna Majumdar, *It Takes Courage to Let a Girl Child Be Born*, Hindustan Times (Feb. 28, 2014), http://www.hindustantimes.com/analysis/it-takes-courage-to-let-a-girl-child-be-born/article1-1189470.aspx.

113. Bus. Leaders Initiative for Hum. Rts., The Millennium Development Goals and Human Rights: Companies Taking a Rights-Aware Approach to Development 47–52 (2010), http://www.hks.harvard.edu/m-rcbg/CSRI/publications/report_44.pdf.

114. Arindam Nandi, *The Unintended Effects of a Ban on Sex-Selective Abortion on Infant Mortality: Evidence from India*, Oxford Dev. Stud. 1, 10–11 (2013), http://www.tandfonline.com/doi/full/10.1080/13600818.2014.973390.

115. John, *supra* note 20, at 16.

116. India Pen. Code, No. 45 of 1860, §§ 312–16.

117. John, *supra* note 20, at 15.

118. John, *supra* note 20, at 16.

119. UNFPA, Doctors for Daughters: Doctors' Dilemmas 11, http://countryoffice.unfpa.org/india/drive/Doctors'Dilemmas.pdf.

120. *See, e.g.*, *Know the Issue*, Girls Count, http://www.girlscount.in/know-the-issue/ (last visited Aug. 8, 2016).

121. Stillman et al., *supra* note 15, at 28.

122. Stillman et al., *supra* note 15, at 28.

123. Stillman et al., *supra* note 15, at 28–29.

124. Stillman et al., *supra* note 15, at 28–29.

125. Jill Filipovic, *The Unintended Consequences of India's War on Sex Selection*, Int'l Reporting Project (Mar. 31, 2016), http://internationalreportingproject.org/stories/view/the-unintended-consequences-of-indias-war-on-sex-selection.

126. Patel, *supra* note 75.

127. John et al., *supra* note 60, at 19.

128. Nivedita Menon, *Abortion as a Feminist Issue—Who Decides, and What?*, Kafila (May 11, 2012), https://kafila.online/2012/05/11/abortion-as-a-feminist-issue-who-decides-and-what/.

129. Vinod, *supra* note 3, at 104.

130. John, *supra* note 20, at 11–12.

131. *See generally* Sunita Bose et al., *The Effect of a Male Surplus on Intimate Partner Violence in India*, 48 Econ. & Pol. Wkly. 53 (2013).

132. Judith G. Greenberg, *Criminalizing Dowry Deaths: The Indian Experience*, 11 Am. U. J. Gender, Soc. Pol'y & L. 801, 805–09 (2003).

133. Consider, for example, the Beti Utsav programs organized by Action India. *Beti Utsav*, Action India, http://www.action-india.org/beti_utsav.html (last visited Aug. 8, 2015).

134. John, *supra* note 20, at 13.

135. John, *supra* note 20, at 13.

136. Kim Barker, *Fewer Girls, and Few Will Discuss Why*, Chi. Trib. (May 12, 2006), http://articles.chicagotribune.com/2006-05-12/news/0605120135_1_female-fetuses-sex-selective-abortions-fewer-girls (stating that activists hold mourning ceremonies outside the homes of couples suspected of aborting females in one district in Punjab).

137. John, *supra* note 20, at 8.

138. *See, e.g.*, *India Donation: Invisible Girl Project*, Causes, https://www.causes.com/indiadonation (last visited June 15, 2015).

139. John, *supra* note 20, at 14.

140. *Ladli Scheme*, New Delhi Mun. Council, http://www.ndmc.gov.in/departments/education/LADLI SCHEME.pdf (last visited June 15, 2015).

141. Barker, *supra* note 136.

142. John, *supra* note 20, at 15.

143. John, *supra* note 20, at 14.

144. Stephanie A. Devaney et al., *Noninvasive Fetal Sex Determination Using Cell-Free Fetal DNA*, 306 JAMA 627, 636 (2011); *see* Ceara O'Brien, *Social Implications of Non-Invasive Blood Tests to Determine the Sex of Fetuses*, Embryo Project Encyclopedia (Mar. 24, 2014), http://embryo.asu.edu/handle/10776/7648 (last visited May 29, 2015).

Chapter 6

1. CEHAT v. Union of India, 2003 SOL Case No. 547 (2003), *in* The Lawyer's Collective: Women's Rights Initiative, Pre-conception & Pre-natal Diagnostic Techniques Act: A Users Guide to the Law 1, 109–16 (Indira Jaising ed., 2004).

2. The Pre-Natal Diagnostic Techniques (Regulation and Prevention of Misuse) Amendment Act, No. 14 of 2003, India Code (2003) [hereinafter 2003 PNDT Amendment Act].

3. 2003 PNDT Amendment Act, *supra* note 2.

4. Medical Termination of Pregnancy (MTP) Act, No. 34 of 1971, India Code (1971).

5. *See e.g.*, Bombay High Court, Writ Petition No. 2777 of 2005 (June 6, 2007).

6. One Indian woman stated, "Our society makes you feel so bad if you don't have a son. . . . Especially when I go out for parties, people say 'How many children?' I say, 'Two girls,' and they say 'Oh, too bad, no boy.' And I feel very bad." RUTH MACKLIN, AGAINST RELATIVISM: CULTURAL DIVERSITY AND THE SEARCH FOR ETHICAL UNIVERSALS IN MEDICINE 149 (Oxford Univ. Press 1999).

7. Jill Filipovic, *The Unintended Consequences of India's War on Sex Selection*, 33 WORLD POL'Y J. 71, 72 (2016).

8. MELISSA STILLMAN ET AL., GUTTMACHER INST., ABORTION IN INDIA: A LITERATURE REVIEW 1, 18 (2014), https://www.guttmacher.org/pubs/Abortion-India-Lit-Review.pdf.

9. Christophe Z. Guilmoto, *Skewed Sex Ratios at Birth and Future Marriage Squeeze in China and India, 2005–2100*, 49 DEMOGRAPHY 77 (2012).

10. *The Marriage Squeeze in India and China: Bare Branches, Redundant Males*, ECONOMIST, Apr. 18, 2015, http://www.economist.com/news/asia/21648715-distorted-sex-ratios-birth-generation-ago-are-changing-marriage-and-damaging-societies-asias [hereinafter *The Marriage Squeeze*].

11. *The Marriage Squeeze*, *supra* note 10.

12. *The Marriage Squeeze*, *supra* note 10.

13. ANALIA SCHLOSSER & LUOJIA HU, DOES PRENATAL SEX SELECTION IMPROVE GIRLS' WELL-BEING? EVIDENCE FROM INDIA 18 (2010), http://www.biu.ac.il/soc/ec/seminar/data/29_11_10/Hu_Schlosser_Nov18_2010.pdf.

14. Arindam Nandi, *The Unintended Effects of a Ban on Sex-Selective Abortion on Infant Mortality: Evidence from India*, OXFORD DEV. STUD. 1, 11 (2013), http://www.tandfonline.com/doi/full/10.1080/13600818.2014.973390.

15. VALERIE M. HUDSON & ANDREA M. DEN BOER, BARE BRANCHES: THE SECURITY IMPLICATIONS OF ASIA'S SURPLUS MALE POPULATION 264 (2004).

16. *See generally* Lena Edlund et al., *More Men, More Crime: Evidence from China's One-Child Policy* (IZA, Working Paper No. 3214, 2008), http://papers.ssrn.com/sol3/papers.cfm?abstract_id=1136376 [hereinafter *More Men, More Crime*].

17. *More Men, More Crime*, *supra* note 16, at 9.

18. Jean Drèze & Reetika Khera, *Crime, Gender, and Society in India: Insights from Homicide Data*, 26 POPULATION & DEV. REV. 335, 342 (2000).

19. Shareen Joshi, *Missing Women and Violent Crimes in India: More Than a Correlation?*, 15 GEO. J. INT'L AFF. 35, 38 (2014).

20. Joshi, *supra* note 19, at 39.

21. Allan Mazur & Joel Michalek, *Marriage, Divorce, and Male Testosterone*, 77 SOC. FORCES 315, 315 (1998), http://sf.oxfordjournals.org/content/77/1/315.full.pdf. *See also* James M. Dabbs Jr. & Robin Morris, *Testosterone, Social Class, and Antisocial Behavior in a Sample of 4,462 Men*, 1 PSYCHOL. SCI. 209 (1990), http://pss.sagepub.com/content/1/3/209.full.pdf.

22. John M.W. Bradford & D. McLean, *Sexual Offenders, Violence and Testosterone: A Clinical Study*, 29 CAN. J. PSYCHIATRY 335 (1984).

23. Robert Epstein, *How the Woman/Man Ratio Affects Sex, Facial Hair, and Politics*, DISCOVER (Oct. 4, 2012), http://discovermagazine.com/2012/oct/21-sex-ratio-women-men-affects-attitudes-facial-hair-politics.

24. Scott J. South et al., *Skewed Sex Ratios and Criminal Victimization in India*, 51 DEMOGRAPHY 1019, 1021–35 (2014), http://link.springer.com/article/10.1007%2Fs13524-014-0289-6.

25. South et al., *supra* note 24, at 1035.

26. Kaare Svalastoga, *Rape and Social Structure*, 5 PAC. SOC. REV. 48, 51 (1962).

27. Sunita Bose et al., *The Effect of a Male Surplus on Intimate Partner Violence in India*, 48 ECON. & POL. WKLY. 53, 57 (2013) [hereinafter *The Effect of a Male Surplus*].

28. *The Effect of a Male Surplus*, *supra* note 27, at 58.

29. *The Effect of a Male Surplus*, *supra* note 27, at 59.

30. One study of certain U.S. metropolitan areas found an association between a surplus of men and homicide and rape rates, but not robbery rates. Steven F. Messner & Judith R. Blau, *Routine Leisure Activities and Rates of Crime: A Macro-Level Analysis*, 65 SOC. FORCES 1035 (1987). Similarly, a study conducted in 1962 of 141 rape cases brought before a court from 1946 to 1958 found that the number of rape cases was higher in regions within Denmark (primarily rural areas) where there was a surplus of men. Svalastoga, *supra* note 26, at 49. Another study undertaken decades earlier, on the other hand, found that arrest rates for rape decrease as sex ratios are more male-skewed. Robert M. O'Brien, *Sex Ratios and Rape Rates: A Power-Control Theory*, 29 CRIMINOLOGY 99 (1991). That study, however, used rape arrests as a dependent variable—the problem with that method is that if the society is male-dominated, police officers might make fewer arrests for rape. Thus, fewer arrests for rape does not mean that fewer rapes are occurring in society as sex ratios become more male-skewed.

31. Mattias Larsen & Ravinder Kaur, *Signs of Change? Sex Ratio Imbalance and Shifting Social Practices in Northern India*, 48 ECON. & POL. WKLY. 45, 48 (2013).

32. Larsen & Kaur, *supra* note 31, at 50.

33. Larsen & Kaur, *supra* note 31, at 51.

34. Larsen & Kaur, *supra* note 31, at 51.

35. Paro Mishra, *Sex Ratios, Cross-Region Marriages and the Challenge to Caste Endogamy in Haryana*, 48 ECON. & POL. WKLY. 70, 71 (2013).

36. Mishra, *supra* note 35, at 72.

37. Mishra, *supra* note 35, at 72.

38. Mishra, *supra* note 35, at 78.

39. UNICEF, ENDING CHILD MARRIAGE: PROGRESS AND PROSPECTS 2 (2014), http://data.unicef.org/corecode/uploads/document6/uploaded_pdfs/corecode/Child-Marriage-Brochure-HR_164.pdf.

40. Mara Hvistendahl, for example, notes that rich men in South Korea and Taiwan are able to import wives from poorer regions, but poor men are more likely to use sex workers (who are often coerced). MARA HVISTENDAHL, UNNATURAL SELECTION 15 (2011). The committee that monitors the implementation of the UN Convention on the Elimination of All Forms of Discrimination against Women also warns China that it "is concerned about the impact of the adverse sex ratio, which may contribute to the increase in trafficking in women and girls." Comm. on the Elimination of Discrimination Against Women, Concluding Comments of the Committee on the Elimination of Discrimination against Women: China, ¶ 31, U.N. Doc. CEDAW/C/CHN/CO/6 (Aug. 25, 2006).

41. *Gender Inequality Index (GII)*, UNITED NATIONS DEVELOPMENT PROGRAMME: HUMAN DEVELOPMENT REPORTS, http://hdr.undp.org/en/content/gender-inequality-index-gii (last visited July 12, 2016).

42. UNITED NATIONS DEV. PROGRAMME, HUMAN DEVELOPMENT REPORT 2015: WORK FOR HUMAN DEVELOPMENT 226 (2015), http://hdr.undp.org/en/composite/GII.

43. Nandi, *supra* note 14, at 10-11.

44. Vibhuti Patel, *Sex Tests Endanger Women's Rights*, TIMES INDIA, Jan. 14, 1989, at 12.

45. MARY JOHN, U.N. POPULATION FUND (UNFPA), SEX RATIOS AND GENDER BIASED SEX SELECTION HISTORY, DEBATES AND FUTURE DIRECTIONS 18 (2014), http://asiapacific.unfpa.org/webdav/site/asiapacific/shared/Publications/2014/Sex-Ratios-and-Gender-Biased-Sex-Selection.pdf.

46. I describe in Chapter 4 the results of a national survey on parents' gender preference for their children.

47. Prenatal Nondiscrimination Act of 2016, H.R. 4924, 114th Cong. § 2(a)(1)(I) (2016); Prenatal Nondiscrimination Act of 2015, S. 48, 114th Cong. § 2(a)(9) (2015).

48. H.R. 4924, at § 2(a)(1)(J); S. 48, at § 2(a)(10).

49. H.R. 4924, at § 2(a)(1)(E); S. 48, at § 2(a)(5).

50. *See, e.g.*, S.B. 56, 69th Gen. Assemb., Reg. Sess. (Colo. 2013), http://www.leg.state.co.us/clics/clics2013a/csl.nsf/billcontainers/7F8D8BCADA17D73C87257AEE0057B52C/$FILE/056_01.pdf.

51. Complaint, Ex. A at 86-7, NAACP, et al. v. Tom Horne, et al., No. CV13-01079-PHX-DGC (D. Ariz. Oct. 3, 2013), *appeal docketed*, No. 13-17247 (9th Cir. Nov. 4, 2013), https://www.aclu.org/sites/default/files/field_document/arizona_exhibits_a-e.pdf.

52. *Field Listing: Sex Ratio*, in THE WORLD FACTBOOK, CIA, https://www.cia.gov/library/publications/the-world-factbook/fields/2018.html (last visited May 31, 2015).

53. Jennifer Hickes Lundquist & Eiko Strader, *Does Europe Have a Sex Selection Problem?*, SOC. PAGES (Sept. 13, 2013), http://thesocietypages.org/socimages/2013/09/13/does-europe-have-a-sex-selection-problem/?utm_source=feedburner&utm_medium=feed&utm_campaign=Feed%3A+SociologicalImagesSeeingIsBelieving+%28Sociological+Images%3A+Seeing+Is+Believing%29.

54. *See* Associated Press, *Liechtenstein Rejects Plan to Legalize Abortion*, YAHOO NEWS (Sept. 18, 2011), http://news.yahoo.com/liechtenstein-rejects-plan-legalize-abortion-133712436.html.

55. *Field Listing: Sex Ratio*, *supra* note 52.

56. *Field Listing: Sex Ratio*, *supra* note 52.

57. S.D. CODIFIED LAWS § 34-23A-56 (4A) (2014).

58. OKLA. STAT. ANN. tit. 63, § 1-738k (2013).

59. ARIZ. REV. STAT. ANN. § 36-2157 (2011).

60. ARIZ. REV. STAT. § 13-3603.02 (2013).

61. *See, e.g.*, THE CUSTOM-MADE CHILD?: WOMEN-CENTERED PERSPECTIVES (Helen B. Holmes et al. eds., 1981); Jodi Danis, *Sexism and "The Superfluous Female": Arguments for Regulating Preimplantation Sex Selection*, 18 HARV. WOMEN'S L.J. 219, 234–35 (1995) (describing the consequentialist argument that people in the United States would use sex selection technology to select against females); Norma J. Wikler, *Society's Response to the New Reproductive Technologies: The Feminist Perspectives*, 59 S. CAL. L. REV. 1043, 1044–46 (1986).

62. PETER SINGER & DEANE WELLS, MAKING BABIES: THE NEW SCIENCE AND ETHICS OF CONCEPTION 152–53 (1985). Additionally, Mary Anne Warren, who coined the phrase "gendercide," described the extreme form of this position: men would use sex selection to eliminate all women. But she quickly dismissed this position by pointing out that "[i]t is not in men's interest to eliminate women, and even if it were, the economic resources necessary to replace women as child-bearers with artificial gestation machines are unlikely to be available for a very long time." MARY ANN WARREN, GENDERCIDE: THE IMPLICATIONS OF SEX SELECTION ch. 3 (1985).

63. Danis, *supra* note 61, at 236.

64. Roberta Steinbacher, *Futuristic Implications of Sex Preselection*, *in* THE CUSTOM-MADE CHILD?: WOMEN-CENTERED PERSPECTIVES 187–89 (Helen B. Holmes et al. eds., 1981). *See also* Amitai Etzioni, *Sex Control, Science, and Society*, 161 SCI. 1107, 1107 (1968) (saying male-skewed sex ratios will result in women in purdah).

65. Steinbacher, *supra* note 64, at 188.

66. Frank Newport, *Americans Prefer Boys to Girls, Just as They Did in 1941: Men Tend to Want Boys; Women Are Divided in Their Gender Preferences*, GALLUP (June 23, 2011), http://www.gallup.com/poll/148187/americans-prefer-boys-girls-1941.aspx.

67. See Chapter 4 for a discussion of the Cornell Survey Research Institute poll.

68. Norbert Gleicher & David H. Barad, *The Choice of Gender: Is Elective Gender Selection Indeed Sexist?*, 22 HUM. REPROD. 3038, 3040 (2007). *See also* HANNA ROSIN, THE END OF MEN: AND THE RISE OF WOMEN (2012) (arguing that there is a "girl preference" in America).

69. Edgar Dahl, *Sex Selection Will Not Lead to Gender Discrimination*, *in* SHOULD PARENTS BE ALLOWED TO CHOOSE THE SEX OF THEIR CHILDREN? 40, 44 (Tamara Thompson ed., 2012).

70. Sital Kalantry & Miriam Yeung, U. Chi. L. Sch. Int'l Hum. Rts. Clinic, Nat'l Asian Pac. Women's F. & Advancing New Standards for Reprod. Just., Replacing Myths with Facts: Sex Selective Abortion Laws in the United States 25 (2014), https://ihrclinic.uchicago.edu/page/replacing-myths-facts-sex-selective-abortion-laws-united-states.

71. *See supra* Chapter 5.

72. Sneha Barot, *A Problem-and-Solution Mismatch: Son Preference and Sex-Selective Abortion Bans,* 15 Guttmacher Pol'y Rev. 20 (2012), https://www.guttmacher.org/pubs/gpr/15/2/gpr150218.html ("Moreover, an ultrasound may be performed in one location and an abortion obtained in another, where a woman can provide alternative reasons for the procedure."); Lauren Vogel, *Sex-Selective Abortions: No Simple Solution,* 184 Canadian Med. Ass'n J. 287 (2012) ("Several countries that have prohibited sex-selective abortions have found that the law is difficult to enforce and that people determined to have boys find ways of skirting the law", "People who are dramatically committed to aborting a little girl could simply lie.").

73. Arindam Nandi et al., *Sex-Selective Abortion Bans Are Not Associated with Changes in Sex Ratios at Birth among Asian Populations in Illinois and Pennsylvania,* 18 F. Health Econ. & Pol'y 41 (2015).

74. Planned Parenthood v. Casey, 744 F. Supp. 1323 (E.D. Pa. 1990).

75. Mitch Smith & Erik Eckholm, *Federal Judge Blocks Indiana Abortion Law,* N.Y. Times (June 30, 2016), http://www.nytimes.com/2016/07/01/us/federal-judge-blocks-indiana-abortion-law.html?_r=0.

76. Planned Parenthood of Ind. & Ky. v. Comm'r, No. 1:16-cv-00763-TWP-DML, 2016 U.S. Dist. LEXIS 84917 (S.D. Ind. June 30, 2016).

77. Planned Parenthood v. Casey, 505 U.S. 833, 878 (1992).

78. *Casey,* 505 U.S. at 886-87, 899.

79. *Casey,* 505 U.S. at 898.

80. Gonzales v. Carhart, 550 U.S. 124, 156 (2007).

81. *Gonzales,* 550 U.S. at 156.

82. Whole Woman's Health v. Hellerstedt, 136 S. Ct. 2292, 2311-12 (2016).

83. *Whole Woman's Health,* 136 S. Ct. at 2311-12, 2315.

84. *Whole Woman's Health,* 136 S. Ct. at 2311-12.

85. Roe v. Wade, 410 U.S. 113 (1973).

86. Mitch Smith & Erik Eckholm, *Federal Judge Blocks Indiana Abortion Law,* N.Y. Times (June 30, 2016), http://www.nytimes.com/2016/07/01/us/federal-judge-blocks-indiana-abortion-law.html?_r=0.

87. Planned Parenthood of Ind. & Ky. v. Comm'r, No. 1:16-cv-00763-TWP-DML, 2016 U.S. Dist. LEXIS 84917, at *16 (S.D. Ind. June 30, 2016) (internal quotations omitted).

88. Herbst v. O'Malley, No. 84 C 5602, 1993 WL 59142 (N.D. Ill. Mar. 2, 1993).

89. *Herbst,* 1993 WL 59142, at *9.

90. Isaacson v. Horne, 716 F.3d 1213 (9th Cir. 2013).

91. *Horne*, 716 F.3d at 1217 (emphasis in original).

92. Planned Parenthood v. Casey, 505 U.S. 833, 846 (1992).

Chapter 7

1. Law No. 2004-228 of Mar. 15, 2004, Journal Officiel de la République Française [J.O.] [Official Gazette of France], Mar. 17, 2004, p. 5190. The English-language media has translated this law as follows: "in schools, junior high schools and high schools, signs and dress that conspicuously show the religious affiliation of students are forbidden." *French Cabinet Backs Scarf Ban*, BBCNews (Jan. 28, 2004), http://news.bbc.co.uk/2/hi/europe/3437133.stm.

2. Loi 2010-776 11 octobre 2010 interdisant la dissimulation du visage dans l'espace public [law 2010-1192 of 11 October 2010 prohibiting the concealment of the face in public], Journal Officiel de la Republique Francaise [J.O.] [Official Gazette of France], Oct. 12, 2010, p. 18344 (cited in the ECHR opinion, para 28).

3. Case of S.A.S. v. France, Grand Chamber, European Court of Human Rights, July, 1, 2014, Application No. 43835/11, ¶ 82.

4. S.A.S. v. France, E.C.H.R. no. 43835/11 ¶ 82 (2014).

5. S.A.S. v. France ¶ 16.

6. Eva Brems, *Face Veil Bans in the European Court of Human Rights: The Importance of Empirical Findings*, 22 J.L. & Pol'y 517, 517-18 (2014).

7. Saba Mahmood, Politics of Piety: The Islamic Revival and the Feminist Subject 16 (Princeton Univ. Press, 2d ed. 2011).

8. Leila Ahmed, The Veil's Resurgence from the Middle East to America: The Quiet Revolution (Yale University Press, 2011).

9. Joan Wallach Scott, The Politics of the Veil 129 (2010).

10. Scott, *supra* note 9, at 129.

11. Scott, *supra* note 9, at 129.

12. Scott, *supra* note 9, at 132.

13. Scott, *supra* note 9, at 129.

14. Loi 2010-1192, art. 4.

15. Scott, *supra* note 9, at 137.

16. Scott, *supra* note 9, at 138–39.

17. Karima Bennoune, *Secularism and Human Rights: A Contextual Analysis of Headscarves, Religious Expression, and Women's Equality under International Law*, 45 Colum. J. Transnat'l L. 367, 391 (citing Fadela Amara, Breaking the Silence: French Women's Voices from the Ghetto 79 (Helen Chenut trans., 2003)).

18. Swati Sharma, *MAP: Where Islamic Veils Are Banned—and Where They Are Mandatory*, Wash. Post: WorldViews (July 1, 2014), https://www.washingtonpost.com/news/worldviews/wp/2014/07/01/map-where-islamic-veils-are-banned-and-where-they-are-mandatory/; Ramin Mostaghim, *Protest over Islamic Dress Code Clogs Tehran*

Streets, L.A. Times (May 7, 2014), http://www.latimes.com/world/middleeast/la-fg-iran-dress-code-protest-20140507-story.html; *Reasons Vary for Wearing a Veil*, ABCNews (Oct. 11, 2001), http://abcnews.go.com/GMA/story?id=126666&page=1.

19. S.A.S. v. France ¶ 42 (emphasis added).

20. Vanessa Friedman, *What Freedom Looks Like*, N.Y. Times (Apr. 13, 2016), https://www.nytimes.com/2016/04/14/fashion/islamic-fashion-france.html; Richard Hartley-Parkinson, *French Minister Compares Muslims Who Wear Veils to "Negroes Who Supported Slavery,"* Metro (Mar. 31, 2016), http://metro.co.uk/2016/03/31/french-minister-compares-muslims-who-wear-veils-to-negroes-who-supported-slavery-5785783/.

21. Katie Mettler, *Burkini Beach Brawl Leads Third French City in a Week to Ban the Swimsuit for Muslim Women*, Wash. Post (Aug. 16, 2016), https://www.washingtonpost.com/news/morning-mix/wp/2016/08/16/burkini-beach-brawl-leads-third-french-city-in-a-week-to-ban-the-swimsuit-for-muslim-women/.

22. Scott, *supra* note 9, at 176.

23. *European Court of Human Rights (ECtHR)*, Council Eur., http://www.coe.int/t/democracy/migration/bodies/echr_en.asp (last visited Aug 4, 2016).

24. S.A.S. v. France ¶ 37.

25. Convention for the Protection of Human Rights and Fundamental Freedoms, art. 8(2), Nov. 4, 1950, 213 U.N.T.S. 222.

26. S.A.S. v. France ¶ 139.

27. S.A.S. v. France ¶ 119.

28. S.A.S. v. France ¶ 119.

29. S.A.S. v. France ¶ 122.

30. S.A.S. v. France ¶ 153.

31. S.A.S. v. France ¶ 157.

32. S.A.S. v. France dissent ¶ 5.

33. Brems, *supra* note 6, at 531.

34. Brems, *supra* note 6, at 517–18.

35. Brems, *supra* note 6, at 537–40.

36. S.A.S. v. France ¶ 129.

37. S.A.S. v. France ¶ 37.

38. S.A.S. v. France ¶ 47.

39. S.A.S. v. France ¶ 137.

40. S.A.S. v. France ¶ 139.

41. S.A.S. v. France ¶ 47.

42. *See* Yonatan Lupu & Erik Voeten, *Precedent in International Courts: A Network Analysis of Case Citations by the European Court of Human Rights*, 42 Brit. J. Pol. Sci. 413 (2012).

43. Lupu & Voeten, *supra* note 42, at 433.

44. S.A.S. v. France ¶ 126.

45. S.A.S. v. France ¶ 133.

46. S.A.S. v. France ¶ 130 ("It observed that the rules in this sphere would consequently vary from one country to another according to national traditions and the requirements imposed by the need to protect the rights and freedoms of others and to maintain public order. It concluded from this that the choice of the extent and form of such rules must inevitably be left up to a point to the State concerned, as it would depend on the specific domestic context" (citing Sahin at § 109)).

47. Leyla Sahin v. Turkey, E.C.H.R. no. 44774/98 ¶ 115 (2005), http://www.tjsl.edu/slomansonb/SahinTurk.pdf.

48. Bennoune, *supra* note 17, at 386.

49. Bennoune, *supra* note 17, at 387.

50. Bennoune, *supra* note 17, at 386.

51. Jacco Bomhoff, *Leyla Sahin v. Turkey: ECHR Grand Chamber Judgment*, ComparativeLawBlog (Nov. 11, 2005, 1:36 PM), http://comparativelawblog.blogspot.com/2005/11/leyla-sahin-v-turkey-echr-grand.html.

52. Russell Goldman, *What's That You're Wearing? A Guide to Muslim Veils*, N.Y. Times: What in the World (May 3, 2016), http://www.nytimes.com/2016/05/04/world/what-in-the-world/burqa-hijab-abaya-chador.html; James Vyver, *Explainer: Why Do Muslim Women Wear a Burka, Niqab or Hijab?*, Austl. Broadcasting Corp.: News (Oct. 2, 2014), http://www.abc.net.au/news/2014-09-23/why-do-muslim-women-wear-a-burka-niqab-or-hijab/5761510.

53. Bennoune, *supra* note 17, at 369.

54. *European Court Ruling on Full-Face Veils Punishes Women for Expressing Their Beliefs*, Amnesty Int'l (July 1, 2014), https://www.amnesty.org/en/latest/news/2014/07/european-court-ruling-full-face-veils-punishes-women-expressing-their-religion/.

55. S.A.S. v. France ¶ 24.

56. *See Women in Afghanistan: The Back Story*, Amnesty Int'l (Oct. 25, 2013), http://www.amnesty.org.uk/womens-rights-afghanistan-history#.VbkuUfN_Oko.

57. Juhie Bhatia, *Overturn of Canada's Niqab Ban Reignites Controversy*, Women's eNews, (Sep. 25, 2015), http://womensenews.org/story/religion/150924/overturn-canadas-niqab-ban-reignites-controversy.

Conclusion

1. Peer Zumbansen, *Defining the Space of Transnational Law: Legal Theory, Global Governance, and Legal Pluralism*, 21 Transnat'l L. & Contemp. Probs. 305, 307 (2012).

2. Richard A. Shweder, *"What About Female Genital Mutilation?" and Why Understanding Culture Matters in the First Place*, *in* Engaging Cultural Differences: The Multicultural Challenge in Liberal Democracies 216, 239–42 (Richard A. Shweder et al. eds. 2002).

3. Canada and the United Kingdom have considered bans on sex selection. *See, e.g.*, Michel Viatteau, *Keep Sex of Fetuses a Secret to Prevent Selective Abortion of Girls: Journal*, Nat'l Post (Jan. 16, 2012), http://news.nationalpost.com/news/canada/canada-is

-haven-for-parents-seeking-sex-selective-abortions-medical-journal; Sheetal Parmar, *MPs Back Ban on Sex-Selective Abortion*, BBC (Nov. 4, 2014), http://www.bbc.com/news/uk-politics-29891005.

4. Harry Yorke, *Doctors Could Be Prosecuted for Gender-Based Abortion Following British Lawyers Appeal to European Court of Human Rights*, Telegraph (June 18, 2016, 8:15 PM), http://www.telegraph.co.uk/news/2016/06/18/doctors-could-be-prosecuted-for-gender-based-abortion-following/.

INDEX

ACKNOWLEDGMENTS

I could not have produced this work without the collaboration, guidance, and feedback of so many wonderful people. I would like to thank my reviewers Hila Shamir and Sonia Katyal for their insightful and thoughtful comments. This book would not exist were it not for my collaboration with Brian Citro, Arindam Nandi, Alexander Persaud, Miriam Yeung, Sujatha Jesudason, and Shivana Jorwar. Marty Wells provided guidance on the statistical analysis of the sex-selective abortion bills. Zillah Eisenstein read many draft chapters and I am grateful for her guidance and mentorship throughout this process. I conceived of this as a book project from my discussion with Martha Nussbaum and her comments on an article where I developed the idea for a contextualized approach. Nur Kara opened the doors to this project for me by the invitation to moderate the film discussion.

I am grateful for comments and feedback on draft chapters by participants of Cornell's summer faculty workshop series, including: Sherry Colb, Chantal Thomas, Aziz Rana, Cynthia Bowman, Elizabeth Anker, Eduardo Peñalver, Jeff Rachlinski, Jed Stiglitz, Odette Lienau, Valerie Hans, and Jens Ohlin. I appreciate Mary Katzenstein's comments to draft chapters; she has been a mentor since she supervised my college thesis. There are many other people who gave me thought-provoking comments who I would like to acknowledge—Aziza Ahmed, Anindita Banerjee, Priya Gupta, Jocelyn Getgen, Maithili Pradhan, and Rachael Rebouche. I am grateful to Peer Zumbansen for his tremendous guidance and comments. I benefited greatly from comments I received on the chapters I presented at the University of Baltimore Law School's Center for Applied Feminism conference and the Law & Society Conference in 2016. I am also grateful to the Cornell Survey Research Institute for including my questions in their national poll.

There are many research assistants who worked on different iterations of the manuscript. I appreciate the dedicated work provided by John Ready, Evan Johnson, James Kraemer, Sonia Gupta, Rebecca Helm, Kimberly

Rhoten, and Hannah Zwetsloot. Thank you to Thomas Mills for his invaluable support in finding and suggesting materials for me to use in this book. I want to recognize clinic students and research assistants at the University of Chicago Law School—Jeff Gilson, Kelsey Stricker, Frederick Watson, Lindsay Gus, and Marlow Svatek.

I am indebted to Bert Lockwood and Peter Agree for their support and faith in me throughout the editorial process.